The Armenian Genocide and Turkey

Armenians in the Modern and Early Modern World

Recent decades have seen the expansion of Armenian Studies from insular history to a broader, more interactive field within an inter-regional and global context. This series, Armenians in the Modern and Early Modern World, responds to this growth by promoting innovative and interdisciplinary approaches to Armenian history, politics, and culture in the period between 1500-2000. Focusing on the geographies of the Mediterranean, Middle East, and Contemporary Russia [Eastern Armenia], it directs specific attention to imperial and post-imperial frameworks: from the Ottoman Empire to Modern Turkey/Arab Middle East; the Safavid/Qajar Empires to Iran; and the Russian Empire to Soviet Union/Post-Soviet territories.

Series Editor

Bedross Der Matossian, *University of Nebraska, Lincoln, USA*

Advisory Board

Levon Abrahamian, *Yerevan State University, Armenia*
Sylvie Alajaji, *Franklin & Marshal College, USA*
Sebouh Aslanian, *University of California, Los Angeles, USA*
Stephan Astourian, *University of California, Berkley, USA*
Houri Berberian, *University of California, Irvine, USA*
Talar Chahinian, *University of California, Irvine, USA*
Rachel Goshgarian, *Lafayette College, USA*
Ronald Grigor Suny, *University of Michigan, USA*
Sossie Kasbarian, *University of Stirling, UK*
Christina Maranci, *Tufts University, USA*
Tsolin Nalbantian, *Leiden University, the Netherlands*
Anna Ohanyan, *Stonehill College, USA*
Hratch Tchilingirian, *University of Oxford, UK*

Published and Forthcoming Titles

The Politics of Naming the Armenian Genocide: Language, History and 'Medz Yeghern', Vartan Matiossian
Picturing the Ottoman Armenian World: Photography in Erzerum, Kharpert, Van and Beyond, David Low

The Armenian Genocide and Turkey

Public Memory and Institutionalized Denial

Hakan Seckinelgin

I.B. TAURIS
LONDON • NEW YORK • OXFORD • NEW DELHI • SYDNEY

I.B. TAURIS
Bloomsbury Publishing Plc, 50 Bedford Square, London, WC1B 3DP, UK
Bloomsbury Publishing Inc, 1359 Broadway, 12th Floor, New York, NY 10018, USA
Bloomsbury Publishing Ireland, 29 Earlsfort Terrace, Dublin 2, D02 AY28, Ireland

BLOOMSBURY, I.B. TAURIS and the I.B. Tauris logo are trademarks of Bloomsbury Publishing Plc

First published in Great Britain 2024
This paperback edition published 2025

Copyright © Hakan Seckinelgin, 2024, 2025

Hakan Seckinelgin has asserted his rights under the Copyright, Designs and Patents Act, 1988, to be identified as Author of this work.

For legal purposes the Acknowledgements on p. viii constitute an extension of this copyright page.

Cover design: Adriana Brioso
Cover image © Hakan Seckinelgin

All rights reserved. No part of this publication may be: i) reproduced or transmitted in any form, electronic or mechanical, including photocopying, recording or by means of any information storage or retrieval system without prior permission in writing from the publishers; or ii) used or reproduced in any way for the training, development or operation of artificial intelligence (AI) technologies, including generative AI technologies. The rights holders expressly reserve this publication from the text and data mining exception as per Article 4(3) of the Digital Single Market Directive (EU) 2019/790.

Bloomsbury Publishing Inc does not have any control over, or responsibility for, any third-party websites referred to or in this book. All internet addresses given in this book were correct at the time of going to press. The author and publisher regret any inconvenience caused if addresses have changed or sites have ceased to exist, but can accept no responsibility for any such changes.

Library of Congress Cataloging-in-Publication Data
Names: Seckinelgin, Hakan, 1969- author.
Title: The Armenian genocide and Turkey: public memory and institutionalized denial / Hakan Seckinelgin.
Other titles: Public memory and institutionalized denial
Description: London; New York: I. B. Tauris, 2024. | Series: Armenians in the modern and early modern world | Includes bibliographical references and index.
Identifiers: LCCN 2023036820 (print) | LCCN 2023036821 (ebook) | ISBN 9780755653614 (hb) | ISBN 9780755653652 (paperback) | ISBN 9780755653621 (ebook) | ISBN 9780755653638 (epdf) | ISBN 9780755653645
Subjects: LCSH: Armenian Genocide, 1915-1923. | Armenian Genocide, 1915-1923–Public opinion. | Public opinion–Turkey. | Armenian Genocide, 1915-1923–Anniversaries, etc. | Armenian Genocide, 1915-1923–Press coverage–Turkey. | Armenian Genocide, 1915-1923–Censorship–Turkey. | Collective memory–Turkey. | Denialism–Turkey.
Classification: LCC DS195.5 .S43 2024 (print) | LCC DS195.5 (ebook) | DDC 956.6/20154–dc23/eng/20230812
LC record available at https://lccn.loc.gov/2023036820
LC ebook record available at https://lccn.loc.gov/2023036821

ISBN: HB: 978-0-7556-5361-4
PB: 978-0-7556-5365-2
ePDF: 978-0-7556-5363-8
eBook: 978-0-7556-5362-1

Typeset by Deanta Global Publishing Services, Chennai, India

For product safety related questions contact productsafety@bloomsbury.com.

To find out more about our authors and books visit www.bloomsbury.com and sign up for our newsletters.

To Claire and Riva

Contents

Acknowledgements		viii
1	Introduction	1
2	The memory machine: The Armenian genocide in Turkey	27
3	Commemorating the centennial of the Armenian genocide: 24 April 2015	57
4	Public memory and the mass media	87
5	Formal education: Creating citizens	113
6	Educating the public	141
7	Conclusion	169
References		189
Index		203

Acknowledgements

Many have heard me talk about the book over the years. I am now very happy to tell them that the book is done! The writing of this book was an emotionally demanding task, and it was interrupted by the Covid-19 pandemic with its confinements, health concerns and online teaching procedures. With hindsight, I think the argument of the book matured through these challenges and the book arrives *when it is meant to arrive*.

Of course, in some ways writing a book is a collective endeavour. Many inspiring scholars in this field require clear acknowledgement. I have met or heard some of them speak, but many I have never met and yet inspired by their research and by their resolute drive to establish the facts about the genocide in their pursuit for justice. It is hard to produce this book without their significant contributions in this field. Furthermore, along the way, I met many people in different places in Istanbul, Paris, London and elsewhere; they shared with me their experiences and their thinking about the everyday experiences of denial. I decided to maintain their anonymity in this text for various reasons but I am very much indebted to them for sharing their views and experiences with me. They provided the material triggering and informing my thinking out of which the book's analysis emerged. Similarly, over the years parts of the research were presented in different venues, including Sciences Po, L'École des hautes études en sciences sociales (EHESS), the American University of Paris, *Mémorial de la Shoah in Paris* and the London School of Economics (LSE). I thank for all the invitations to present my work and for all the questions that were asked during these presentations. I still would like to acknowledge some of the colleagues I met during my research and friends as over the years on different occasions I benefited from their views, questions and conversations in Istanbul, London and Paris: Boris Adjemian, Claire Andrieu, Serge Avedikian, Seyhan Bayraktar, Nazlı Temir Beyleryan, Hamit Bozarslan, Cloé Drieu, Bernard George, Sema Kaygusuz, Marie-Claire Lavabre, Mark Levene, Johann Michel, Claire Mouradian, Gretty Mirdal, Karoline Postel-Vinay, Pınar Selek, Emmanuel Szurek, Sebla Selin Ok, Sena Ok, Mark Osiel, Ara Sarafian, Brian Schiff, Uğur Ümit Üngör, Nurdan Türker, Julien Zarifian.

As I was doing research from January to July 2015, I was a visiting researcher in Paris at the Centre for International Studies (CERI), Sciences Po. The first draft of the book was developed from February to July 2019 when I was a fellow at the Institute d'études avacées de Paris (The Paris Institute for Advanced Study). The institute provided intellectually stimulating environment with its extensive network of French and international researchers. Both Saadi Lahlou, as director, and Gretty Mirdal, previous director, were generous with their time and engagement with the fellows, creating a vibrant research context. We were also very much supported by other colleagues in the institute and a special acknowledgement is required for Simon Luck. I was very happy to be a fellow at the institute as there were several other fellows who were interested in analysis of violence. I was very privileged to be a fellow at the same time as Joachim S. Savelsberg who was working on his last book *Knowing about Genocide* at the time (2021). Special thanks are due to him as we had so many discussions over the months, co-organized workshops (*Genocide and Collective Memory: Social Science of the Armenian Case and beyond* and *Recognition Versus Denial of Genocide: Art Films, Documentaries and Graphic Novels*) and more broadly supported each other's work. Similarly, Penny Roberts, another fellow, has become someone I talked to about many things, including violence, given her expertise in the history of violence in sixteenth-century France. The institute created an intellectual space for all fellows to share conversations informed by their different research interests and disciplines. I thank all the fellows for their engagement in these conversations that certainly had enriched my thinking: Gregory Bochner, Adam Frank, Kei Hiruta, Michael Jonik, Andrew Kahn, Marylène Lieber, Adam Mestyan, Buket Türkmen and Denis Walsh.

Both the research and writing of the book facilitated by several sabbatical periods and research leaves. Therefore, I also would like to thank many colleagues in my department at the LSE. They took over my teaching and other duties number of times. Without, of course, their willingness to do so, I would not have been able to produce this work. I deeply thank specifically Liam Beiser-McGrath, the late Tony Hall, Tim Hildebrandt, Armine Ishkanian, Hayley Jones, Sunil Kumar, David Lewis, Robtel Neajai Payley and Vicente Silva.

The book is the outcome of the research that began in 2014 and developed around the centennial commemorations of the Armenian genocide leading to 24 April 2015 in Turkey. But my interest on the Armenian genocide and denial emerges from earlier discussions that have been important. Two good friends, fellow PhD students at the LSE in the 1990s, are important to mention: Ayla Göl and Razmik Panossian. Their PhD work focused on different aspects of this field. Their enthusiasm for their subjects and discussions they had over many years sparked an ongoing discussion among number of us as we worked on our PhDs. Nonetheless, different questions on the Armenian genocide for me remained informal research questions that I followed through the years. It was only in 2008 through joint research with my colleague, Armine Ishkanian, I formally focused on this area. Our research at the time explored civil society relations between Armenia and Turkey (funded by the British Academy). This research, as I discuss later, was challenging but in many ways a productive process. We conducted our field research together in Yerevan and in Istanbul and then organized a number of workshops in London to understand the dynamics of the issues involved in civil society relations emerging at the time across borders. I am grateful to Armine as I learned a lot in this joint research.

I would also like to thank Rory Gormley from Bloomsbury Academic and Bedross Der Matossian, series editor for Armenians in the Modern and Early Modern World in I.B. Tauris/Bloomsbury Academic, for their enthusiasm for the book. I also thank two anonymous reviewers for their insightful comments on an earlier draft of the manuscript.

The book is dedicated to an inspiring scholar: Claire Mouradian. She is always intellectually curious, a critical and engaging scholar. She generously shares her own vast, encyclopaedic, knowledge on her specializations. During my research and the writing process she provided a very warm welcome to me and my research, and was always ready to provide critical comments and suggestions to push me further. She also very generously and enthusiastically included me in her networks that provided me with an intellectual context.

I am also grateful to my parents-in-law, Francoise and William Fennell, who have been enthusiastic about my research. They very generously allowed me to stay in their flat in Paris while I was a visiting scholar at CERI in 2015. As to my partner Damien, I am grateful as I feel his support in everything I do, though on this occasion he has been rather cautiously supportive. As I was writing about public memory, my mother, Beyhan, unfortunately has gradually moved to the threshold of her own memories. As a result, it has not been possible to talk about the book with her, although I know she would have been very interested in it. Ironically one of the last *conversations* we had was in early September 2022 when she talked about her own experience of the 6–7 September 1955 Istanbul Anti-Greek pogrom. At the time she was a witness to the terror and the destruction in the centre of Istanbul, in Beyoğlu. This was, of course, a story she shared with us many times as we were growing up. But this time she talked about the memory of bloodthirsty and terrorizing eyes of the perpetrators that remained with her even though she was not the direct target of their terror.

At the end, of course the responsibility for the shortcomings of this book remains mine alone.

1

Introduction

On 14 January 2017, during politically contentious discussions in the Turkish parliament about a change to the Constitution, Garo Paylan, an Armenian-Turkish member of parliament (MP) from Istanbul for the People's Democratic Party (Halklarin Demokratik Partisi, HDP), gave a speech (Paylan 2017). Another MP during the same session had described the Constitution as a 'Constitution for Turks', and Paylan's speech was about the importance of thinking about the Constitution as an inclusive document rather than as for the majority only. In the speech, Paylan made historical comparisons to the first Ottoman Constitution, produced under Abdülhamit II, pointing out that one of the drafters had been the Armenian lawmaker Krikor Odyan. Paylan's aim was clearly to highlight the implications of moving away from a multicultural Constitution. Talking about the constitutional changes initiated in 1908, he said: 'In that decade of long chaos between 1913 and 1923, we lost four peoples, Armenians, Greeks, Assyrians and Jews, to great massacres and genocides. They were either deported from these lands or exposed to population exchanges' (Paylan 2017). His speech was immediately interrupted by shouts in the chamber as MPs from various political parties insisted that 'in these lands [i.e. Turkey] there were no genocides'. Amid these disruptions, the deputy speaker was called upon to stop Paylan's speech. The deputy speaker asked Paylan to correct his wording and say that 'there was no genocide, although many had painful experiences'. Nevertheless, Paylan tried to carry on with his speech:

> In the past we were 40%, today we are one in 1000. Something must have happened to us. I call this genocide. You are free to call whatever you want. Today we are one in 1000. . . . Let's name it together and move on. (Paylan 2017)

Finally he was warned by the deputy speaker to watch his language: 'Know what you are saying [*ne konustugunuzu bilin*]' (Paylan 2017). The disruptions and shouts of outrage continued. The session was adjourned for an hour.

The constitutional change under discussion during this extraordinary occurrence concerned the introduction of a presidential governance system to the Republic of Turkey. The topic was highly contentious, and the political discussions the most fractious Turkey had seen in decades; society and parliament were divided, and the political fallout for the country was dramatic. Yet, with the exception of the HDP, parliament suddenly became united in its reaction to the claim of genocide, calling on the speaker to ban Paylan from parliamentary debate in accordance with the internal regulations of the legislature. Subsequently, thanks to votes by three large parties – the Justice and Development Party (Adalet ve Kalkinma Partisi), the Nationalist Movement Party (Milliyetci Hareket Partisi) and the Republican People's Party (Cumhuriyet Halk Partisi, CHP) – which were at loggerheads on the issue of constitutional change – Paylan was temporarily banned from three parliamentary sessions under Article 163 of the parliamentary bylaws. Then, in accordance with Article 83 of the Constitution, his words were removed from the record of the session.

This event in parliament is representative of the ways in which public talk about the Armenian genocide is often received in Turkey. This was a complex situation where an Armenian-Turkish MP, with obvious political agency, had his voice stifled by the expectations of public discourse about the events of 1915. He was challenged for talking about history in a way that did not follow the accepted narrative. He was also challenged for having suggested the possibility of another history when he stated that it was *his* history: 'I know what happened to my grandfathers' (Paylan 2017). The MPs' disruptive challenge to such talk about history was fervently opposed to considering the events of 1915 as a genocide. The challenge was a move to negate Paylan's being by delegitimating the historical and sociocultural narrative he was presenting in the eyes of the public. The position underwriting this exchange in parliament was not about whether to have a conversation or a discussion on the issue; it was about asserting a historical truth, and the importance of that truth, to determine public discourse, speech and action in Turkey. It was about regulating the limits of other ways of thinking, if indeed thinking was allowed at all.

In this book, I am interested in analysing the mechanisms through which this public discourse about the events of 1915 in Turkey is produced and maintained. Thus, the book is neither a historical account nor an attempt to collect the right kind of evidence to determine whether the events of 1915 were or were not a genocide. A great number of previous studies have looked very closely at the events of 1915 in order to understand what happened. These studies have also produced a very rich literature on the experiences of Armenian subjects of the

Ottoman Empire. On the basis of this significant historiography, I consider the events of 1915 to have been a genocide, as I will explain later.

Although this book certainly engages with the existing literature, my work is more concerned with how discussions and debates in Turkey about the Armenian genocide are understood by the majority of the Turkish public. What are the conditions of the understanding that is evident in the reactions to Paylan? The book also examines the mechanism that creates the specific pattern of this public understanding, which involves producing what Fatma Müge Göçek (2014) calls 'publicly manufactured emotions', or what I call manufactured public memories. This approach is a way of thinking about the refusal to engage in a discussion of the Armenian genocide as well as the context of the public's understanding of the idea of the genocide when it is introduced in public debates. I try to comprehend and unpack reactions in Turkish public discussions to the idea that the events of 1915 were a genocide. In the case of the parliamentary debate reported above, for example, it is important to understand the cognitive resources through which MPs articulated their reactions to Paylan.

Thus, this book is based on research that focuses on these cognitive resources and how they frame the public's perceptions of the Armenian genocide in Turkey. The book has a number of origins, and I will now talk about these in order to locate the development of the question that drives the book. I will also offer some theoretical and methodological delineations to introduce the book's content.

The research journey

I have followed public discussions about Armenians in Turkey since the 1980s. In the 1970s and 1980s, the argument about the impossibility of genocide emerged in Turkey in reaction to the attacks on Turkish diplomats by the Armenian Secret Army for the Liberation of Armenia (ASALA). Later, in the 1990s, when I was a Turkish postgraduate student in social sciences at the London School of Economics (LSE), my fellow students would constantly ask me what I thought about the Armenian genocide. I had to think about that question closely. Some of this thinking was part of an ongoing discussion with colleagues who came from different countries with different traditions of thought about violence and nationalism.

The opportunity to conduct research only arrived in 2009. As social scientists interested in civil society, my LSE colleague Armine Ishkanian and I wanted to look at how civil society groups from Armenia and Turkey engaged with each other across physical and ideological borders. This research involved us doing fieldwork together in Yerevan and Istanbul, conducting interviews with various civil society organizations, including those taking part in joint work across borders, and with civil society groups that were facilitating communities from the two countries to engage with each other. The research process was challenging and very productive, and it yielded many rich and at times unexpected discussions. One of the outcomes for us was the clear realization that it was absolutely impossible to engage in these civil society relationships or discussions today without having a debate about the past. It seemed to me that the context of present-day relationships was the events of 1915 or how one thought about those events. This was highlighted by comments I heard during two interviews, one in Yerevan and the other in Istanbul.

The interview in Yerevan was at the Armenian Genocide Museum-Institute. It took place against the backdrop of the apology campaign that had been initiated by civil society actors in Turkey in December 2008 (CNN.Türk 2008). Our conversation touched on this issue. Our interviewee said that for him, the Turkish apology campaign in the main was a positive gesture towards recognition of the events of 1915. But his response was cautious. He said:

> We now get many requests to visit the memorial and to apologise. They are welcome to come, but before that, I have questions. What are they apologising for, and to whom? Do they know who we are? What will happen once they apologise?

The Istanbul interview was with a leader of the Armenian community in Turkey. After a long conversation, he reflected on the real challenge as he saw it: 'Look, we are at most 70,000 people in Turkey, and we have to teach over 72 million people that we are here. Most of the population does not even know we exist.' He identified this as a challenge not only because most people did not know the Armenian community existed but also because everyone in Turkey had opinions about Armenians. He also mentioned that traditionally the Armenian community had been inward-looking and reluctant to engage. Of course, the 'tradition' he was talking about applied to the period after the 1915 genocide, covering the time from the establishment of the Republic of Turkey to the present day.

The cautious but firm questions in Yerevan concerned the apology process: What would happen once people apologized? Was there an intention to get to know who the addressees were in this process? What were the boundaries of this relationship? The unease was about whether this attempt to relate would lead to a relationship or not. Would those who were ready to apologize be prepared to hear about people's experiences? If a new relationship were forged, how would people understand each other and each other's histories? These questions about relationships concerned both memory and the future. An apology is a gesture of remembrance. But what happens when an event is publicly remembered – what is remembered and by whom? What is the next step, and does it also create a new relationship between the communities involved? The apology process operates in two registers: an event in the past and the moment of the apology in the present. It also presents a challenge: it is one thing to remember a past event, but it is quite another to process that event's implications for the present. The question put to us in Yerevan was about the orientation of the groups that wanted to apologize. Did they want to do more than just apologize – did they want to remember? It is at this juncture that the issue raised in Istanbul becomes material to this discussion. The question is still about a relationship. But this time it reveals another aspect of the issue: the existing public discourse about Armenians in Turkey, and how that discourse frames social relations between Armenians and the Muslim-Sunni Turkish majority. Furthermore, there is also the issue of how this framing informs the majority's understanding of Armenians' experiences and whether that understanding limits processes such as the apology campaign.

Similarly, one of the focus groups we held in Yerevan revealed that individuals had many different views about the relationship between the two countries. The interesting point here was the ambiguity in older generations' views about the issue from an international perspective. For some participants, even if they had been born in Armenia, their links with Kars or Van – from where their parents or in many cases grandparents had originated – had a deeper emotional resonance than their national belonging according to territorial borders. At the end of our analysis of cross-border civil society relations, we decided at the time not to publish on the topic, due to the difficulty of maintaining some research participants' anonymity.

I learned a lot from this research on civil society work in the two countries, and my focus changed as a result of the questions posed during the research process. I realized that another issue underwriting civil society relationships went beyond the forms of engagement I had observed: the issue of the memory of 1915. As our research had revealed, the failure to address this underlying issue constituted a fundamental obstacle to change in civil society relationships. The insights we had gained in Istanbul were about *not* remembering. At the same time, they called into question the usefulness of the concept of *forgetting* for understanding sociocultural and political life between an event in the past and the moment of the present. It was clear that the situation was not about forgetting, particularly not in the present, over a hundred years after the genocide. This was more than merely forgetting: the existence and history of a whole community seemed to have 'disappeared' (Benjamin 1968: 255), in such a way that remembrance of the past did not leave traces in Turkey's everyday life that might enable new generations to remember anything about those who had disappeared. If something has been forgotten, it must once have existed; but if something disappears without trace, then for subsequent generations it never existed at all – there is only an absence. Despite this situation, our Istanbul interviewee's words were delivered not with a psychological attitude of resignation, but as describing a real sociopolitical challenge in the present. The challenge is to engage with the consequences of this disappearance of the Armenians and their experiences, and with the production and reproduction of its conditions in everyday life.

The statements made by our interviewees in Yerevan and Istanbul are related. They link an event – such as an apology – with the process within which that event takes place. It is in this context that this particular apology process creates its own meaning regarding what apology is supposed to achieve as a civil society action. The idea of apology clearly involves an attempt to remember. However, the remembrance that underpins the various moves to apologize is generated within the context of the disappearance, perhaps even obliteration, of societal knowledge in Turkey since 1915. The questions asked in Yerevan highlight this relationship, forcing us to reflect on whether *just* remembering, and signing a short statement, is a good enough outcome if the everyday lives of Armenians in Turkey before and after 1915 are still not remembered. I came to the realization that unless this underlying process of partial remembering – remembering only 'us' – that mediates social relations is unpacked and considered, it will be extremely difficult to engage in the process of bringing different groups together.

Let me give an example from personal experience of how this disappearance works. In Yerevan, while waiting to conduct an interview in the office of a civil society organization, I noticed a copy of Osman Köker's book *100 Years Ago: Armenians in Turkey* (*100 yıl önce Türkiyede Ermeniler*) lying on the coffee table. I knew about the book because in January 2005 there had been an exhibition based on it in Istanbul. Although I had missed the exhibition, I had followed the debate it had generated in various media, and I was keen to see the book. The book provides a unique window into the lives of Armenians in Turkey between 1900 and 1914, using over 700 postcards from the period to present Armenian lives in many different contexts. I immediately began to flick through it. The images were absorbing and thought-provoking. It included some postcards showing Armenian lives in Ankara. This was unexpected and unsettling for me. I thought: What Armenians? I had lived in Ankara for years as a university student, but I was not even aware that there had been a vibrant Armenian community in Ankara at the turn of the twentieth century. Our interviewee arrived, and I had to put the book down, but this unsettling thought about the Armenians in Ankara stuck with me. I am from Istanbul, and of course I had always been familiar with Armenians in everyday life. I had had Armenian neighbours, schoolfriends and many others. For instance, Dr Jirayr's name had been part of our daily routine for years; my maternal grandmother turned to him as the medical authority whenever she had any kind of health problem, and she would repeat the refrain 'but this is prescribed by Dr Jirayr' to stop us children refusing our medicine. Material aspects of Armenian culture were part of life in the city too: we would regularly see churches, schools and many palaces built by the members of the Balyan family. But I was shocked by the book's revelations because I had met no Armenian people in Ankara while I was studying there, and nor did I remember seeing any material evidence that the city had had an Armenian community relatively recently (a central explanation for the absence of such evidence is given in Taylan Esin and Zeliha Etöz's (2015) book on the 1916 Ankara fire). Subsequently, I have often wondered why, when I was living and studying in the comparatively small city of Ankara in the late 1980s and early 1990s, I had not thought to ask about the possibility of an Armenian past in the city. But at the time, and indeed long afterwards, such a question would never have occurred to me as relevant.

This experience in Yerevan raised critical questions about my own experience of Ankara, throwing it into confusion. I have a particular memory of the city. That memory is built on an experience that was framed by a specific understanding of the city as the dusty town that came to symbolize the foundation of the Turkish republic. The popular story of Ankara on which individual memories are based begins with 27 December 1919, when Mustafa Kemal arrived in the city. Photos of the city commonly show the modern city centre around Kızılay towards Kavaklıdere and further on as empty fields leading to Çankaya, where Mustafa Kemal lived in a farmhouse from 1921 onwards. In this way, the story of the city merges with the struggle to establish the new republic, creating the grounds on which the memory of the city is constituted. The memory of the city before Mustafa Kemal's arrival has been gradually removed from view. But what happened in Ankara before that date? What are the implications of that past, which is not a part of our present knowledge?

These reflections in turn produced my next question, which orientated the initial stages of the research that led to this book: How can we think about the implications of the 1915 Armenian genocide for sociopolitical relations in Turkey today? At first, I focused on thinking theoretically about the epistemological practices that are used in Turkey to help people understand the issues in this debate. My aim was to grasp the implications of these epistemological practices for thinking, acting and being today. I refined the question further while I was in Turkey to do my research. I was initially interested in conducting interviews with different groups to produce a map of views on the Armenian genocide. In a number of discussions and preliminary interviews, my Armenian-Turkish interlocutors asked me why I thought anyone would be interested in what Armenians thought. This was a challenging question. I also noticed the availability of translated literature on Armenians and the genocide. I started to have misgivings that even if I were to produce a work based on my interviews, I still would not really know what any of it meant to the general public in Turkey.

So, I thought about what people would make of the existing books on the Armenian genocide if they read them, and why they would be interested in Armenians' views. I thought that my expectations about engagement presumed that people would choose to pick such books up in a bookshop and read them. This then generated other questions, similar to some of those posed by our interviewee in Yerevan: If and when people read these books, how would they understand them? Would they want to engage with the experiences they had read about in the books? Even if people did read the material, I was not sure how they would reflect on the content. This finally clarified my real central concern: to understand what cognitive resources were available to the public that would both allow people to choose to read about certain issues and provide them with grounds from which to form judgements about what they had read. As a result, my research focus shifted towards uncovering the mechanisms of memory and remembering as knowledge practices that facilitate how Armenians and studies of the genocide can be understood at present in Turkey.

In this book, therefore, I focus on the constitution of a knowledge base that guides the public to engage with questions about the events of 1915. In other words, the book is about the sources of public understanding that aim to inform the majority of the public in Turkey. In more general terms, the book is about how the 'we' is claimed in Turkey in instances such as that which opened this introduction. The issue is how the 'we' is reproduced on the basis of what 'we' can remember, in such a way as to constitute the 'we' in contradistinction to some Other. The starting point of my thinking is the following question: What does the 1915 genocide mean to Turkish people today? I also consider corollary questions: Does it mean anything at all? Should it mean anything? To provide direct answers to these questions, I must unpack existing attempts in Turkish public discussions to explain what these events were (or were not). From there I can then move on to answer my last question about what it should mean. None of these steps to answer my questions are easy or straightforward in a Turkish context that expects discussions of the issue to be guided by existing conventions. These conventions require the use of the language of the 'Armenian issue/problem' (*Ermeni Meselesi*) as the prescribed entry point into the discussion. This is also an injunction to remember history in a specific way, both implicitly and officially (Michel 2018: 50–51). As Johann Michel (2018: 4) points out, this is in the form of 'you *have* to remember [tu *dois* te souvenir]', which of course carries a moral imperative in relation to *that which* you have to remember. It immediately and explicitly limits the possibility of an open discussion by providing cognitive guidance for the practice of remembering. According to the conventions, the concept of genocide is certainly not a part of the discussion; the discussion needs to be about 1915 and the Ottoman administration of the day; and the claims about genocide must be treated as demands made by the Armenian diaspora. If one agrees with these reference points, then one can have a discussion of the events of 1915. This is also a monitoring device: for instance, calling the events of 1915 a genocide locates one outside the limits of public acceptability in Turkey.

The existence of this injunction to remember as a diffused sociocultural understanding somewhat calls into question Göçek's (2014) position. Reflecting on her initial reservations about using 'genocide' to refer to the events of 1915–17, she writes: 'What I objected to was the almost total ignorance of contemporary Turkish society about what happened to the Armenians in the past due to the nationalist educational system' (Göçek 2014: 19). This position seems to suggest that the public first needs to be properly informed so that it can understand why the term 'genocide' is used. Of course, her point about ignorance is correct. There is ample evidence to demonstrate that ignorance. I argue, however, that this ignorance does not imply a lack of opinions. As discussed above, the public seems to have views about Armenians. These views are not only about what might have happened in 1915 but also about Armenian lives in the intervening period until the present. The existence of this cognitive context motivates my research. The questions I pose seek to understand the content of the repertoire used in public to understand both Armenians and the Armenian genocide, and the mechanisms that underpin that understanding within present-day social relations.

I will dwell on this framing in the coming chapters. Here, I need to attend to two critical issues raised by use of the language of *Ermeni Meselesi* as a rule, a boundary condition, that regulates how one can take part in discussions in Turkey (also see Turan and Öztan 2018: 17–18). First, why, as a member of the Muslim-Sunni Turkish majority, am I talking about this topic – what is it to me? Second, why do I think it's appropriate to call the events of 1915 a genocide? While I approach this study as a trained social scientist using a multidisciplinary lens, the issues that are material to it have been at the centre of significant academic and political confrontations, and many participants in these debates have emotional and professional commitments to particular positions. Discussing one's positionality is part of the process. I will now unpack what motivates my work and in doing so I will highlight my thinking about the question of the use of 'genocide' as a term. This will hopefully satisfy some concerns, although it will certainly exacerbate others.

What is it to you?

I need to answer this question, which more or less everyone in this field is asked, directly or indirectly, when they begin their research: What is it to you? When people ask this question, they mean: What is it to you *personally*? The field – studying and discussing the 1915 genocide, and looking at Armenian-Turkish relations more broadly – is a difficult one. The difficulty is not only about historically understanding and unpacking people's experiences of the events of 1915. There are different academic and political networks, and to a degree these networks act as boundary control mechanisms to determine who belongs to which group. In some sense, all of these networks are working on the events of 1915. Probably the most contentious of all these highly contentious issues is the language one should use to talk about the events. There are also many discussions regarding the exact number of people massacred, what this number does or does not indicate and who should be considered responsible for the atrocities. Many people find their own way into these debates.

When you are a researcher, who will challenge you about what is always a little unpredictable. For instance, in Yerevan we went into an interview with the head of a local civil society group that works on historical documents and narratives and aims to keep the archive alive to think about the 'Armenian homeland'. As we shook hands to greet the director of the organization, he realized I was Turkish, and he said: 'The only good Turk is a dead Turk.' This was unexpected, to say the least; up to that point, no one in Yerevan had engaged with me personally in such a manner. However, we carried on discussing various issues as if nothing had happened. During the same period, as we talked to a highly respected civil society leader in Istanbul, my Armenian colleague was ignored entirely, and I was addressed in Turkish, in the full knowledge that my colleague did not speak Turkish. I was told that 'all these Armenian claims are unsupportable' and 'they are the product of diaspora, which is trying to undermine the integrity of the country'. There was also an underlying suspicion as to why I was working with an Armenian on this topic. It is hard to say which of these two experiences was worse. Both were unpleasant, but they were also very informative. Implicit in these individual positions was the measure used by various groups to judge the intentions behind one's engagement in the debate. People's own positions – as either majority Turkish or Armenian – lead to significant suspicions in relation to the Other, at least in the initial stages of the conversation. One gains some recognition only when one provides more insights into one's thinking, although sometimes even that is not straightforward.

After conducting our research in Yerevan and Istanbul in 2009, we organized two invitation-only workshops at the LSE in London. The aim was to present our findings to scholarly groups and also to bring together civil society representatives from each research site and elsewhere to have in-depth discussions about the challenges they faced. At one of these meetings, a London-based Armenian participant asked me: 'What is it to you, why do you work on this topic?' She asked, 'Do you have Armenian connection?', by which she meant a family connection. I said no. Then she asked: 'Do you have anyone involved in the genocide?' This time she was asking whether the older generations of my family had been involved in the genocide in some way and whether this was my way of coming to terms with that family history. I said not to my knowledge. Still she insisted, asking further questions about my family. I told her my knowledge was partial – although I knew my paternal family had a long history in Istanbul, I did not know about their positions or actions in 1915 or the period immediately afterwards, as that generation had died well before I was born, and my father had died when I was seven; as the last in my paternal family line, I did not have much information. On the maternal side too, I told her, the answer was no. Then I added that in any case I was interested in the issue regardless of my family past, because it mattered to me as a human being in relation to other human beings. As part of a society that had turned forgetting into a sociocultural factory for memory-making, I said, I was implicated in the issue. The woman's questions appeared to be very direct, but they were very useful in helping me to reflect on myself. I said I had certainly been educated by the process of thinking with absence, both in everyday life and within the education system. This made me party to the debate. Furthermore, as someone who – like most people in Turkey – had been formally trained in denialism, the national view claimed a position for me as a citizen; whether I agreed with it or not, I was implicated in Turkey's denialist position simply by virtue of being a Turkish citizen. When asked my views about the genocide claims, I told her, I was expected to answer in a particular way – regardless of what I really thought – if I wanted to signal and confirm my belonging to the national community. This made me responsible for thinking about my answer and disagreeing with the expectation. While this answer was acceptable to the woman at the workshop, many others may find it unsatisfactory.

There are various possible and typical attacks on scholars who take this public stance on the issues. These include a legal charge under Article 301 of the Turkish Penal Code on 'defamation of Turkish identity', which has been used against number of Turkish scholars and public intellectuals, although its use was limited by a revision in 2008 (see Tate 2014). Particularly because I use the concept of genocide immediately and directly, this raises questions, independently of the reasons I present for my own use of the concept. A typical claim is that as a Turkish scholar living outside Turkey, I might be trying to gain success by criticizing Turkey, playing into the hands of foreign powers for personal gain (see Gürsel 2015). In a different version of this claim, I might be asked why I am talking about this to foreigners, as doing so undermines the integrity of national solidarity and my implied belonging to it as a Turk. Other typical claims might move into more personalized attacks, undermining the scholar's integrity and insinuating bias by revealing some family link to Armenians in the distant past – or if that does not work, family links to some other, preferably non-Muslim minority in Turkey. For the accusers, this is arguably an attempt to show that one is producing this kind of work because one is genetically defective. The implication is that if you were 'really' Turkish, you would not ask these questions. The status of being 'really' Turkish seems to provide presumptive objectivity on these issues. It also carries the implicit claim that if we can show you are not Turkish, not one of us, what you say will not count. Most of these positions are attempts to assert a group identity in order to maintain or enforce solidarity with the public discourse.

This approach and its claims are based on an essentialized 'Turkishness' – on what Turks would or would not do. For individuals in the public eye, this creates a burden of responsibility to accord with the homogenized claims being made on their behalf. In other words, by being Turkish one is co-opted into the national position. One's supposed responsibility to share a discourse about forgetting and denial indicates another responsibility: the responsibility to resist and repudiate such positions of violence. For a critical social scientist who was brought up within the denialist ontology, this responsibility means studying the issues with an open mind and questioning supposedly natural truths about the events that are publicly endorsed.

Statements about *Ermeni Meselesi* and the presentation of the 1915 events as deportations (*tehcir*) are attempts to make parts of the past disappear from the public understanding. They attempt to create a memory that allows partial remembering. A consideration of the issue from the perspective of the genocidal process calls for different memories to be publicly available so as to enable the majority of Turkish society to think about 'others' and how they become Other through constitutive exclusion. One central issue is the fact that when part of a society disappears together with its history, the rest of the society not only intergenerationally forgets but also becomes involved in the reproduction of that forgetting. Intergenerationally, the public remembers memories from nowhere, as it were, about things it is sure *did not happen*. For me, this invokes a responsibility to think and act differently, implicit in Primo Levi's (2013: 231) statement: 'It happened, therefore it can happen again: this is the core of what we have to say.' I will come back to the implications of this statement later in the book. But now, I would like to focus on the term 'genocide' and why I think what happened in 1915–18 was indeed a genocide.

Were the events experienced by Armenians in 1915 a genocide?

The term 'genocide' was coined by Raphael Lemkin to give meaning to what was happening to the Jewish populations in Europe under the Nazi regime. In his 1944 articulation of the concept, he frames how one needs to think about the issue:

> Genocide does not mean the immediate destruction of a nation, except when accomplished by mass killings of all members of a nation. It is intended rather to signify a coordinated plan of different actions aiming at the destruction of essential foundations of the life of national groups, with the aim of annihilating the groups themselves. The objectives of such a plan would be the disintegration of the political and social institutions, of culture, language, national feelings, religion, and economic existence of national groups and the destruction of personal security, liberty, health, dignity, and even the lives of individuals belonging to such groups. (Lemkin 1944: 79–95)

Lemkin's work was important for the post-war engagement with crimes committed by the Nazis. It also led to the United Nations' (UN) Convention on the Prevention and Punishment of the Crime of Genocide (CPPCG), which was adopted by the UN General Assembly in 1948 and has been in force since 1951. The CPPCG has become part of international law, and its provisions have formed part of the legal discussions of various crimes committed since then. At present, over 140 states are party to the CPPCG. The Republic of Turkey acceded to it in 1950.

One of the main arguments of successive Turkish governments in relation to the events of 1915 has been that the CPPCG as a legal instrument cannot be applied to them retrospectively, particularly given that the Ottoman state ceased to exist once the republic was founded in 1923. The CPPCG is a legally binding document, but at the same time this generates two limitations. First, the definition of genocide has become closely linked to the convention, but most international conventions represent a compromised political outcome. Given that the CPPCG requires its signatories to involve themselves in steps to prevent any genocide, signatories are reluctant to use the concept to describe an ongoing situation. The case of Rwanda in 1994 is instructive in this regard. Second, given the chronology of events, the CPPCG and its encapsulation of the concept of genocide are closely associated with the Holocaust, and this gives the impression that the concept refers specifically to Jewish lives in Europe during the Second World War. In a different version of this, some denialists even insist that there must be similarities between the dynamics of the Holocaust and the dynamics of other political persecutions and violence if the latter are to be called genocide.

This second point imposes limitations on the perspectives of many commentators when they are asked to think about the Armenian genocide from this perspective. In addition to the chronological limitation, they regard the concept of genocide enshrined in the convention to be specific to the Holocaust. For instance, in an interesting book published in French as *Dialogue sur le tabou arménien* in 2009, and then in Turkish in 2010, the French scholar Michel Marian and the Turkish-French scholar Ahment İnsel discuss many aspects of the 'taboo' on Armenians in Turkey, providing different perspectives based on different experiences. The book offers a refined discussion by bringing in views from both sides. Although they seem to agree on many aspects of the situation, one issue that divides them is whether 1915 was a genocide, and the nuances of their disagreement are revealing of the impact of how the CPPCG frames the term 'genocide'. İnsel argues:

I don't find using the 'genocide' term appropriate. First, the term genocide is linked with the Jewish Holocaust in my mind, as it were, it is linked with killings that indiscriminately target anyone, from children to the elderly, to destroy a nation intentionally in a systematic and meticulous manner. (İnsel and Marian 2010: 110)

This is interesting, as further on in the discussion İnsel points out that the 'events of 1915 are very serious crimes against humanity, and the Ottoman government is directly responsible for these events' (Marian and İnsel 2010: 113). Nonetheless, he still says that he considers the term 'genocide' to be inappropriate because of its connotation of a confrontation or attempt by one nation to kill another. In the Armenian case, he says, it is hard to demonstrate this, as there were cases during the deportations where many Armenians were saved by Muslim Turks; therefore, he says, 'I can't use the term "genocide"' – although he goes on to say that if one uses Lemkin's definition, then 'this is a genocide' (Marian and İnsel 2010: 114).

This tension, as İnsel himself acknowledges, is about two difficulties: 'using the convention retrospectively', and using it 'to engage with all crimes against humanity' (İnsel and Marian 2010: 114). The tension is a synthetic problem, created by linking the concept of genocide as an analytical tool too closely to the legal framing provided by the UN convention. While there is a relationship between the two, there is no necessity to consider the legal document as embodying the limits of thinking about the term 'genocide'. Moreover, as Marian points out, Lemkin took account of the Armenian experience, and the events of 1915 provided him with material for the articulation of his concept of genocide. Therefore, even if the events of 1915 are chronologically prior to the legalization of the term under the UN convention, 'genocide' still has central value for thinking about the process to which Armenians were exposed in 1915.

It is clear that one needs to differentiate Lemkin's conceptual thinking about genocide from the UN convention's legalistic approach. The legal document restricts the scope of 'genocide' to large-scale massacres and murderous destruction. Moreover, limiting the use of the term to a legal description in an international document hinders us from thinking about the implications of the events of 1915 for Armenians, or for Turkey in general, after 1915. Lemkin's articulation takes account of attacks on a group's sociocultural infrastructure for the assessment of genocidal behaviour. This is important. Lemkin expands the concept by including the socio-economic and cultural sustainability of a community. He introduces a longitudinal perspective. It is in this aspect of the process that one observes the full scale of the issue of genocide: killing biological life is one aspect of the crime, but the attempt to remove any material and immaterial resources of community life is the last step in the creation of disposable people, communities and cultures. People are stripped of the sociological and cultural contexts of their lives, and this arguably targets the sociocultural underpinnings of group life; as a result, the people lose sense of their belonging, even if some of them ultimately survive. In this sense, Lemkin's original articulation provides a more comprehensive understanding than is available in the UN convention. It is on the basis of this broader conceptualization that I use the term 'genocide' in relation to the events of 1915 that targeted the Armenian population in the Ottoman Empire. In this way I do not limit my analysis to the events of 1915 themselves, and I can consider the implications of present-day denialism and how it frames knowledge in Turkey. My reflections on Ankara, discussed above, highlight the relevance of Lemkin's broader conceptualization. For instance, we need to reflect on the question of what it means to forget so comprehensively that Armenians ever lived in Ankara. However, this discussion will neither satisfy nor win agreement from those who are determined to disagree. Conceptual discussion is one thing, they will say, but why are you calling the events of 1915 a genocide when they were internal and planned movements of people, deportations carried out for security reasons?

Some might still argue that the arrests of 24 April 1915, which targeted sociopolitically and economically prominent Armenians in Istanbul, were purely custodial with no intention to kill, and that this is demonstrated by the fact that a few of those who had been arrested were sent back to Istanbul. However, the arrests sent a clear message to the Armenian community about the government's intentions. This message speaks to Lemkin's criteria: it was an attempt to break up sociopolitical and cultural institutions, with a clear threat to individual security. It is also important to acknowledge that Lemkin's conceptualization of genocide is about a process and what happens to a target group over time. In this regard, 24 April 1915 was a pivotal moment in that process, in relation to what happened to Armenian communities across Anatolia and their sustainability as living and functioning social structures and cultures for the next hundred years. This was both more evident and more drastic outside Istanbul, where whole populations were removed from the places where they lived, regardless of age, gender or social status. The issue of security is used as a historical justification for the deportations, on the grounds that Armenian gangs linked to the Armenian Revolutionary Federation (Dashnaktsutyun) were terrorizing people on the Eastern Front. There were indeed many such cases along the Ottoman Empire's Russian border and elsewhere, but it is hard to use this explanation to justify the removal of an entire religious (ethnic) community from the heart of the empire. In any case, not everyone supported or was affiliated with the Dashnaktsutyun, and even within the Dashnaktsutyun it was not the case that all members shared a common political understanding. There were many different views about the possible future political directions of Armenians in the empire (Tachjian, Adjemian and Davidian 2021). Previous research on these issues, which I will discuss later in this chapter, is persuasive in showing the different ways in which Armenian communities existed across the empire. This previous research is very much in line with the Lemkin-inspired view that the targeting of the Armenian population not only indicates genocidal intent but also provides evidence that the intention was carried out, as many of these publications map the absence of communities and lives. It is important to look more closely at Lemkin's conceptualization, as it is important to thinking through the temporality of the genocide as a process that was not limited to killings.

Lemkin's conceptualization of genocide not only gives us an appropriate lens to consider the events of 1915 but also challenges us to think about a period when the social and cultural existence of a whole community could be targeted. Thus, it can prevent our analysis from creating a superficial compartmentalization that focuses exclusively on what happened between 1915 and 1918 and takes little interest in what happened to Armenian life in Anatolia during the century that followed those violent events. Lemkin writes:

> Genocide has two phases: one, destruction of the national pattern of the oppressed group; the other, the imposition of the national pattern of the oppressor. This imposition, in turn, may be made upon the oppressed population which is allowed to remain or upon the territory alone, after the removal of the population and the colonization of the oppressor's own nationals. (Lemkin 1944: 74–5)

This conceptualization is much more challenging: rather than being an instance in time and space, it considers genocide as a longer process of the assimilation and disappearance of a group. Furthermore, it moves away from treating instances of mass killing (which are certainly crimes against humanity) as the only criterion to ascertain whether an event is or is not a genocide. Instead, it includes other long-term policies – such as use of particular language or educational and religious practices before and after the murderous moment – to undermine the survival of a social group or culture (see Sands 2017). This position allows us to evaluate policy practices before and after mass killings as parts of the genocidal process.

To summarize, Lemkin's critical contribution is to conceptualize genocide as a process that is not limited to the moment of its mass-murderous manifestation. This position also questions attempts to limit responsibility to those who are actually involved in mass killings. It looks at the process of killing the 'foundations of life' of a given community and at policies that seek to dismantle 'the political and social institutions, of culture, language, national feelings, religion, and economic existence of national groups and the destruction of personal security, liberty, health, dignity' (Lemkin 1944: 74–5). This also provides a way to understand conceptually where the issue of intentionality may be observed. The observation of intentionality is not only about identifying policies that directly planned and implemented mass murders. Intentionality is also found, for instance, in policies that were designed to absorb Armenian property and economic resources and to deal with the remaining sociocultural infrastructure. From this perspective, the 1915 events were part of a genocide not only because of the numbers of people killed but also because policies both before and afterwards targeted the existence of the community and the things that sustained the community's life (Polatel et al. 2012; Gust 2013; Ter Minassian 2015). Scholarship on the post-1915 Armenian experience has demonstrated the absence of this community and the disappearance of its economic and sociocultural infrastructure from the wider Turkey (Akçam and Kurt 2017; Kurt 2021). Furthermore, Lemkin's formulation suggests that part of the intentionality was about how Armenians were treated after the First World War. Under what conditions was survival possible? Were survivors allowed to return? Were those who did return allowed to reclaim their property? Previous research has answered these questions, sufficiently demonstrating for instance that after the deportations Armenian property was absorbed and 'Turkified' to such an extent that it would have been quite impossible for any returning survivors to have any kind of economic future (Esin and Etöz 2015). Lemkin's argument uncomfortably locates the discussion in the broader political context of the experiences of the victims of the 1915 events. This political context is a complex one and includes the disintegration of the Ottoman Empire, the upheavals of the Turkish War of Independence between 1919 and 1923 and the foundation of the Turkish republic at the end of that war through the Lausanne treaty. The treaty, which established the new Turkish republic, also recognized the minority rights of its non-Muslim population as citizens. Lemkin's conceptualization of genocide is most challenging of all for the *Ermeni Meselesi* framing, which has come to dominate the discussion in

Turkey today. It thus brings a whole set of post-1915 policy practices across the political continuum into the discussion, even though many commentators try to position the 1915 genocide as a self-contained event, the responsibility for which remains with the Ottoman administration of the day.

Methodology

How should I answer my central concern: to understand what cognitive resources were available to the public that would allow them to engage in the discussions on the Armenian genocide. My initial analysis of different aspects of the research had revealed that there was a grammar for speaking about Armenians and the Armenian genocide in Turkey. The grammatical analogy is important, as it highlights that there are norms and rules, just as in any linguistic system that one uses to make sense to others who use the same language. Certain ways of speaking – using specific language and conceptual reference points to conceptualize an issue – allow speech to become comprehensible to a given audience. The grammatical structure signals linguistic reference points that enable comprehensibility and allow the speaker to be categorized as belonging (or not) to a group. I had observed this grammatical or linguistic structure when speaking or writing on the Armenian genocide in ways that would be comprehensible (or incomprehensible) to the public in Turkey. Language use mattered. It was through the language used that people in Turkey learned what they knew about these issues, and it was through the language they heard that they remembered what they knew. Thus, my initial analysis motivated me to think about how the understanding of these issues in Turkey was structured within a specific language that signified knowledge about those issues. Furthermore, the idea of grammar allows analysis of intergenerational reproduction of denialism and how it is maintained, and monitored, through norms and values embedded in specific use (in speaking, thinking and writing) of linguistic constructions. Therefore, I focused on public memory as the domain of this knowledge signified by language use, and on how public memory facilitated individuals' and the wider public's recall of what was known about specific issues that mattered in society. In the next chapter I will outline this approach as the conceptual apparatus guiding this study. Here, I will discuss the research process that refined both my question and the orientation of my methods.

As a qualitative social scientist working on current social issues, I normally conduct interviews of various kinds, collect oral histories and conduct focus groups and workshops, in addition to literature reviews and documentary analyses. In these ways I aim to understand people's experiences of policies that target their well-being. However, as I began new fieldwork in Istanbul in October 2014, during which I intended to study the run-up to the centennial of the genocide in April 2015, I realized that my usual approach would be difficult to utilize, as the events and their initial implications would be hard to trace on the basis of interviews with individuals. For instance, it was not possible to conduct interviews with people who had relocated to Istanbul after 1918, after the deportations and massacres, in order to understand the environment within which they had found themselves. How had they been received, and had they been able to talk about their experiences? What had happened after 1923, with the advent of the new republic? My usual methods would not answer these questions.

Instead, I decided to conduct a set of interviews with Armenian Turks in Turkey, to produce oral history-based information about their experiences of everyday life. I thought this would be a good starting point to position the research. However, a number of issues made me adjust this approach too. One issue was the difficulty I quickly encountered when I tried to interview people within the Armenian community in Turkey. There were important questions about trust, and this in itself yielded important insights about the community's current experience. The trust issue was partially associated, sometimes implicitly and sometimes explicitly, with fears about the implications of any engagement with my research. This was of course a serious concern for me too. Whatever I did should not have negative effects on the community.

Another initial research finding that reorientated my thinking was the availability of publications in Turkish, including those arising from a number of oral history research projects during the last decade in Turkey. Many books have been published and/or translated in Turkey on the question of the genocide (see Akçam 2008, 2010, 2014; Göçek 2014; Suny, Göçek and Naimark 2015). These include books on the dynamics of the Union and Progress Party, which constituted the political leadership of the Ottoman government at the time and whose decision-making led to the genocidal violence. Some books, for instance, consider the role of Talat Pasha as grand vizier, and of figures such as Enver Pasha and Cemal Pasha, the party and government's other leaders at the time. Even Talat Pasha's personal documents have been published (Bardakçı 2008; Sarafian 2011). Other publications focus on the Armenian population in Anatolia in the early part of the twentieth century. These include the above-mentioned work by Köker, and his subsequent work, demonstrating the wide spread of the Armenian population across Anatolia. Raymond H. Kévorkian and Paul B. Paboudjian's book is also very important. Originally published in France in 1992 as *Les Arméniens dans l'Empire Ottoman à la veille du génocide*, it appeared in Turkish translation in 2012 under the title *Armenians in the Pre-1915 Ottoman Empire* (also see Der Matossian 2022).

While Köker's volumes provide a wide-ranging sense of everyday life in Armenian communities across Anatolia and link people to locations, Kévorkian and Paboudjian's work gives in-depth substance to these communities' lives. It painstakingly documents the Armenian existence in Anatolia in terms of its social and cultural infrastructure, providing numbers of households (as far as this is possible) for each community as well as numbers of institutions such as churches, orphanages, schools and hospitals, in addition to actual maps. The authors manage to create an almost three-dimensional understanding of Armenian life. Similarly, studies produced by the Hrant Dink Foundation on sociocultural heritage in specific cities in Turkey, which have been brought together in a project entitled *Turkey Cultural Heritage Map*, demonstrate the wealth of Armenian culture and social relations that existed across Anatolia before 1915 (HDV 2018). The foundation has also published oral history-based accounts of Armenian lives in different cities in Turkey, drawing on interviews with a cross-section of the population – young and old, male and female and from different professions. These accounts provide well-formed and in-depth data to pinpoint the issues people face today (see Balancar 2012, 2013, 2015, 2016). Together with these, number of publications on denialism in Turkey were also available. In this, Göçek's *Denial of Violence* (2014) is a seminal work. It significantly shows that the denial of genocidal violence began in 1915 and was subsequently reproduced in different stages of the foundation of the Turkish republic until today. The analysis provides an important corrective against the official historiography that had emerged to construct the national imagination of the new Turkish republic. Göçek's focus also allows many researchers, like me, to understand the implications of the continuities between the late Ottoman period and early Republican period. The book by considering the trajectory of the denial in Turkey highlights multiple pathways for the enculturation of the public into denialist existence. In this regard Seyhan Bayraktar's work is also relevant (2015). She aims to identify shifts in denialist discourse by studying 'critical discourse moments' at the juncture of international events/discussions impacting Turkey. Through this lens she develops a periodization of denial discourses. Assassination of Turkish diplomats by ASALA from 1974 onwards is identified as the critical moment, as a watershed for 'a new era in Turkish denialism' as 'ASALA managed to break Turkish silence about Armenian issue' (Bayraktar in Savelsberg 2021: 99). No doubt this periodization allows researchers to map out different discourses (for instance see Turan and Öztan 2018). However, used as a heuristic to understand the genocide denialism in Turkey, I argue, the periodization does not allow understanding denialist continuity and the structural sources of reproduction of the denialist positions in Turkey. Reflecting on my own analysis I diverge from considering the pre-1974 period as a period of some kind of silence about the Armenian genocide. I argue that the assumed silence observed in Turkey was and is produced for decades through public policies designed to exclude, marginalize and penalize minorities in Turkey. The period in which the assumed silence is observed in fact was a deeply dynamic period for public policy in producing and reproducing denialist and racist conditions of institutionalized denialism in Turkey. I think not only this silence observed needs to be explained, as Göçek argues (2014: 54), but also impact of such apparent silence at the present needs to be studied.

Another publication worth mentioning here is Ahmet Tetik and Cihan Güneş's (2014) translation of *Karen Jeppe's Documents on Aleppo Refuges 1922–1927*. The book provides direct translations of entry documents, with photos of the Armenians in question, including large numbers of children, who ended up in Aleppo. Many of the children's entries contain a brief story about how they ended up in the orphanage. The book contains information about 1,184 people. Reading through these individual cases, contra the framing provided by the authors (who frame them as inevitable results of the war, rather than as a population that was being targeted), reveals the process that led to the destruction of lives and communities, as a collective picture of events gradually emerges from each individual story. There are of course many other books, and all of these taken together provide a very comprehensive view of Armenian lives. As fascinating historical documents, they create an effective challenge to most Turkish people's sense of reality, in which Armenians are marginal or mentioned only as aggregate numbers. The broader research reported in these publications immediately raises a number of questions. Where now are the communities that created these sociocultural relations and institutions, these structures and the life associated with them? What happened to the material existence of these thousands of sociocultural institutions? As in Akçam's (2008, 2010, 2014) work, Tetik and Güneş (2014) hint at the calamitous answer to these questions. There are also publications based on personal accounts by various people who were arrested on 24 April 1915 and survived to tell their stories, and these provide important insights (Balakyan 2014; Odyan 2022). Another aspect of these publications is their ability to provide discussions, sometimes implicitly, of whether what happened in 1915 was a deportation policy or – as the titles suggest – a matter of genocide (see Suny et al. 2015). In the run-up to the centennial yet more volumes were published, including Kévorkian's comprehensive 2006 work *Le Génocide des Arméniens*, translated in full into Turkish under the title *Ermeni Soykırımı* in 2015. Further questions have been raised in relation to the overall process – including the deportations, the patterns of violence many Armenian communities experienced and the way in which communities were destroyed – which throw doubt on the justifications given for the deportations (see Adanır and Özel 2015; Çelik and Dinç 2015; Çubukçu et al. 2015).

The existence of these books altered how I wanted to conduct my research. I decided to collect as many books as I could on Armenian topics published in Turkey, in order to establish an archive. This included the books mentioned above, and also books that broadly objected to the genocide claims in order to establish the Turkish position on the issue – that is, denialist books. As the research began to focus more on the cognitive resources that facilitated the thinking of the Turkish majority about the Armenian genocide, I decided to follow public print and visual media in the run-up to the centennial. Another approach I decided to take was to attend public discussions of 1915, such as conferences and meetings. This was very interesting, as it allowed me to sit in places where the public discourse was operationalized to affirm denialism by reproducing particular lines of discussion. Again, this was a rather difficult process.

I cannot claim that this was pure or standard participant observation. Indeed, in a number of cases it was impossible for me to inform the organizers about the research I was conducting or to seek their consent for my participation in their conference or discussion. To do so would at best have disqualified me from participating and at worst provoked hostile reactions. Nonetheless, I decided that these public events were too important to miss and that I would participate as an interested social scientist. This was an ambiguous position, given the content of the discussions, and I struggled to find a way of thinking about my position during these events. Should I intervene and object to the discussion taking place, or was I there just to observe the nature of the discussion as a researcher? In such situations, I felt morally challenged, as most of the time the discussions assumed the audience's agreement about the content, soliciting complicity. Notwithstanding this, these events were informative not only about the language of the discussion, which provided a part of the cognitive resources, but also about the mechanisms of their use in public. During and after this period, I also attended a number of events organized by different people, including Armenian Turks, non-Turkish Armenians and members of the Muslim-Sunni Turkish majority who agreed with the view that the events of 1915 amounted to genocide. At these events I followed the same procedure and did not inform the organizers about my research, so that there would be some parity in the way I observed the different types of events. It was interesting to compare what I observed with the ways in which the media reported (or in most cases did not report) these events, which helped me to understand the deployment of a particular public language to inform the non-Armenian majority. Another part of the research involved following Turkish media, documents and debates to trace the conceptual framing of the discussions.

The archive I developed through these pathways included news items collected over time from Turkish media that attempted to show that the genocide claim did not stand up to scrutiny. In their claims and their use of material to develop their arguments, I found different memories compared with those narrated in oral histories published in Turkey about Armenian life, then and now. My engagement with the mass media was also motivated by its importance for access to news in Turkey. According to a survey conducted in Turkey in 2018, 'when asked "how often do you read newspapers?", 57.5 % of respondents replied "I do not read newspapers"' (Aydın et al. 2019). The report observed a shift towards accessing news on the internet. It also highlighted that over 90 per cent of people watched television every day, ranging from less than an hour (5.7 per cent) to more than five hours (21.3 per cent), with most respondents falling between those extremes (67.3 per cent) (Aydın et al. 2019). These findings confirmed the gradual decline already observed in the 2014 report *Citizenship in Turkey and in the World*, which had stated that 20 per cent of Turkish citizens read a newspaper every day, and 16 per cent did so three or four times a week. This earlier report had also found a shift from newspapers to television as a news source, pointing out that 61 per cent of citizens watched political news on television every day, and 17 per cent did so three or four days a week (Kalaycıoğlu and Çarkoğlu 2014). However, the observed decline in newspaper reading does not mean that newspaper content does not reach a significant number of people. The link between newspaper ownership and TV channel ownership in Turkey, in addition to the participation of many journalists in TV discussion programmes, allows newspaper content to inform what is communicated on television. This is particularly evident in political news. The two wings of my research – participant observation on one hand, and media analysis on the other – allowed me to develop my analysis of the ways in which the public discourse constructed a view of Armenians that negated their memories.

My analysis in this book looks at the public discourse on the Armenian genocide in Turkey through this lens. It focuses on the language used to discuss these issues. The language not only provides the norms and rules of comprehensibility but also silences and erases. The book focuses on spaces where this language is enacted in normalized ways to communicate with the public so as to facilitate their understanding of the questions raised above. In turn, the use of specific language can also be seen as a mechanism to monitor the conditions of membership of the national community in Turkey.

An outline of the book

The book seeks to understand how denialism is produced intergenerationally for the majority, who are also in some ways descendants of the perpetrators of the genocide. Given the refinements to the project discussed above, in Chapter 2, I take a theoretical look at the mechanism of how 'we' retrieve what 'we' know about 'our' history in Turkey. In this way, I outline the theoretical apparatus that structures my analysis in the book. I argue that the relationship between public memory, the mechanisms of recall/remembering and what is remembered frames how Armenians and the events of 1915 are understood in Turkey. This understanding is based on the construction of the majority's identity, that is, Turkishness. I develop a view of a set of narratives that constitute the memory repertoire that is available for the public to remember the events of 1915 in Turkey (also see Savelsberg 2021). Given my positionality discussed above, I put 'we', 'us' and 'our' in scare quotes to highlight the significant tension and disagreement between my own position as an individual social researcher and the language used in these debates in Turkey, which enforces belonging regardless of what one thinks about these questions.

Another way to think about this is to use the analogy of the iron cage, in this case the iron cage of denialism. I consider these narratives as constitutive of the repertoire that underwrites the rationality of denialism. This is diffused and sedimented by the use of specific language that comes to represent rules and norms of speaking, thinking and acting on the basis of public memory. In its repetitive deployment, this limits what can be known and thought in this field. In what follows, I focus on the mechanisms within which people as members of the public find themselves as the context of their sociability.

Before I look closely at the specific mechanisms of denialism, I begin in Chapter 3 with the way in which denialism manifested itself around the commemoration of the genocide on 24 April 2015. Empirically, I focus on the period leading up to the commemoration, the commemoration day itself and subsequent days, to present the deployment of public memory narratives around this period. Chapter 4 focuses on the role of the media, which reproduced some of the narratives in order to prompt the public to think in particular ways through received knowledge. I consider how what people remember through the mass media reinforces the public memory repertoire, facilitating their engagement with or resistance to discussions of the genocide. Chapter 5 moves on to analyse the grounds of these narratives for public use as previously given knowledge that is then recalled at particular times. The focus of this chapter is on the formal education system and its central role in the intergenerational reproduction of denialism. Chapter 6, the penultimate chapter, analyses how academic research in Turkey, and its framing of what we need to know about the events of 1915, is publicly communicated through a number of spaces, including academic conferences and documentaries developed for TV audiences in Turkey. Chapter 7 concludes the book by first summarizing its argument. This summary highlights that in each public engagement, solidarity with the public memory repertoire is expected and required as a performance of being Turkish. This chapter also answers several questions that might be asked about the book. Finally, it provides a set of policy suggestions to tackle the rationality created by the naturalization of denialism in Turkish society.

The aim of the book is not to provide an all-encompassing analysis of the different ways in which questions about the Armenian genocide might be answered in Turkey. Instead, it focuses on the conditions that create the public understanding. It essentially focuses on the central mechanisms that create denialism, by providing a close reading of different materials that claim to provide the public with knowledge about these issues. Even when one is analysing different media and spaces of communication, the provision of knowledge in those spaces simply repeats the same narratives in different configurations in different instances. No doubt this approach conveys a sense of the claustrophobic social context. I use extensive resources in Turkish throughout the text. I have translated these myself, as a native Turkish speaker educated in Turkey. My approach to analysing how the public's understanding is framed by knowledge practices will also have broader applications beyond the Turkish case.

2

The memory machine
The Armenian genocide in Turkey

On 24 April 2015, the day of the centennial of the Armenian genocide, the commemorations began with a gathering of people in the Harbiye district of Istanbul. Those who wanted to attend were asked to arrive in the morning in front of a pharmacy called Republic (Cumhuriyet) on the broad, tree-lined Republic Avenue (Cumhuriyet Caddesi), which connects Taksim Square with the city's Şişli, Nişantaşi and Kurtuluş districts. The building was indistinguishable from the other apartment buildings along the avenue. The crowd was large enough for people to spill over into the road, narrowing the space available for traffic. The gathering filled the pavement in front of the pharmacy. Some people held placards showing photos of Armenians who had been arrested in Istanbul on the night of 24 April 1915 (the cover photo of this book was taken at this event). Some of the placards were being carried by descendants of those who had been arrested and died. Many people took photos of the placards that lined the pavement as those carrying them moved about and talked to one another. There was a megaphone to inform attendees about the proceedings in Turkish and English. People waited to see what the next steps would be. Passing cars honked their horns, but their reasons were not clear: some drivers may have heard about the event and were honking in support, some may have been honking in protest and some perhaps simply did not know what was happening and were honking because people were standing in the road. A speech by an Armenian Turk was delivered in Turkish and then translated into Armenian. He talked about the significance of the gathering to remember on that day, and about why the meeting was taking place in front of this particular building: it was the building where Gomidas Vartabet, an important priest and musician, and Dr Avedis Nakhashian, a well-known doctor, had been arrested on the night of 24 April 1915. The two arrested men were later sent into exile. There were two temporary black plaques bearing their names on the pavement, and people left flowers around them. We were also told that Şişli district's local authority had agreed to erect permanent plaques to commemorate them (although on subsequent visits I saw no sign of these). Then we were asked to follow the speakers for 100 metres, to a street just off the main avenue, and gather in front of a building that looked like old houses newly converted into a hotel. An elderly woman introduced this location as the house where her great uncle Dr Rupen Sevag (Çilingiryan) had lived and from which he had been taken on the night of 24 April 1915. Again, there was a temporary black plaque on the ground, next to a placard bearing his photo. As we were told about his short life – he had been born in 1885 and killed in 1915 – tourists looked out of some of the windows of the new hotel. It was a surreal situation: there we were, commemorating a catastrophic event, listening to deeply sad reflections on what had happened to a young man in 1915; but we were in a side street with loud traffic passing along the avenue, pedestrians walking past us and tourists looking down from their hotel windows at what for them seemed to be just another interesting event in Istanbul.

When I reflected later on this particular act of commemoration at the pharmacy and the hotel, I realized it had been yet another moment of coming to terms with what is publicly unknown in the everyday life of Istanbul. These were not unknown locations per se: Republic Avenue is one of Istanbul's central thoroughfares, and people go along it regularly – albeit perhaps without paying much attention to the pharmacy that stands there. The pharmacy is no different from any of the other pharmacies in Istanbul. I personally must have passed by it many times while walking to Taksim Square or to Şişli via Harbiye. When I had heard that the gathering was going to be at this pharmacy, I had remembered where it was only as a physical space; I had not recalled anything significant about the location. But as I heard the speakers' words, it became clear that for some people living in the city, these apparently nondescript buildings and streets held different, significant memories imbued with sociocultural and political meanings, and those memories and meanings were part of who they were. For Armenians, things in Istanbul that appear nondescript to me and most other non-Armenians are reminders not only of the past but also of a present in which that past is not easy to broach publicly.

Interestingly, these instances of remembering – the memories of the general public, and the memories of the Armenian speakers – were not independent of each other. Each said something about the other. The content of what they said was contentious, as each provided a commentary both on the past and on present-day belonging. I reflected that the public memory that was available to and used by the majority acted as a master narrative to evaluate and control the other memories that existed in Turkish society. It was clear that what I had learned about the city had been insufficient to give me the capacity to remember what the Armenians had remembered in this instance. This is about the politics of creating a public memory that underpins the idea of shared history, which in turn suggests the existence of a community, in this case, a national community. At the same time, this attempt to create a shared history obliterates other possibilities – in this case, Armenian histories that relate to Armenians' own experiences as part of that shared past. Thus, it is also a demand by Others to become part of the public memory that is being created. To think alongside Marc Nichanian (2015), remembering and becoming a subject in relation to what is remembered publicly can be seen as the destruction of another way of being. The creation of a public memory that demands compliance is a process of negating any other alternatives. It also constructs those whose different memories resist it as strangers that do not belong. Being of the place and yet not considered to belong, they cannot be perceived by the majority.

A conversation I overheard while standing in front of the Cumhuriyet pharmacy during the commemoration event provides an interesting insight into this. While the speeches were being delivered amid the numerous images of people who had been arrested and deported on 24 April 1915, I heard a low voice immediately behind me talking in Turkish to someone on the phone. The speaker addressed the other person as *amirim*, which corresponds to 'chief' or 'sir' – a way of addressing a superior officer. He was probably a plain-clothes police officer reporting on what was going on. He said:

> Yes, it seems these are all foreigners here. Just that woman, the lawyer woman, is Turkish. No, all of them are like foreigners, holding up pictures of some men. Oh, all these men apparently were born around 1878 and died in 1915. It is written like that [referring to the placards]. They must have died around same age, very young. No, they are just reading some things.

He carried on making his report, and towards the end of the event he informed the other person that he was going to follow some of the participants to the Armenian cemetery in Şişli for another centennial event. The interesting issue for me was how he read the crowd as foreigners participating in the event. This was made all the more interesting by his reference to 'the lawyer woman' as the only Turkish person in the crowd. This indicates that he had probably recognized her from his previous observations of other demonstrations – perhaps those taking place around the ongoing trial of Hrant Dink's killers. So, he recognized 'the lawyer woman', but he did not have the cognitive resources to understand who these others were, why they were participating in the event or what the event was about. No doubt there were many people from outside the country who had come to participate in the centennial events. However, the police officer did not understand that the main speech was by a local Armenian-Turkish person, given in Armenian and translated into Turkish. He did not even mention the presence of another Turkish citizen: Garo Paylan, an Armenian-Turkish politician and activist, a hard-to-miss tall person who stood next to the speaker throughout the speech. The officer clearly did not perceive that many of the participants were locals and were in fact engaging with their own history, which was also about claiming their belonging as an integral part of the history of the city and the society. Perhaps he did not perceive that Armenians could be local people. While the officer expressed surprise at the short lives of the deported, he again had no way of contextualizing who these people had been and why they had died so young. He clearly did not have the cognitive resources to remember these people or this community as part of 'our' society and history. He did not know.

I am often asked why I even want to talk about memories. I am told that they are subjective. I am also told that the concept of memory is far too imprecise and unhelpful, because it treats subjective emotions as the basis for remembering, rather than what might really have happened in the past. Therefore, it is suggested, memory is too ambiguous a concept to use to study how people think about the Armenian genocide in Turkey. My response to these criticisms and suggestions is inspired by Paul Ricoeur's (2004: 21) view that 'we have nothing better than memory to signify that something has taken place, has occurred, has happened before we declare we remember it'. This view has moved my thinking towards looking at memory as a public process. The process helps one to make sense of one's position as belonging (or not) in a community, a position that is clear to one's fellow community members. In this process, the content of what is remembered is created for the public to use.

Ricoeur thinks about memory not only as a snapshot of the past but also as a process in which people make sense of how that past unfolds in a particular way. He considers memory to be about the 'social representation of the past, understanding an unfolding of events, conjectures and structures that punctuate this historical past' (Ricoeur 2004). If this is a reasonable way of thinking, then the question is what happens when there is a gap or even a contradiction between the public memory through which most members of society identify with each other in public and the memories of a specific community in relation to the history of their relationships within that society. The question here is about the role of public memory as a process or filter that signifies something as an absence, as something that did not happen and therefore cannot be represented or remembered. Moreover, this concerns not only events that happened but also people that lived and whether the question of what happened to those lives can be asked or not. The above-identified gap between public memory and collective or group memory is not accidental. It is politically constituted to think about and differentiate between what the public majority remembers and what the community targeted by genocidal violence remembers. The public memory is constituted to invalidate the latter.

On balance, therefore, I think that an analysis of public memory is a relevant entry point to understand how remembering (or forgetting), which gradually creates an absence, actively constitutes discussions of the Armenian genocide in Turkey. Ricoeur's (2004: 56) argument is informative: 'The verb "to remember" stands in for the substantive "memory." What the verb designates is the fact that memory is "exercised".' The idea of *memory exercised* suggests that remembering is an activity and a process, and as such there is an intentionality to remembering. It involves people wanting to recall something, and their capacity to recall it. Thus, one can talk about people's ability to recognize the content of what is being recalled in order for that thing to be remembered.

The relationship between what prompts one to recall and what can be remembered is important. It is questionable whether one can remember something unless it is a part of the social comprehensibility that frames one's capacity to understand – even in cases where the question that prompts the activity challenges those social considerations. Nonetheless, in order to understand how and what people apprehend in discussions of the Armenian genocide in Turkey, it is important to unpack what is remembered as memory, and how the activity of remembering is guided in these discussions towards privileged 'things' as 'generalities that can be termed as "state of affairs"' (Ricoeur 2004: 23). This also requires a focus on the mechanisms that reproduce the 'what' of the remembered. In this chapter, I first elaborate on how I think about the processes of memory and memory-making, that is, remembering. I take remembering, and what is constructed as memory, as a social and political process within which people are located as the agents of remembering. This centrally suggests that there is something to remember. Forgetting, in this process, does not mean the absence of something to remember. If one tries to remember, one can reach out or be guided towards what might have been forgotten. I argue that in the act of remembering, a public memory is reiterated as an understanding of a given event by individuals. However, it is also the case that there may be absences – not a simple forgetfulness but the non-existence of something to remember. One cannot be guided towards an absence without knowing what might be absent in the first place (see Navaro 2020).

I therefore argue that public memory in Turkey is about creating absences of Armenians (and others) that contain nothing about events or people who lived and died to be recalled or remembered. There is nothing in the public memory to signify that they ever existed. But this applies to the Sunni-Muslim Turks that constitute the public majority. For Armenian Turks, the situation manifests itself differently, as a process of silencing (see Trouillot 2015). They remember those who lived and were murdered, and how it all happened. These memories are silenced in the context of the national memorialization of the past, as I will discuss later in this chapter. However, what is silenced – as opposed to what is erased – can be voiced and publicly remembered. In this sense, for me, the discussion of memory and remembering is inflected by thinking about forgetting, silencing and erasing – who forgets what, who is silenced, who erases what and why.

Public memory and remembering as a process

The process of remembering is no doubt an individual one, but it is not an isolated exercise that takes place in a vacuum. In an individual's act of remembering, the memories that are produced are inherently social and contextual. As Maurice Halbwachs (1997: 94) argues, 'all individuals remember as members of a group'. His point here is not that everyone has the same memory, but that 'each individual memory represents a point of view on the collective memory [*un point de vue sur la mémoire collective*]' (Halbwachs 1997: 94). This importantly highlights the general framing provided by collective memory as the source for individuals' remembering, depending on their position in the group. For instance, when reflecting on Armenians in general, or answering questions about what happened during 1915 or whether those events constituted a genocide, individuals produce answers that are related to the memory of these events that is available to them. In the process of answering or participating in a discussion, they reiterate group thinking in public. This in turn publicly legitimates what is remembered as the source for others in the same group to use to answer similar questions. The role of significant public figures in this reiteration process is important, as their discussions can become part of the memory of the issue: public figures socialize certain ways of remembering. Let me give two examples.

The first took place on 6 August 2014, during the run-up to the Turkish presidential elections. At this time, Recep Tayyip Erdoğan was the prime minister. Talking during a TV interview about unfounded political attacks on him, and on a particularly personal note, he said: 'Well, excuse me [*afedersiniz*], but they said even uglier things [*çirkin şeyler*] and said that I was Armenian' (Bianet 2014). In addition to the explicitness of 'even uglier', his tone clearly highlighted his great surprise and feeling of insult at being called Armenian. The second example dates from March 2015. The Justice and Development Party's (Adalet and Kalkinma Partisi, AKP) Melih Gökçek, who at the time was the mayor of Greater Ankara, decided to sue the Armenian-Turkish journalist Hayko Bağdat because of his suggestion in a tweet that Gökçek might be Armenian (Diken 2015). The court case was based on the accusation that Bağdat's tweet had led to 'libel and slander together with incitement of hatred and hostility towards the mayor and his electorate'. The mayor's lawyer argued that the accused had targeted a well-loved public personality by using 'a word that has a disgusting meaning and infringed his rights'. The court found the journalist guilty and issued him with a fine (Onedio 2015). The first of these examples gains importance because the statement was made by a socially and politically popular politician. He was clearly making a statement about the inappropriateness of being called Armenian. What is described as inappropriate is being a thing – Armenian – that Erdoğan seems unable even to mention without saying 'excuse me' (*afedersiniz*). The description not only positions being Armenian as a questionable state but also publicly establishes the label as an insult. The second example is a more explicit manifestation of this situation: the court formally decided that suggesting that someone was Armenian was punishable because it was slander.

Erdoğan, the court, Gökçek and his lawyers were reproducing sentiments and ways of thinking that pinpointed how to remember Armenians in Turkish society. Given the social positions they occupied, they were also providing legitimacy to that kind of thinking and authorizing others in society to use similar language. While their statements were based on existing tropes, by reiterating them in this way they reinforced the reference points of public memory related to Armenians in Turkey. These reference points in turn became habitual for others who might try to remember what they know about Armenians in order to engage in such discussions. The social process I am describing here closely relates to Halbwachs's account of how the reconstruction of memory works:

Reconstruction must operate on the basis of shared information or notions, to be found both in our minds and those of others, because they move ceaselessly and reciprocally from one to another, which is only possible if they have both been and continue to be part of the same society. (Halbwachs 1997: 63)

In this sense, the above statements reiterate shared information, making it familiar to others, with regard to a memory of belonging to society that is established against Armenians. This approach also homogenizes peoples on both sides of the debate.

When one hears a conversation about the events of 1915 or is asked a direct question about them, one tries to find a way of replying. The reply is often based on the repertoire one has about those events in one's mind. Statements such as those discussed earlier, and more importantly the sentiments they embody, become part of the repertoire one uses when one wants to take part in such discussions. Looking at the process of remembering in terms of the content and where that content comes from helps me to reflect on the capacity that available sources of apprehending the Armenian genocide provide in public debates in Turkey. One reaches out metaphorically to something to produce one's responses in those debates. If we follow Ricoeur's (2004: 4) statement that 'to remember is to have a memory or to set off in search of a memory', answering a question or taking part in a discussion involves searching for something about the subject. One searches for a memory of that subject. The above-discussed utterances of the word 'Armenian' (*Ermeni*) create reference points that become habitual guides in this search for a memory. Similarities in the language used and the sentiments communicated provide ideas that guide one's search for the available memory of Armenians or the Armenian genocide to inform one's views (Halbwachs 1997: 177). When I say that I reach out for a memory, this is about trying to find what is known to *me* on a subject, but it is also about finding the right language to form an answer to a question that will be comprehensible in my group or community. There is a sense of the givenness of knowledge about an event and its comprehensibility in my context. It is in this givenness of the knowledge about both the subject matter and the appropriate language that we observe the social nature of memory as a collective public activity. It is public, but it produces an impact when it is operationalized by individuals' remembering. I agree with Sarah Gensburger (2016: 403) that the analytical approach is about 'considering the individual as the site through which society exists and therefore the place where the social dynamic of memory takes place'.

Another way of thinking about the social nature of remembering is to consider what we can understand from individuals' statements about what they remember. Elizabeth Anscombe's (2000) work on intentional action 'under the description' is relevant here. She argues that 'a human action is intentional if the question of "why?", taken in a certain sense (and evidently conceived as addressed to him), has application' (Anscombe 2000: paras 5–8). If in response to 'why' I can give the reasons behind my action, then my action is intentional. Thus, answering a question or taking a particular position in a discussion is an intentional action: I give an answer in the way I want to express my thoughts about a discussion or a question concerning the events of 1915. Someone can ask why I answered that question in that way – the 'why' of the content of my answer. For instance, hypothetically, why did I say it was not a genocide but a security measure that led to many people dying? I can explain why I answered the question in that way by utilizing what I know to be the facts of the matter, for which I reached to produce my answer. So, in Anscombe's sense, these facts known to me describe why I answered the question in that way. What I know is framed by what I remember and consider to be appropriate on the basis of what I have been taught, experienced, observed and heard in my everyday life. Ultimately, my answer is produced through this socially framed memory – and given the sources of my knowing the facts of the matter, my answer is certainly underwritten by collective or public knowledge. Reflecting on the sources of the descriptions we use to provide reasons for our actions, Ian Hacking (1995) argues that 'the array of descriptions available to an individual depend on the descriptions available to the society in which the individual resides'. He then lists those who provide the descriptions available in a society: 'The media, the expertise of psychologists, physicians and scientist as well as the folk understanding of cultural communities' (Hacking 1995).

In an interview, Jan Assmann describes a similar process:

> Cultural memory is not the same as personal memory; it's a kind of collective memory that develops through communication, through language, or, in other words, within a context of socialization. . . . Cultural memory is manifested in communication and participation in living memory, in a process which takes different forms, encompassing rituals, meals, the landscape. (2013)

So, both in reaching out for a memory and in what gets remembered at the end of that process, we observe an activity that is socially grounded, as Halbwachs (2015: 175) argues. In this, it is not only the content of what is remembered that is socially constructed; the reaching out, the possibility of remembering, is also conditioned by the shared reference points that are available to, comprehensible to and authorized for people to use in a community. It is this kind of memory that I call public memory. Perhaps it is similar to what Ricoeur (2004: 85) describes as 'trained memory . . . instructed memory . . . thus enlisted in the service of remembrance of those events belonging to the common history that are held to be remarkable, even founding, with respect to the common identity'. This view of memory enables me to analyse the contours of public memory related to the Armenian genocide, which is allowed limited space to be remembered in Turkey. It enables my analysis to focus on the manifestations of remembering and forgetting that are implicit in the language people use in public. It also opens up a possibility to trace the mechanisms that reproduce and maintain this public memory by limiting what can be remembered in public discussions.

What do I remember through the public memory?

In order to highlight the use of memory as an entry point to understand the content of what is remembered, I will look at two public declarations that came as unexpected interventions in public debates on Armenians and the Armenian genocide. My aim is to show how the two public statements used existing sources of memory to develop a position that in turn became a guide for others in society to remember. The first declaration was by Erdoğan as prime minister in 2014; the second was by Ahmet Davutoğlu as prime minister in 2015. Watching Turkish TV on the evening of 23 April 2014, we suddenly saw a news ticker on our screens announcing a statement by Erdoğan to mark 24 April that was addressed to Turkish Armenians. The statement said:

> 24 April carries particular significance for our Armenian citizens and for all Armenians around the world, and it provides a valuable opportunity to freely share opinions on a historical matter. It is indisputable that the last years of the Ottoman Empire were a difficult period, full of suffering for Turks, Kurds, Arabs, Armenians and millions of other Ottoman citizens, regardless of their religion or ethnic origin. Any conscientious, fair and humanistic approach to these issues requires an understanding of all the sufferings endured in this period, without discrimination as to religion or ethnicity.... Nevertheless, using the events of 1915 as an excuse for hostility against Turkey and turning this issue into a matter of political conflict is inadmissible. The incidents of World War I are our shared pain. To evaluate this painful period of history from the perspective of just memory is a humane and scholarly responsibility. Millions of people of all religions and ethnicities lost their lives in World War I. Having experienced events that had inhumane consequences – such as relocation – during World War I should not prevent Turks and Armenians from establishing

compassion and mutually humane attitudes towards one another. . . . We extend our sympathy. It is our hope and belief that the peoples of an ancient and unique geography, who share similar customs and manners, will be able to talk to each other about the past with maturity and to remember together their losses in a decent manner. And it is with this hope and belief that we wish the Armenians who lost their lives in the context of the early 20th century will rest in peace, and we convey our condolences to their grandchildren. Regardless of their ethnic or religious origins, we pay tribute, with compassion and respect, to all Ottoman citizens who lost their lives in the same period and under similar conditions. (Erdoğan 2014)

The other statement was issued by Davutoğlu on 20 January 2015 to commemorate Dink's murder. The statement was issued in a number of languages, including Armenian and French:

> Hrant Dink was an invaluable Anatolian intellectual who, without compromising either his Armenian heritage or his loyalty to Turkey, sought to help find the ways and means through which Turks and Armenians may build a common future. As someone who personified Turkish–Armenian friendship, he worked selflessly and gave his all so that the bonds of a historic coexistence could be remembered and deep-rooted suffering overcome. As we commemorate the anniversary of his demise, and guided by the seeds of friendship he sowed, we wish to open new paths into hearts and minds. With this understanding, we call on all Armenians and invite all those who believe in Turkish–Armenian friendship to contribute to a new beginning. Having already underscored the inhumane consequences of the relocation policies essentially enforced by wartime circumstances, including those of 1915, Turkey shares the suffering of Armenians and with patience and resolve is endeavouring to re-establish empathy between the two peoples. Our 23 April 2014 message of condolence, which included elements of how, primarily through dialogue, we may together bring an end to the enmity that has kept our relations captive, was a testament to this determination. Only by breaking taboos can we hope to begin addressing the great trauma that froze time in 1915. For its part, Turkey has transcended this critical threshold and relinquished the generalisations and stereotypical assertions of the past. (Davutoğlu 2015)

Both formal statements were acts of remembering, and in remembering they legitimated particular memories that they used to delineate how to think about the events of 1915. Both statements were direct interventions in memory-making, as they used sets of existing public memories to create particular reference points to guide others who were searching for a way to discuss these issues. Thus, the statements engineered public memory not by denying the deportations, deaths and losses but by reframing those events in such a way that their significance for the Armenian population in 1915 was negated. The events of 1915 were thus reframed in reference to the larger context of the First World War. They were remembered as vagaries of war that impacted on all the peoples of the Ottoman Empire. This aimed to establish the memory of an equivalence of suffering across the Ottoman region. Such reference points both invite and allow others to remember those events in similar ways. Erdoğan's statement made clear that talking about the events of 1915 as a genocide was not only unacceptable but would also be considered an act of aggression against Turkey in the light of 'shared suffering'. This particular language, together with the language of 'all Ottoman citizens', set out a claim to be an equal victim. This move deflected the question of political responsibility for the targeting of a particular community. It was also a gesture to limit the discussion to the period 1915–18 – that is, to limit it to a historical concern. Then, the statement called for these events to be considered from the perspective of something called 'just memory'. To a degree, the justness being considered seemed to be implicit in the statement itself: on one hand, it explicitly showed sympathy; on the other, by using the language of victimhood, it resisted being victimized again today by attempts to use the events of 1915 against Turkey. This made anyone who raised these questions a possible enemy, thereby providing evidence of 'our' vulnerability. However, on the whole it was not clear what was meant by 'just memory', given that the statement had already negated any possibility of remembering these events differently, outside its own narrative structure and had established that any other way of engaging in the debate would be indecent.

The Davutoğlu statement built on this and seemed to use the commemoration of Dink's assassination as the moment to argue that Erdoğan's earlier statement constituted the new approach to relations with Armenians. It claimed to show a great understanding of suffering, which was of course the suffering of all. This was an interesting move, using Erdoğan's statement of 23 April 2014 as intertextual evidence to show that things had changed in Turkey. It turned that statement into a public memory that delineated historical facts and informed the country's sentiment of goodwill towards Armenians. These statements attempted to memorialize a certain way of remembering. They were 'claim[s] to collective memory to subjugate history by means of abuses of memory' (Ricoeur 2004: 393), initiated by a political agency. The subjugation, however, concerned not only the past but also the present. The statements were attempts to engineer an agreed public memory by soliciting Armenians' conformity with the understanding of the events of 1915 while negating history as they remembered it. Thus, the remembering practised in these statements worked at two levels: it set reference points for others – that is, non-Armenian Turks – to remember 1915 as a particular history, and it was also an invitation to Armenians to forget.

Paying attention to the content of these public pronouncements and discussions reveals the sources of thinking that underwrite them. It exposes the nature of the public memory that is maintained and reproduced. I argue that the production and reproduction of public memory is a political process that creates a mechanism for a community or society to reflect on itself. By unpacking this mechanism, it is perhaps possible to engage with the question posed by Ricoeur concerning the nature of 'the *praxis* in which the search for memories consists' (2004: 93).

I interpret the formal statements analysed above and their use of language as attempts to shape the public memory. This demonstrates the working of public memory as praxis. I consider this praxiological process of remembering to be an action. This action is facilitated by the existing public memory for people to reach out to those narratives of memory to further diffuse/naturalize them. For me, the critical issue concerns how public memory as praxis delegitimates and displaces other sources of memory. Not only is what is displaced silenced in this process but also its very existence as a source of remembering is gradually erased from public memory, leading to an intergenerational absence of knowledge. It is sufficient to say that this process normalizes the remembering of certain things insofar as it is prompted by language 'automatically', as Halbwachs (2015: 176) puts it. At the same time, this praxis maintains a different memory repertoire that allows a remembering that is compatible with itself as public memory. I argue that in this process individuals reach out to remember, but remembering becomes independent of the experience of the thing remembered (see Halbwachs 1997: 107). The experience of the thing remembered thus becomes a function of public memory. Ricoeur poses an interesting question:

> Does there not exist an intermediate level of reference between the poles of individual memory and collective memory, where concrete exchanges operate between the living memory of individual persons and the public memory of the communities to which they belong? (Ricoeur 2004: 131)

This is a critical question about the nature of what Ricoeur calls 'the living memory of individual persons' and its relationship to public memory, or the capacity of individuals to operationalize such memories to take part in public discussions. This is highly pertinent to discussions of the Armenian genocide in Turkey.

Both the vignette that opened this chapter and publications that have appeared in Turkey since 2004 on (among other topics) the converted Armenians who became 'grandmothers' highlight the existence of a living memory on Armenians and the Armenian genocide in Turkey (Çetin 2004; Çetin and Altinay 2009; HDV 2015; also see Biner 2010; Çelik and Dinç 2015; Beyleryan 2019; Mouradian 2021). However, as my Armenian interviewee from Istanbul (discussed in the previous chapter) pointed out, most Turkish people have never met an Armenian but still seem to have opinions about Armenians in general, and it seems that the majority of Muslim Sunni Turkish individuals have no living memory of Armenians in Turkey. In this case, Ricoeur's 'intermediary level' exists but does not constitute a reference point for the majority to remember as something they have experienced. In the absence of living memory, people's opinions are based broadly on the remembering that is facilitated by public memory. Furthermore, the lack of everyday experiences of others limits individuals' ability to interpret or think about what they remember. Thus, what they remember through this memory machine limits their conditions of apprehension when they encounter expressions of remembering differently, such as the expressions found in questions, experiences and publications concerning the genocide. These considerations allow me to focus on the public manifestations of the repertoire of memory, in order to understand the registers it uses to locate Armenians and the question of genocide in public discussions. Since the possibilities for thinking are located in a set of narratives in public discussions about Turks ('us') and Armenians ('them'), the public's ability to think is conditioned to reach out to the most publicly repeated memories as their own.

The repertoire of public memory

In this section, I present a central finding of the research that grounds this book. The finding concerns the existence in Turkey of a language and a set of narratives that are used repeatedly over time to talk about Armenians and the Armenian genocide. I will present a typology of these narratives which constitutes the public memory that facilitates people's remembering when they encounter discussions and questions about the genocide. These narratives do not only facilitate public thinking; through their repetition, they also reproduce the boundaries of what can be known. There are many books published that normalize these narratives. In addition to individual books, a five-volume series published from September 2014 until December 2014 by the New Turkey: Centre for Strategic Research (Yeni

Türkiye: Stratejik Araştırma Merkezi) on the Armenian Issue (*Ermeni Meselesi*). This series provides significant material in which the typology I develop below is evident. Over time, this repertoire becomes the ontological grounds of knowing for the Turkish public. I have developed the typology through a content analysis of public statements and discussions that are available in diverse media and books, in addition to my observations and analyses of public debates in academic and non-academic forums, including statements by public figures. From this analysis, it is clear that these narratives and statements use similar language that constructs a set of reference points to guide the public through discussions by linking them to a repertoire of public memory. These linguistic reference points – such as the language of 'the so-called (*sözde*) Armenian genocide', 'the Armenian issue' (*Meselesi*) or 'the Armenian diaspora' (*Ermeni diasporası*) – signify specific knowledge embedded in narratives that are then used to frame answers and discussions. By looking at the typology, one can unpack what is being maintained and reproduced for the public to remember. What is being remembered also directs the public's comprehension of discussions about the Armenian genocide.

Following Ricoeur, I argue that the different parts of the typology and the reference points therein allow 'us', members of the public, to search for memory in these narratives. 'We' follow these reference points and remember together with them. So what exactly do these statements guide us to remember in our quest to understand? My typology is based on six publicly used, repeatedly deployed statements that are linked to various narratives that create the memory repertoire. What they all share is that they are grounded in claims about the nature of being Turkish and the values of Turkishness. While I set out the typology in a way that looks at each part of the repertoire separately, they should not be regarded as mutually exclusive. Indeed, it is often the case that they are used together to strengthen the persuasiveness of public memory. I will now outline each narrative in relation to a typical statement that aims to trigger engagement with that narrative. Whenever one of these six statements is used, it provides reference points that allow remembering in a particular manner.

1. 'These Are All Lies, and the So-Called Genocide Could Not Have Taken Place'

This statement (or variations of it) reaches out to a narrative that guides us about history. The narrative is that Armenians were always treated fairly, properly and with consideration in the Ottoman Empire; that there were not enough

Armenians in Anatolia for the numbers presented by the Armenian diaspora to justify their genocide claim to make sense and that the stories they use when presenting their claims are historically inaccurate because they draw on the politically motivated views of foreign missionaries who were agitating against the Ottomans at the time (see Ayverdi 2005; Tuncer 2004; Ata 2017; Sertçelik 2015; Şimşir 2014). The narrative thus aims to historically discredit discussions of the genocide in various registers, ranging from harmonious coexistence within the empire to factual inaccuracy on the part of the Armenian diaspora. For instance, it questions the veracity of claims about the numbers of Armenians killed by asserting that there were not significant numbers of Armenians in Anatolia at the time. This works by asserting the factual accuracy of what 'we' know about Anatolia and Armenians against the claims presented by others (see Karayumak 2007; Adıgüzel 2015; Çiçek 2020). It also turns the debate around to assert that these historically inaccurate genocide claims are attempts to hide the real victims of the First World War, that is, the Turks who successfully created a new republic. The narrative then turns to the period of terror attacks by the Armenian Secret Army for the Liberation of Armenia (ASALA) in the 1970s and 1980s, establishing this violent period as a pathway to remember that Turks are still under threat from external enemies, linking ASALA terrorism with Armenians' historical victimization of Turks in Anatolia during the First World War (see Gürün 1988). In its more extreme versions, this historical narrative also draws parallels between discussions of the Armenian genocide and the 'Sèvres spirit' embodied in the 1920 Treaty of Sèvres, which the Ottoman Empire signed with the Allies at the end of the First World War (see Tekin 2013). Both the genocide discussions and the treaty are represented as attempts to divide Anatolia and push the Turks out, thereby informing Turkey's victimization in both the past and the present.

2. 'Security Problems During the First World War Forced the Ottoman Government to Relocate the Armenian Population, and People Died Due Various Problems That Arose During Those Relocations, Including Outbreaks of Disease'

This part of the repertoire builds memory based on the imperatives of the security and defence of the empire in the face of threats by the Armenian militia. This is a reuse of an older narrative that seems to have first emerged alraedy during 1915 and then bewteen 1919–22 Constantinople trials, which were established to prosecute the perpetrators of crimes committed against Armenians (Dadrian and Akçam 2011). It is broadly narrated as a threat in the East, particularly in stories about the Armenian Revolutionary Federation (Dashnaktsutyun) raiding villages and killing Turkish villagers. Armenians from other areas are also presented as having associated or at least sympathized with Russian interests to destroy the integrity of the Ottoman Empire. For instance, for many people, Mehmet Perinçek's (2007 and 2012; also see Serdar 2015; Seyrek 2015) work provides comprehensive evidence of the danger the empire faced during this period. Thus, the memory one acquires here is about existential insecurity and the inevitability of the government's response in defence of the country. The Ottoman government's ruthlessness towards the Armenian population in general is explained by the nature of the Armenian threat as an 'enemy within' that undermined the government's authority when it was at its weakest (see Mısıroğlu 2015). Here again, the sense is conveyed of victimhood, of having been betrayed. This narrative also provides and interprets a set of historical 'facts' to guide remembering for the public. In fact, there are two versions of this particular narrative:

1. The anti-Ottoman, more republican version argues that the situation was a result of the misguided, power-hungry governance of the Committee of Union and Progress (CUP), the party that led the country at the time. This presents yet another example of the weakness of the empire's administration in general. It then adds in passing that in the end the Armenians got what was coming to them.
2. The long-standing pro-Ottoman version presents what happened in 1915 as a patriotic endeavour by the leaders of the CUP (see Över 2007).

The latter version of the narrative is embodied in the symbolism of the memorials to the CUP's leaders. Talat Pasha was reburied after his body was returned to Istanbul from Berlin in 1943; Enver Pasha's body was brought back to Istanbul from Tajikistan in 1996 and buried next to Talat Pasha at the Monument of Liberty (Abide-i Hürriyet) in Şişli. These symbolic references have been used to guide public memory even more directly since the AKP became the dominant political voice in Turkey. In this narrative, the main political figures involved in decisions regarding the genocide – Enver, Talat and Cemal Pashas – are presented as martyrs who acted to save the destiny of their people but were tragically betrayed and slain in vain. This betrayal is evidenced by the 1919–22 Constantinople trials, which are presented as a foreign plot based on the Treaty of Sèvres (see Bilgi 2006). Again, the memory being constructed here includes the representation of Armenians as an enemy within. The memory is also that Ottoman leaders after the First World War were weak and broadly controlled by the occupying forces. The important issue that this version of the memory settles is the centrality of the security imperative during this period. 'We' remember the inevitably of the decision to deport Armenians to protect the country. Thus, 'we' remember that it was not a decision to kill Armenians; it was just a measure to protect the country. This logic is summed up in a slogan that has become common since April 2015 and is often reiterated on posters: 'We did not commit genocide, we defended our country'. This public policy praxis contextualizes historical events to assert an interpretation for the public to remember (see Arslan, Bal and Demirhan 2012; Deli 2015). The security and defence arguments ground the debate in an existential survival story about the Turkish people who remained in Anatolia.

3. 'The Republic of Turkey Is Not the Addressee in This Matter'

This is a general statement used by politicians, academics and lawyers. The aim is to maintain a historical distance between the empire and the republic. This is both to avoid the responsibility of engaging in discussions of the Armenian genocide and to limit any discussion of the genocide to a historical past demarcated by the lifespan of the Ottoman Empire (Halaçoğlu 2008). The narrative constructs a view of the new Turkish republic by sharply delinking it from the empire. It utilizes a common historical trope that presents the republic as a modernizing polity that broke with the empire and was built in contradistinction to the empire's backwardness. Many of those who reach out to this narrative state that as citizens of the republic, 'we' are not party to debates about the genocide. Therefore, any formal response to a discussion about the genocide would be an unnecessary engagement with other people's problem. In this way, the narrative not only limits the discussion to a specific historical period, but it also limits its relevance to the Armenian diaspora and Western powers. It is possible to find statements that argue that 'this issue has nothing to do with us'.

4. 'Genocide Is a Legal Concept That Was Invented in 1948, and It Cannot Apply to Events Before That Time'

This narrative frames its story by defining 'genocide' and then establishing whether the events of 1915 constitute a genocide from a legal perspective. It delimits what we remember about genocide strictly in relation to the 1948 United Nations (UN) Convention on the Prevention and Punishment of the Crime of Genocide (some versions of the narrative even state that 'genocide' does not apply before 'our' time, thereby emphasizing the distinction between the Ottoman Empire and the Republic of Turkey) (see Ekşi 2010). The narrative presents the following arguments:

1. The UN definition cannot be used to describe events that predate its first articulation.
2. As a legal document, the 1948 UN convention cannot be used to judge or punish events that happened before its ratification.
3. Given that a clear intention of mass murder is legally required to establish that the killings in question were indeed planned to target an entire group, the convention does not apply in the Ottoman case, as the events took place under wartime conditions and the deaths were unintentional outcomes.

Thus, when people reach for this narrative, it reminds them of a number of things:

1. The events of 1915 predate the 1948 UN convention, and therefore those events cannot be retroactively considered a genocide.
2. Legally, there is no case to answer.
3. No court of law has considered and judged the events to have been a genocide under the UN convention.

The last point was demonstrated in 2016 in a statement by the Turkish political leader Doğu Perinçek. Swiss courts had previously found him guilty of the crime of denying the Armenian genocide. Subsequently, the European Court of Human Rights ruled on appeal in favour of his right to free speech. In response to the European court ruling, Perinçek (2016) explicitly stated: 'There is no court decision, there is no genocide [*Mahkeme kararı yok, soykırım yok*]' (see Perinçek 2012; Pazarcı 2014; Akçay 2016). This position considers genocide as a legal issue that can only be decided by a court to establish an event as a genocide, as a crime according to the 1948 UN Convention. Another part of this narrative also suggests that even if the Armenian genocide claims were to be heard in court, the claims would fail the legal tests set by the UN convention, since there is no evidence to establish the *intention* to exterminate a population group. By limiting the discussion to its legal form, this narrative reminds people that there is no reason to answer the question why an entire community was targeted indiscriminately and independently of individuals' links with security concerns. The narrative silences the implications of the 1919–22 Constantinople trials, which established the events of 1915–18 as crimes against humanity. By focusing on the UN convention as a legal text, the narrative invalidates the relationship between the 1915–18 events and the term 'genocide' – a term that Raphael Lemkin (1944) developed on the basis of his study of Armenians' fate during 1915–18.

5. 'This Issue Is Not a Problem in Turkey'

This narrative reminds people that the Turkish state has treated its minorities responsibly ever since its foundation. The 1923 Treaty of Lausanne underwrites this position as the foundational document of the Republic of Turkey. It is argued that of course the Turkish state recognizes the country's minorities, who have always been treated in accordance with their rights as citizens and the Lausanne treaty. Most of the time one hears the argument that 'we' have no problem with Armenians or other minorities in Turkey. According to this narrative, all other issues concerning 1915 – whether it was a genocide or not, the numbers involved, the reasons for the population movements – have been created by the diaspora, who are opposed to 'our' existence, and 'we' cannot give in to such external pressure. Every year for the past decade or more, this narrative has been used particularly extensively in the run-up to 24 April, as the Turkish public debate focuses on whether the US president will use the 'G-word' and whether the US House of Representatives will pass a resolution recognizing 1915 as a genocide. Each iteration of this public discussion implies a victimhood, a state of existential insecurity, created by the Armenian diaspora to undermine individual Turks' self-confidence and consciousness. Thus, the narrative creates a need to reach out to defensive memories to protect the Turkish public (see Özdemir 2021). For example, on 31 July 2018, in response to international questions about pressures on religious minorities in Turkey, all the leaders of minority religious groups issued a statement saying that the claims they were under pressure were untrue and politically misguided, and that they had good and cordial relations with the Turkish government, with whom they worked to resolve any issues or problems (Daily Sabah 2018). This statement was clearly an operationalization of this narrative to remember publicly that 'we' do not have problems with 'our' minorities. The narrative builds on the distinction between the Ottoman past and the Turkish republic. It also externalizes questions about the genocide as a matter of external pressure on the country and thus as not related to 'our' Armenians (Bayraktar 2015). The use of the pronoun 'our' is also a trope to remind people of what is expected of minorities in Turkey when they engage with the public, and thus of how 'they' should evaluate their own public engagements.

6. 'We Are All Brothers of the Same Land – Let Us Recognize Each Other's Suffering and Move On'

This narrative presents a way of remembering that has been increasingly valorized by the AKP government, although Turgut Özal moved in this direction in the 1980s to claim that all cultures that had ever lived in Anatolia were a part of Turkish culture. The narrative facilitates a shared memory of the Ottoman period that leads to remembering the shared suffering of the peoples of the Ottoman region during the First World War (see Palabıyık 2015; Sakin 2015). It selectively presents the Ottoman regime as a benevolent rule that created a society of harmonious relations that were only derailed by external interference. This fits well with the AKP's overall reframing of Turkish society as a neo-Ottoman polity governed by top-down benevolence and tolerance. Minorities are considered to be homogenous religious communities that are allowed to practise their own rituals. Thus, the narrative remembers the existence of Armenians in Anatolia among many other groups. For instance, when it allowed the renovation of the Armenian Cathedral of the Holy Cross on Aghtamar Island in Lake Van, the government operationalized this narrative by turning the restoration into a reference point for the public. However, remembering through this narrative first locates Armenians in pre-1915 Anatolia, ignoring the massacres of 1894–6 and 1909, and then relocates them in 1915 in an undifferentiated manner as subject to the overall consequences of the war, in the same way as other groups – such as, say, the people who suffered greatly in the Balkans. What people are being encouraged to remember here is the disruption of the harmonious Ottoman society due to the interference of foreign powers. This memory negates memories of the events of 1915, but it does so with benevolence, expressing sympathy for the dead of all communities, as demonstrated in the statement by Erdoğan I discussed above. There is nothing in this narrative that reflects on the general life experiences of the two or three generations of Armenian citizens that Turkey has had since 1915. This aspect is subsumed by the use of the pronoun 'our', as mentioned earlier. Interestingly, this narrative of benevolence underpinned by an equivalence of victimhood is functional for more liberal-leaning people in Turkey too. It allows them to acknowledge the pain that 1915 must have caused and the importance of sharing it by acknowledging the existence of that pain. It motivates people to tell Armenians that 'we understand your pain, as many people in our own communities were also killed in World War I'. The conversation seems to end with the standard benevolent acknowledgement that 'honestly, everywhere must have been a mess [*vallahi, cok karısıklık olmuş heryerde*]'.

This sharing informs a depoliticized acknowledgement without reaching out to remember what the events of 1915 and their aftermath were about (see Dixon 2015). It allows 'us' to move on without thinking deeply about what needs to be acknowledged. Another aspect of this is the fact that once an equivalence of victimhood is created and used to share the pain, there is an immediate view that the events of 1915 were different from those of the Holocaust. Therefore, 1915 cannot be considered a genocide. Furthermore, in this narrative one is not willing to go beyond the shared pain, as 'unfortunately neither side can prove it historically'. Underwriting this is the common sentiment that 'if it was genocide, does that mean our grandfathers were killers?'

These narratives, and the different statements through which they are reached, reveal the architecture of the repertoire of public memory. By providing alternative ways to remember, the narratives limit what can be remembered and whose memories matter for the Turkish public. For instance, on the whole there is little in this repertoire with which to remember Armenians positively. The possibility of reaching out to a memory to recall traces of actual Armenian lives, then or now, is severely limited. The idea of 'the enemy within' is one of two central signs in the repertoire that facilitate the process of remembering. Armenians are always remembered as associated with foreign powers and as working against the interests of the 'Turkish' people, who are generically defined contra Armenians. In this way the repertoire provides the content for denialism in Turkey.

The repertoire fits well with Stan Cohen's (2001) typology of denial, which moves from factual denials to interpretive and cultural forms of denial. In Cohen's (2001: 9) terms, the situation can be described as creating conditions for 'cultural not-noticing' by creating 'taken-for-granted' parts of everyday life for the general public that are reproduced over time through 'calculated forms of lying, deception or disinformation'. Cohen's understanding of interpretive and cultural denial is pertinent. He points out that 'societies arrive at unwritten agreements about what can be publicly remembered and acknowledged', and that 'these denials may be initiated by the state, but then acquire lives of their own' (Cohen 2001: 11). The public memory of the Armenians and the genocide is one such process, and it is maintained not only by an unwritten agreement but also by becoming a condition for solidarity, for belonging, in Turkey. Remembering through this repertoire establishes denialist narratives as the baseline knowledge for the Turkish public to use to remember and be citizens (Cohen 2001). While the language used enables people to reach out for these narratives to remember, as a part of the repertoire it negates the political and moral implications of mass murder (Cohen 2001: 8). This process is how Eviatar Zerubavel consider silencing to be 'a collective endeavour, and it involves a collaborative effort on the parts of both the potential generator and recipient of a given piece of information to stay away from it' (2007: 48).

By providing these denial narratives, the repertoire does not only create conditions for the silencing of Armenian memories of Armenian lives and experiences in Anatolia. These people and their experiences are also erased over time and intergenerationally, as the repertoire becomes the exclusive grounds on which new generations remember. For these new generations, there is nothing to remember Armenians with. The narratives that would allow that remembering do not exist in the public memory repertoire. Furthermore, through this repertoire, the general repeated use of 'Armenian' in significantly negative terms attributes qualities that transform the word. It becomes an insult, as I observed earlier. This in itself is a mechanism to emotionally distance oneself from hearing different voices with different memories, since those voices are morally distanced as signifiers of the insult (Guyyonet 2011/2012: 189). Furthermore, the insult also works on the stigmatization of Armenian identity as a socially acceptable status (Goffman 1990). The other central sign in the repertoire is the constant evocation of the existential insecurity of being Turkish. This not only communicates a generalized anxiety and feeling of existential threat, but also constructs memories of Turkish victimhood in various forms. It provides a memory of a bounded descriptive world that informs people's thinking and gives meaning to what they hear and read, without Armenian lives in present-day Turkey appearing in it. In this way the repertoire emotionally externalizes both Armenians in everyday life in today's Turkey and questions about the genocide. These externalizations support attempts to justify mass murder as self-defence.

The structure of this repertoire is analogous to a grammar. Through norms that construct and order linguistic signs, the comprehensibility of speech in a culture is created (see Lemieux 2009). This repertoire, in an analogous manner, normalizes the rules and signs of acceptable forms of thinking and speaking about Armenians and the genocide. The stereotypical statements outlined above act as signs. On one hand, they facilitate people to reach out to memories, as I have discussed. On the other hand, they act as automatic, naturalized monitoring devices: they consider the language people use in everyday life to judge each act of remembering, validating or invalidating each such act on the basis of its acceptability to the values expressed in the public memory. As they are deployed in public discussions, these signs become markers of group belonging and not-belonging. Therefore, the practice of public memory is also about solidarity.

Reaching out to public memory to remember in a particular way becomes a sign of solidarity. It is also a demonstration of one's understanding that one is being called into solidarity in the face of a constantly amplified existential insecurity. One's use of the repertoire's denialist language marks one's belonging to the community.

Turkishness and the public memory repertoire

By now I imagine that readers might be wondering what it is that enables the public memory repertoire to be as robust as I claim in communicating knowledge. Perhaps one can think about this by paraphrasing Joachim J. Savelsberg (2021: 61): what allows 'knowledge entrepreneurs' to 'succeed best in certifying or modifying knowledge' is their '*epistemic power*' (Savelsberg's italics; also see Göçek 2014: 49). So, what is the source of the epistemic power that gives this public memory repertoire its resilience in Turkey, even while different knowledge entrepreneurs reproduce and adjust it as necessary, without changing its robustly denialist overall epistemological framework? As I argued above, the repertoire's narratives relate to the founding imaginary of the Republic of Turkey as a nation. The repertoire's epistemic power rests within that imaginary and its framing of the epistemology of being Turkish. This imaginary is built on the sociocultural and political transformation initiated contra the Ottoman Empire to forge a national community. A central part of this transformation involved a two-stage language revolution (*devrimi*) that prescribed first how to write and then how to speak. It was a total 'language planning' as part of a 'social planning', managed from the top of the political hierarchy to create a new nation (Rubin and Jernudd 1971: xi; see also Cooper 2000; Sadoğlu 2003).

Beginning in 1928 with the Alphabet Revolution (Harf Devrimi), which introduced a new Romanized alphabet and ended the use of the Arabic-based Ottoman script, this process reached its pinnacle with the language revolution (Dil Devrimi) of 1932 (see Szurek 2013). The latter initiated a deeper change than just a change of the script used for writing and reading. It initiated a lexical change that would underwrite how linguistic meanings were constructed and communicated. In order to disseminate this fundamental change in how society communicated, in 1932 a new state institution was created: the Turkish Linguistic Association (Türk Dil Kurumu) (see Szurek 2014). It was given the formal linguistic authority to create various dictionaries to introduce new words, meanings and usages as well as new grammatical rules. It was also tasked with conducting research on the sources of the Turkish language (Lewis 1961: 433). Another important aim was to purge the foreign words that had been adopted into Turkish from various other languages, including Arabic and Persian. Atatürk launched these changes on 26 October 1932 at the opening of the first Language Convention, which later became an annual Language Festival that has continued to be celebrated ever since (albeit not always on the same date). Additionally, these linguistic changes shared common roots in the drive to create a national history, which led to the creation of the Turkish Historical Society (Türk Tarih Kurumu) on 29 May 1931. The overall aim was to produce research from the standpoint of being Turkish and for the new linguistic community that was emerging.

Charles F. Gallagher (1971: 153) describes all this as an attempt to 'form a community on the basis of being primarily Turkish and only incidentally Muslim'. He adds that the linguistic changes were not only revolutionary but also 'paralleled fundamental societal change under way in political, economic and social fields' (Gallagher 1971: 165). The link between national language and national history was seen at the time as central for building the new republic. For instance, on 26 September 1934, the well-known linguist and language reformer İbrahim Necmi marked the Language Festival in a piece for the daily *Zaman*. Talking about the reasons behind the linguistic changes, he stated: 'Language means Nation. . . . Those who speak one language are also one in their being [*varlık*]. Those who speak different languages, even if they are under one flag, they are different beings' (Necmi 1934: 2). He then pointed out that this was why the Turkish language was so central to the work of the new republic, and he ended the piece with a call to arms: 'Turkish authors! Turkish scientists! Come and join the war! Come and join the war for pure (*öz*) language' (Necmi 1934: 2). On the occasion of the fourth Language Festival, in 1936, in an editorial for the daily *Ulus*, the well-known author and journalist Falih Rıfkı Atay argued that the Kemalism that was leading the foundation of the republic was also about finding our own history to build a new understanding of ourselves: it was not just a war, but also a journey into our history, and 'in order to give order to this research and build it scientifically, to discuss our truths with Western scientists, history and language associations are created' (Atay 1936: 1). He added: 'Language is the base: we will answer the questions of the past as well as the future with it' (Atay 1936: 1). I give these extracts as illustrative examples from the media of the period. They were by no means exceptional in expressing these views. Such views, and the language policies with which they were linked, were also used publicly to educate people, not only to teach them Turkish but also to motivate them to think about themselves from a historically different position as part of the republic.

The views expressed here reveal a political intention to build a national identity based on a national language that framed a national histography. These narratives were constructed against the multilingual Ottoman period (Ersanlı 2011: 104–5). Clearly, the justification given to the public for these language and history policies at the time was framed in a number of ways as a reaction against the darkness of the Ottoman period for Turks as one undistinguished community among many others in the empire. According to Çağla Kubilay (2004: 56), after the foundation of the republic, the state followed 'a policy of monolingualism, independent of the existence of social groups that spoke different languages'. The aim, Kubilay argues, was to create national unity: 'while considering speaking Turkish as one of the main marks of Turkishness', the political authority 'considered speaking in other first languages [in Turkey] as one of the threats to the regime' (Kubilay 2004: 56). She further observes that this view brought in a policy approach that aimed to suppress and assimilate all other languages by restricting their use in public, thereby linguistically homogenizing public space (Kubilay 2004: 56).

This combination of an exclusive, linguistic-based belonging and an exclusively constructed national history determined how to be, think and act as a Turk. Through this specific language and history, the citizens of the republic were and are given the conceptual tools to make sense of themselves and their world. In Anscombe's (2000) terms, they were given a whole new set of descriptions about themselves and others, to make sense of their past and present as Turkish. I argue that this exclusive didactic view is where the epistemic power is located. It is the power of using language policies to forge a national identity that legitimates the narratives which constitute the public memory repertoire. The robustness of this epistemic power, and therefore of the repertoire it legitimates and normalizes, is produced by a central policy mechanism that was initiated as a necessary part of language reforms.

As a first step, the change in the medium of communication – that is, the alphabet – meant that immediately after 1928, students and citizens could not read in Ottoman. Even the immediate past could not be studied in existing written work. As a second step, the language was stripped of its Ottoman syntax and vocabulary. Then, the linguistic reform started to produce new words and meanings for people to communicate within this linguistic community as Turkish citizens. As Kubilay argues, this also required that different communities living under one flag (as Necmi put it) be brought together under this linguistic definition of the nation. If they resisted, their belonging became an open question that invited pressure to conform (see also Sadoğlu 2003; Bali 2005). Many dictionaries and linguistic guides, large and small, were produced throughout this period. Next, a link was established between the national language and the national history, as clearly stated by the authors from the period I quoted above. Writing the national history required using the national language. In this way, the Turkish language became the anchor for historical research and thinking about the past. In her seminal book *Denial of Violence* (2015) Fatma Müge Göçek focuses on how this new thinking on language and history early on was used to ground the new education system with the aim of teaching 'Turkish Nationalism'. She points out that '[t]he teaching of Turkish nationalism pedagogically united the centralized republican education system, highlighting not only Turkish civilizational achievements but also bravery and righteousness of the Muslim Turks at the expense of all other religions and ethnicities' (2015: 288, also see Turan and Öztan 2018:149–56).

This set of moves, which framed policies on education, research and public communication, at the same time delegitimated the public role of other languages from the Ottoman past. As Necmi and Atay indicated, speaking in any other language came to signify otherness, foreignness, not-belonging. There was a general sense that speakers of other languages, particularly in public, were in confrontation with the founding principles of the republic, as they signified the Ottoman past. As Necmi highlighted above, because they had other first languages, their belonging in the new polity was questioned even though they remained part of the country. Historiography was attempting to create a new understanding of Turks' position in the world, both past and present, and those who did not share the Turkish linguistic identity were not seen as relevant contributors to that process. Thus, the foundational link between the national language and the national historiography further delegitimated the participation of people with other languages. This situation also meant that memories of past lives and experiences that were embedded in different communities and constructed in those communities' own languages were delegitimated as irrelevant to Turkish historiography. Over time, those memories became inaccessible to the bulk of society and were erased from the national public memory.

This created an interesting situation: the bulk of the nation could not write, read or comprehend their own past due to the lexical transformation of the language. Thus, their access to the past was mediated by those who could still use the old lexicon. Gradually, of course, those who had been educated in the old lexicon disappeared, leaving only cadres of specially trained historians to make sense of the past for younger generations. People's understanding of their past in this way became linked to the narrow field of national historiography as authorized and memorialized knowledge. Again, this was a dramatic intervention that created a foundational break with the past. It is the epistemological power of that break that creates the robustness of the public memory repertoire. Its narratives as I framed them above were produced by the nationalization of language and history, in a context where the public had no other way to access knowledge about their past.

Conclusion

One of the central sources of denialism in the narratives of the public memory repertoire lies in these national language policies and the way in which a particular history is memorialized to forge a nation. As Paul Ricoeur (2004: 441) points out: 'The core of profound memory consists of marks designating what in one way or another we have seen, heard, felt, learned, acquired.... [A]round this core are assembled the customary manners of thinking, acting and feeling.' The new language was thus also about forging a basis for solidarity – the solidarity of forgetting through acquired memories. This immediately excludes individuals or groups that have their own first languages. It means that society forms its understanding of its past in a way that self-selects what matters to 'us' in Turkey. In addition, as it propagates a public memory of exclusive group solidarity, it makes it problematic for Armenian Turks (and other groups living in Turkey) to take part in discussions as a part of the past or the present. As language use becomes a significant marker of belonging, other groups' use of their own languages – the very fact that they have first languages of their own – is used against the speakers of those languages to mark them as potential strangers to 'us'. Their epistemic position within the national language and history already excludes them from having a voice on issues that are a central part of the national history and identity. In this context, the ability to present alternative or silenced narratives to challenge and restructure the public memory is invalidated and seen as hostile when evaluated against national solidarity tests.

The public memory is a denialist machine that delineates everyday understandings through various parts of a repertoire concerning the Armenian genocide in Turkey. This public memory comprehensively socializes individuals into a denialist process, as its signs are absorbed and inform a way of being and relating to one another in everyday life. The public language describes a world where Armenians remain 'the enemy within' in relation to 'us' and are a 'threat to our national integrity'. Public language and the memories embedded in it reproduce an intergenerational denialist memory in Turkey.

Furthermore, the public memory of Armenians has ensured that something did not take place and some people did not exist by effacing the traces of alternative memory and materiality. Ricoeur (2004: 452) argues that 'obsession is selective and the dominant narratives consecrate the obliteration of part of the field of vision'. Therefore, the concern here is with how the denialist repertoire is installed as the only memory available to new generations who cannot reach out to remember or 'recall' other ways of being (Ricoeur 2004: 454). The normalization of denialist public memory depends not only on its initiation by the state but also on how it is used in different social interactions and reinforced by being reproduced in education, mass media and other spaces of sociability. By educating new generations in this repertoire through formal education, commemorations, celebrations and mass media presentations, the public memory becomes the intergenerational social reflex (Seckinelgin 2006) and provides 'meanings that individual subjects can make their own' (Descombes 2014: 9). In the rest of this book, I analyse these reinforcement and reproduction mechanisms of the public memory of the Armenian genocide in everyday life in Turkey.

3

Commemorating the centennial of the Armenian genocide

24 April 2015

In this chapter, I focus on the genocide centennial commemorations held in Istanbul on 24 April 2015. There were commemoration events in other cities too, notably in Ankara and in Diyarbakir. My analysis is based on field notes I took during my participation in some of the events on the day in Istanbul. I locate these against the backdrop of the mass media coverage of the questions raised by the centennial, both before and after 24 April. My aim is to highlight the way in which the public memory repertoire was diffused across the mass media coverage, constructing what took place in a way that did not allow the public to engage with the centennial outside of a defensive lens. The pertinent question here is who remembered what around that moment in time.

The repertoire presented in the previous chapter constitutes the context of remembrance for the non-Armenian majority in Turkey. Thinking through memorials and their everyday function, Andrew M. Shanken (2022: 18) argues: 'Most memorials are "turned on" only on special days. . . . [A]t these moments they become part of commemorative activity.' This is relevant to the case I am considering in two ways: (1) the repertoire I presented earlier is evidently turned on through the language used and the reference points deployed in the mass media, and thus the media plays an important role; (2) the way in which narratives from the repertoire are turned on during this commemoration process indicates the memorialization of the repertoire itself for the public. The repertoire participates in the commemorations.

People in the public that had no specific experiences of Armenians, or 'no idea' about the issues raised by the centennial, reached out to this memorialized repertoire as the safe ground for their belonging to remember and engage with the questions raised. My aim in this chapter is to show how this 'turning on' around the commemoration unfolded in the mass media to allow representations of the past to be recalled. Paul Ricoeur (2005: 124) states that this reaching out is about 'the present representation of something absent'. According to Ricoeur (2005: 125), this reaching out grasps at whatever is stored (or 'remains') in the public memory. The outcome in this case was remembering through limited representations of Armenians and the events of 1915. These representations appeared as the only ones that were available for recall (Ricoeur 2005: 126). What was remembered also gave one the ability to apprehend oneself as Turkish in relation to Armenians, and one apprehended the questions raised about the genocide by the centennial events in this way too.

Istanbul's centennial commemorations of the genocide provide me with a good focus to consider how the mass media 'turned on' the repertoire. I will look at the coverage of the centennial in three stages: before the commemoration events on 24 April 2015, on the day of the commemoration itself and on the day after the commemoration. The analysis of the latter period is particularly interesting, as it demonstrates that the role of the mass media was even more critical in light of the events I analyse from the day of the commemoration. I take the commemoration as a moment that generated both a lot of interest and a lot of emotion that can be interpreted as anxiety on the part of the non-Armenian majority. The media coverage of the events transmitted that anxiety as a defensive position. While most of the media coverage fell into this category, there were sources that took different positions, questioning this emotion and its manifestations in the deployment of the public memory repertoire to report on the commemorations. Perhaps these voices got lost in the sea of defensive coverage, but I think they are important to highlight in this analysis.

Newspaper coverage in the run-up to the commemorations

The mass media coverage during the period leading up to the commemorations on 24 April 2015 can generally be considered under two broad headings. The first focuses on reports that framed 'the Armenian issue' as an international concern or a foreign policy issue sparked by either the self-interest of individual countries or the interests of the Armenian diaspora, or both. This coverage referenced international reactions to the centennial. It also focused on how Turkish politicians and the government were defending the country against a series of formal recognitions of the genocide by Austria, Belgium, the Czech Republic and Germany in addition the Vatican. The reports deployed the concept of 'diaspora' to explain why Turkey was being pressurized internationally. The second heading focuses on reporting that provided historical narratives in order to determine and justify what 'really' happened in 1915. These reports aimed to remind the public of the cognitive resources that were embedded in the public memory, thereby allowing the public to recall what they might already know in order to think in a specific way and counter the 'so-called Armenian genocide' claims that intensified during this period. Another aspect of the coverage was that some journalists questioned the usefulness of the concept of genocide as a single word to cover a complex historical past. In both strands, the coverage deployed linguistic reference points that linked the public's attention to the public memory repertoire to facilitate further discussion of these issues. In the following, I will look at the coverage on 22 and 23 April 2015. The central reason for my focus here is to see how the mass media guided the public to think what was relevant for them during this period. First, I will consider what I have described as the international focus of the reporting.

On 22 April 2015, the daily *Habertürk* reported the upcoming visit by Volkan Bozkır, the Turkish government's European Union minister and chief negotiator, to Surp Kevork, an Armenian church in the Kocamustafapaşa area of Istanbul. This story was covered by most papers, and they directly referred to his statement. In the statement the minister had said: 'For us, looking to the future means walking together in this way.' Talking about the problem of using history for political ends, he also said: 'I am inviting third parties to withdraw from our discussions [with Armenians].' The tone of the reported message was measured and emphasized togetherness, using the language of 'our' Armenian 'brothers and sisters [*kardeşlerimiz*]': Bozkır had said that these 'third parties' were even 'unable to point to the location of Armenia and have no historical togetherness with our Armenian brothers and sisters' (Bozkır 2015). On the same page, *Habertürk* also reported that according to some White House sources, US president Barack Obama was not going to use the word 'genocide' in his statement. This is interesting in two ways. The minister's statement was rather vague as to what he was talking about and whom he was addressing, given that it was delivered in Istanbul in an Armenian church but seemed implicitly to reference international actors as 'third parties'. It was also ambiguous in relation to the nature of 'our' togetherness with Armenians and the conditions under which 'we' would walk together. The statement could be interpreted as speaking to memories of the imperial gaze, as the use of 'us' and 'our' Armenians seems to imply. It was clearly meant to counter statements on the genocide issued from various European capitals as well as the anticipated US presidential statement in the run-up to the centennial. Complaining about the global rumpus caused by Armenians every April in their quest for recognition of the genocide, Yalçın Bayer's column in the daily *Hürriyet* on 22 April provided a lesson as a historical corrective, arguing that the state had had an imperative to defend itself and punish those who had 'stabbed the empire in the back' Bayer 2015). This seemed to recall some of the reasons behind what had happened to Armenians in 1915. The first reference here, albeit not explicitly, was to the Armenian diaspora, which was seen as unsettling the situation. The other references were more explicit in pointing out views regarding victimhood and the enemy within.

On 23 April 2015, *Habertürk* reported on developments after the Austrian parliament joined others in calling the events of 1915 a genocide. The paper pointed out that Obama was not going to attend the ceremonies in Yerevan but would send another government official to represent him (Aslan 2015). Additionally, it gave information about the centennial commemorations that were going to take place in various stages across Istanbul and in Diyarbakır. It reported that there would be a formal ceremony held by the Armenian patriarchate in Istanbul – a first – during which there would be prayers for all the dead. *Habertürk* also reported that the Turkish president Recep Tayyip Erdoğan had repeated his call for a historic commission, stated that he did not expect Obama to use the language of genocide and directed most of his comments to Armenia by asking whether that country had reciprocated his initiatives such as the restoration of the church on Aghtamar Island in Lake Van. In addition, there was a page-long interview, conducted by Selçuk Tepeli, with the Turkish foreign minister Mevlüt Çavuşoğlu, who observed that there was declining support in the US House of Representatives for the so-called genocide resolution. He said: 'The realisation [in Washington, DC] that we don't deny the suffering of the Armenian people breaks their routine thinking. At the end, for the first time ever, we will commemorate all the Ottoman Armenian dead with a religious ceremony. We would like joint Turkish–Armenian commemorations. This is our humanist approach' (Tepeli 2015). On the same page, the columnist Muharrem Sarıkaya also focused on what Obama might say. He considered the announcement that for the first time ever a government minister would attend a religious ceremony in Istanbul to mark the commemoration to be a positive move by the Turkish government. By contrast, he pointed out the diaspora's unhelpful obsession with calling the events a genocide, and he called for the redevelopment of Turkey–Armenia relations (Sarıkaya 2015).

On the same day, the dailies *Zaman* and *Hürriyet* also focused on the international pressure created by the acceptance of the term 'genocide' by a number of countries and commented on the unlikelihood of Obama using it in his annual statement. In the daily *Aydınlık*, Hakkı Keskin covered this issue in his column and advised the government to use the evidence Turkey had against the international claims, suggesting that the Justice and Development Party (Adalet and Kalkinma Partisi, AKP) government was not acting in Turkey's best interests (Keskin 2015: 8). In the same paper, another writer, Mehmet Ali Güller, argued that while 'Obama is not going to say genocide', the AKP government was taking a softer approach by recognizing joint suffering and expressing condolences following a foreign policy venture to develop relations with Armenia under the direction of the United States. He expressed concern that this approach would lead to a situation where 'Turkey might recognise the genocide' (Güller 2015). In his column in the daily *Sözcü*, Rahmi Turan also focused on why Turkey was so concerned about what Obama might say, given that for the United States this was a rational foreign policy decision and not one about friendship. He also mentioned the issue of the Armenian lobby influencing US politicians (Turan 2015). The daily *Vatan* reported on preparations by 145 Turkish-American civil society groups for a peace march in Washington, DC, on 24 April to protest against Armenian attempts to misrepresent history.

This media focus located the question of the commemorations and the genocide as an international concern. Turkey's concerns seemed to be about defending itself against unfounded claims. The addressees of the concerns were outside Turkey. As a result, the coverage made it clear that Turkish people had nothing to think about the issues that were being commemorated. In this way, the sincerity of the Turkish argument was asserted to demonstrate both the gap and the different moral positions between 'us' – benevolent in recognizing common suffering, renovating churches, giving church services – and 'them' – the self-interested diaspora and international actors. The sense of being pressurized on an issue that had nothing to do with 'us' was implicit in most of this coverage, guiding the public through its reference points towards the public memory repertoire to find the right sources to think about the situation. The media repeated some of the narratives from the repertoire, such as joint suffering and the clear distinction between Turkey today and the Ottoman past. These were 'defensive tactics' to protect the institutional denialist architecture against 'the gaze of the other' and 'disruptive experiences', which in this case were being created by multiple international declarations recognizing the genocide (Gillespie 2020: 382).

The next group of discussions broadly presented similar historical analyses to ward off the possibility of encountering other ways of looking at what had happened in 1915. In his column in the daily *Sözcü* on 22 April 2015, Emin Çölaşan talked about the importance of 24 April specifically for Armenians in the United States and reminded readers that '24 April 1915 is the day when 300 Armenian terrorists were arrested in Istanbul' (Çölaşan 2015a). After mentioning that thousands of Armenians had lived across the country and had thousands of schools, churches and orphanages, he stated: 'Including churches, all of these were used to store weapons, and in many places including Istanbul many Armenian revolts emerged' (Çölaşan 2015a). The rest of the piece went over familiar ground, discussing the conditions of the First World War and the necessity to deport internal enemies for reasons of self-defence: in the end, many people had died on both sides, 'but we saved the nation' (Çölaşan 2015a). The designation of the people arrested in Istanbul on 24 April 1915 as terrorists reproduces the logic of 'the enemy within' to maintain an emotional and moral distance from Armenians and the commemorations. In the same paper, columnist Soner Yalçın followed a similar strategy to talk about history. The Ottoman army, he said, had been fighting on different fronts, ranging from Sarıkamış to Suez to Gallipoli. He informed readers that on 27 February 1915 the Ottoman authorities had become aware of a planned Armenian revolt, and they had ordered caution in relation to Armenians who were soldiers in the army. On 18 April 1915, there had been 'Armenian revolts and massacres in Bitlis, Van, Muş, Erzurum and Zeytun' (Yalçın 2015). Next, Yalçın looked at the arrests on 24 April 1915. The readers were informed that on the back of the revolts, the arrests had been relevant to deal with a larger revolt being planned by the Armenian Revolutionary Federation (Dashnaktsutyun) in case the Ottomans failed to win at Gallipoli. Therefore, Ottoman authorities had arrested the Dashnaktsutyun members who were waiting to revolt in Istanbul. In the last section of his column, Yalçın considered the people who had been arrested in Istanbul, suggesting that many had been released and the overall numbers had not been that high.

Writing in the daily *Cumhuriyet*, Mine G. Kırıkkanat began her column by looking at the Armenian Secret Army for the Liberation of Armenia's (ASALA) attack on Orly airport in Paris on 15 July 1983, in which eight people were killed and sixty others injured. Her column was broadly about ASALA terrorism. However, the photos included in the piece implicitly linked ASALA's actions in the 1980s with the Armenians who had revolted in 1915 (Kırıkkanat 2015). The choice to recount ASALA's terrorism as a central concern during the period leading up to the centennial commemorations focused attention on Armenian violence as a singular event. Doing so in this context reiterated an existential security problem in the face of Armenian demands. On 23 April, the daily *Aydınlık* reported that the Patriotic Party (Vatan Partisi), led by Doğu Perinçek, was organizing a big public demonstration on 24 April 2015 to mark the 100th year of the genocide lie. The same newspaper also issued an extensive supplement entitled 'The Historical Realities of Turkish–Armenian Relations'. Over fifteen pages illustrated with photos, the supplement provided knowledge about the situation in Anatolia during the First World War and the atrocities committed by Armenians, in addition to discussing the assassinations by ASALA in the 1970s. The text repeated the reference points that made the public memory repertoire operational, homogenizing Armenians as generally violent. The visual material aimed to emotionally provoke a realization that 'our' forefathers had suffered to defend 'our' people and now 'we' needed to be no less vigilant in the face of 'so-called genocide' claims. The supplement seemed to be supported by the Talat Pasha Committee (Talat Paşa Komitesi), a civil society group founded in 2005 to fight the 'so-called Armenian genocide claims'. This coverage also used the familiar language of the public memory repertoire to reiterate a sense of betrayal due to the behaviour of the enemy within and the unfair international pressure on Turkey. On the whole, this historical engagement aimed to limit the impact of the upcoming commemorations and to prevent the hearing of Armenian voices according to different registers that were not framed by the public memory. As a result, for vast parts of the population who had never met any Armenians, this media coverage provided a singular representation of Armenians whenever they heard about them, both during this period and afterwards.

In his *Habertürk* column on 22 April, Fehmi Koru asked: 'What's in a name?' Looking at what happened in 1915, he highlighted the international obsession with the word 'genocide' (*soykırım*) and the Turkish hesitation (*tereddüt*) to name that event. Although Turkey did not deny that many people had died, he argued, this obsession with naming the event had become an international obstacle, as it was used to put pressure on Turkey. Moreover, he pointed out that the use of the word 'genocide' created different international expectations. His main point concerned the confusion created by the focus on naming the event. According to him, it created an unnecessary problem that could easily be solved if it were left as a matter to be resolved 'between two neighbouring countries, Turkey and Armenia', and that this would be very helpful for our neighbour. He ended the piece by arguing that 'this happens when the name becomes more important than anything else' (koru 2015). The overall effect of Koru's piece was to remind people that the issue was not about a failure to recognize the war dead but about an insistence on exactly what those deaths should be called.

Writing in *Zaman* on 23 April, Ali Yurttagül focused on the difficulty of prioritizing the use of the term 'genocide' without establishing a mutual understanding to unpack the past. He highlighted the relationship between international processes and the diaspora, which he claimed prioritized the use of 'genocide' regardless of its impact on internal discussions in Turkey. On the same day in the daily *Yeni Şafak*, Merve Şebnem Oruç raised historical questions about the responsibility of the Committee of Union and Progress (CUP) during the First World War, arguing that the past remained undetermined. According to her, relations between Turks and Armenians had got stuck between the 'Turkish denialist mindset, which refuses to even discuss such pain', and 'the Armenian diaspora's use of this situation as an imposition rather than a discussion at the international level'. This led her to ask whether the deportations (*tehcir*) had been a function of the particular circumstances of the war, and to suggest that it was important to understand 'the past rather than get stuck on a word' (Oruç 2015). Such thoughts are positioned in the public memory repertoire around the idea of our shared losses during the First World War and Turkey's willingness to engage in a dialogue to acknowledge shared pain. However, these arguments repeat the public memory repertoire that presents the events of 1915 by creating an equivalence between the Armenian population's violent experiences under the Ottoman Empire and the general casualties of war. While this approach purports to consider the understanding of history as a precondition for naming the events of 1915, it seems to ignore the fact that genocide is not *just a name*. 'Genocide' is a multifaceted concept that is used to explain experiences of mass violence and atrocities that target specific groups and communities. In this case, it describes a sociopolitical, cultural and economic process in order to understand what might have happened in 1915. Furthermore, by claiming that 'we' do not know the history of what happened in the past, the approach also seems to assert 'our' innocence in the present due to 'our' lack of knowledge. This negates what is already known by Armenians and others, knowledge that has led many experts to use the concept of genocide to describe the events of 1915 and their aftermath. The approach gives the impression to the reader that no one really knows what happened. Therefore, no one has any responsibility to accept the 'genocide' label used by the Armenian diaspora. Rather than providing historical arguments similar to some of the other discussions mentioned above, this approach creates doubt about what is known, and it locates its discussion within the narrative that Turkey is being pressurized due to international interests.

There were some voices providing more direct and challenging analyses, although they were far too few in number to be noticed within the broader media communication, which focused on international pressures and the historical argument that the Ottomans had merely been defending themselves. For instance, on 22 April 2015 in the daily *Habertürk*, Soli Özel, writing about international recognition processes and Turkey's response to them, pointed out that relations within Turkey created a problem for Armenian-Turkish citizens, who were often made to feel unsafe and insulted, with no judicial process to defend their rights. While he did not use the word 'genocide', it was clear what he was talking about when he wrote: 'There is a lack of moral responsibility, humane understanding and pain linked with the wiping out an autochthonous people and the disappearance of a culture from Anatolia' (Özel 2015). On 23 April in the daily *Taraf*, Mustafa Paçal stated: 'According to many historical records, one million Armenians faced genocide. Now there are about 60,000 Armenians left, mostly living in Istanbul. This is not only Armenians' pain, this is 100 years of pain for all Anatolian people' (Paçal 2015). These views highlight an important problem that underpins the broader media communication I have considered up to this point. Both international pressure and history-based pieces represented the issue as if the main challenge was to resist the pressure from the international (diasporic) community while simultaneously finding a way to discuss and perhaps negotiate an acceptable historical account that would allow Turks to think about 1915. This gives the impression that the concern was only with what to think about 1915 and only in relation to international claims made by others – thus silencing voices, memories and experiences within Turkey since 1915. Such silencing can lead members of public to think, for instance, that the Armenian Turks they encounter in their everyday lives have recently arrived from Armenia – indeed, Turks often express surprise at Armenians' ability to speak Turkish. Arguably, the media framing of the issues described above implicitly reiterates the question of Armenians' belonging in Turkey.

Newspaper coverage on 24 April 2015

On the actual day of the centennial commemorations, the mainstream media maintained its approach to reporting along the lines described above. The daily *Milliyet* covered a number of aspects of the day. The main feature was the story that Turkish Americans had spent ten days guarding the pavement outside the Turkish embassy in Washington, DC, in order to stop Armenian protestors gaining a foothold on the pavement (Ersoy 2015). Another story focused on the statement by the German president, which had used the word 'genocide', and also reported the views of the Azeri ambassador in Ankara. Interestingly, the same page included a report on 'In Memoriam 24 Nisan', a music concert that had been given in Istanbul on the previous evening to mark the centennial. The report appeared under the headline 'Impressive Concert in Memory of Armenian Intellectuals: We Should Fight Together for Justice'. It described the music played and quoted directly from some of the speeches given, including readings from letters written by the victims of the 24 April 1915 deportations – 'letters that made us cry' (Sarı 2015). The report implied the importance of facing the past and referred to the pain of the unaddressed injustice that underpinned the evening. However, it provided little explanation about the intellectuals themselves, why they had been deported and why people had found the music at the concert to be such an emotional experience. Furthermore, the question of justice was somewhat depoliticized, as no explanation was provided as to what had created the injustice or why it remained unaddressed. This was potentially confusing to the reader: the report provided no reference points to guide the reader to find answers to these questions from within the public memory repertoire, nor did it give any substance to its implied orientation towards justice.

Habertürk reported a speech delivered by Erdoğan at the international peace conference organized on 23 April 2015. The conference had been organized by Turkey and hosted by the president to mark the 100th anniversary of the Gallipoli campaign. In the speech, Erdoğan addressed the European Union about our readiness to open our military archives, and he went on to challenge Armenian claims about 1915, including their claims about the numbers involved. He also spoke of the role of Armenian gangs during the First World War, which had posed a serious security challenge for the Ottoman Empire (see Erdoğan 2015b). A small piece referring to a news item distributed by Anadolu Ajansı (AA-Anatolian News Agency) on the same page highlighted the rich holdings of the military archives. This piece seemed to suggest that the archives shed light on the events of 1915, revealing the Ottoman government's concern about the deported Armenians, how the deportees were cared for during the deportations and how their properties were protected. The piece also mentioned the atrocities committed by Armenian gangs (AA 2015). The use of the news item thus seemed to provide evidence to back Erdoğan's statement. What is curious about this evidence is that rather than providing a translation of the document shown in the accompanying photo, the text merely reproduced the reference points of the public memory repertoire – Ottoman benevolence, internal security threats and Armenian gangs.

Aydınlık used the headline 'Diaspora is in Shock' and stated that Turkey had been vindicated by the international courts: 'The spokesperson for the UN Secretary General issued the statement "there is no genocide decision [by the courts]"' (Aydınlık 2015a). The same page also contained a number of other items that, according to the paper, when taken together with the UN position put an end to the lies about genocide. These items included a piece on Hrant Dink comparing his objections against imperialism to *Aydınlık*'s objections against the genocide claim, since the latter amounted to an imperialist attack on Turkey. Another of these items focused on the 1923 report by Hovhannes Kaçznuni (Katchaznouni), Armenia's first prime minister, arguing that his report had acknowledged the atrocities committed by Armenians and had indicated the Ottomans' innocence in 1915. Together with several other pieces inside the newspaper – including one by Mustafa Solak, who argued that 'there was no genocide, but massacres were reciprocal' – the overall coverage reproduced some deeply sedimented narratives from the public memory repertoire (Solak 2015).

By (re)presenting the victimization of Turks, both in 1915 and in the present, this reporting entirely recast and silenced the events that had created the genocide. *Vatan* reported the statements made by the German and Russian presidents and also informed its readers that 24 April had been declared a school holiday in Armenia. Under the headline 'Blood Lobby [*Kan Lobisi*]', the daily *Takvim* placed all the international politicians who had travelled to Yerevan for the centennial commemorations under one umbrella. Producing a list of the atrocities or crimes each country represented at the event was alleged to have committed in the past, it made accusations against them all and asked, given all this, 'how can you accuse Turkey?' (2015). A number of columnists in *Yeniçağ* questioned the genocide claims. For instance, after quoting from Kaçznuni's 1923 report, Selcan Taşçı ended her column by stating that given his acceptance of guilt, 'there is nothing for Turkey to feel remorse about. I have nothing else to say' (Taşçı 2015). On the same page, under the headline 'I Am the Enemy of Whoever Acts with Hostility to Me', Arslan Tekin presented the demands for recognition as anti-Turkish animosity that the diaspora repeated every year. The main point of his column was to draw a distinction: 'We say "Nazi", not "German"; we say "Hinçak", we say "Taşnak" [pointing out Armenian Political Parties], we say "diaspora", we don't say "Armenian"'. He ended on an emotional note, pointing out that the guilt of those who were responsible during that period is now put on all Turks: 'I am a Turk and I cry out – "I am the enemy of whoever acts with hostility to me . . . enough is enough [*yeter be*]"' (Tekin 2015). In similar manner on the same page, Timuçin Mert asked 'who cares if they say "genocide"', arguing 'we are alone in the world, it would not be an exaggeration to say we have no friends'.

There were some exceptions to this general media reporting. One of these was the weekly Armenian-Turkish newspaper *Agos*, the front page of which on 24 April carried a photo of the long disappeared Huşartsan memorial to the Armenian genocide, alongside the statement in Armenian: 'We will not forget and will walk together to the future.' Huşartsan had been erected in 1919 on the grounds of the old Armenian cemetery near Taksim Square but disappeared in 1922. The newspaper's main headline was 'Never-Ending Denial: The Longest Genocide', and the whole of the paper focused on the pre-1915 lives of Armenians in the Ottoman Empire and what had happened during the genocide. The aim was clearly to give depth to the lives of the murdered Armenians, public memory of whom had been erased after the 1920s. The entire newspaper thus acted as a memory box. It not only provided multiple avenues to think about what had happened in 1915, but it also reflected on what had (or had not) happened in Turkey since then. But while it was a powerful public document, its ability to challenge the deployment of the public memory repertoire was very limited. On one hand, *Agos* has a limited and self-selecting readership; on the other, what it communicated was in no way reinforced by the other publicly available sources that are used to communicate with the public, including television programming. The role of TV broadcasting is important given the numbers of people that use TV news and discussion programmes to inform themselves about politics. TV coverage on the whole reinforced the content of the mainstream print media discussed above. TV broadcasting was thus another space within which the media reproduced the public memory repertoire rather than challenging the public to open a space to rethink conventional or normalized narratives.

On 24 April 2015, however, there were some attempts to reinforce *Agos*'s message. The daily *Taraf* published many columns that directly tackled the public memory repertoire. For instance, an interview with Ayhan Aktar appeared under the front-page headline 'Both Deportation and Genocide' (Aktar 2015). In the interview, Aktar challenged (among other things) the notion that Armenians had been a serious threat to Ottoman security at the time. Elsewhere in the paper, Hadi Uluengin talked about 100 years of solitude due to the long-standing denial that had become sociopolitical instinct in Turkey, while Cengiz Aktar commented that it was important to reflect on the scale of the cultural loss if one wished to understand the scale of the disaster for Turkey. These were challenging reflections that tried to introduce registers different from the narratives that constitute public memory. Again, some of these ideas – such as the loss of a previously productive culture in Turkey – were not reinforced in any way and certainly were not part of the publicly available memory repertoire, which depicts Armenians only through representations of violence. Given the public's unfamiliarity with these perspectives, and in the face of the overwhelming coverage of the 'refusal to be pressured by the diaspora into a position on the genocide', these perspectives were unlikely to attract much attention beyond those who were already interested. The most challenging front page was published by the daily *Cumhuriyet*, a paper that is considered to be centre left but is also seen as a custodian of the republic's founding Kemalist values. Its front page carried a photo of Hrant Dink taken in 2004, which showed him walking alone towards the genocide memorial in Yerevan. An inset in the middle of the photo included a statement by Dink's widow, Rakel Dink, along with a photo of her. Above the main photo, which took up most of the page, were the words 'Never Again' in Armenian (Cumhuriyet 2015a). This was a complex representation that drew a link between the genocide and Dink's assassination, challenging the public. The words 'Never Again' created a shared responsibility to think and act differently, bringing what had happened in the past into conversation with the present. This front page was a bold surprise. However, the rest of the newspaper's reporting broadly diverged from the challenging front page. For instance, while the front page was echoed in a piece written by Rakel Dink under the headline '100 Years of Genocide', two other pieces in the paper provided discussions that were more in tune both with *Cumhuriyet*'s general outlook and with the public memory repertoire. One of these pieces presented a document from the military archives to emphasize the careful treatment of Armenians during the deportations and to explain why the deportations had been necessary (Cumhuriyet 2015b). A tension was observable in the rest of the paper's reporting too. The tension concerned whether the issue of the genocide was about the past or (also) about the present.

Many journalists seemed willing to acknowledge and share the pain the Armenians had suffered, but they wanted to do so in a way that did not commit them to challenging the common understanding of events produced through the memory repertoire. While *Cumhuriyet*'s act of solidarity was remarkable, it did not go far enough to tackle the subtle reproduction of the public memory repertoire by providing a different baseline for use in further communications with the public. Nevertheless, both the paper and its then new editor Can Dündar came under fire in the media in subsequent days, as I will discuss later in this chapter.

What happened at the actual commemorations on the day in Istanbul?

Following the previous evening's memorial concert 'In Memoriam 24 Nisan', 24 April 2015 began early for those who wanted to attend the commemoration programme. The first event was in Harbiye in front of the house from which Gomidas and Avedis Nakkaşyan had been taken. Having discussed this particular event at length in Chapter 2, I will not repeat the details here. At the end of that event, participants were reminded of the day's other events. One was to be held in Sultanahmet Square in the heart of the old city, in front of the Museum of Turkish and Islamic Arts, which in 1915 had been a prison where the arrested Armenians had initially been kept. After that, the commemorations were going to move across the Bosporus to Haydarpaşa railway station, where in 1915 the Armenian arrestees had been put on trains to be sent to Anatolia. There was also another event scheduled in the Armenian cemetery in Şişli. I decided to go to Sultanahmet Square. On arrival in the area, in addition to the normal tourist crowds, I found a gathering of people holding posters outside the museum. Lined up in front of the old prison, the posters all repeated the same message in Turkish, English and Armenian: '100 Years of the Genocide. Recognise! Apologise! Compensate!' Other people stood behind the posters, holding photos of some of the Armenians arrested on 24 April 1915. A sizeable group waited in solidarity while the protestors took their time to protest in this memory space. There was also a clear police presence, and the museum's security guards were trying to make sure that people could still enter and exit the building. The protestors were a mixed group of people, including a few recognizable Turkish intellectuals. Many wore stickers or pins with purple forget-me-not flowers, the symbol of the centennial commemorations. This was interesting, because it signalled who was in the group of protestors and who was not, at times creating some wariness.

People chatted together in various languages, and they were evidently aware of their surroundings. Some were wondering whether any of those who had gathered to watch the protest presented any danger. An Armenian Turkish group was giving out its own commemorative pamphlet to those who were interested. There was a speech by a representative of the human rights association Dur De, which had organized this part of the day together with other groups working on the Armenian genocide from outside Turkey. By this time, the crowd was sizeable – about 300 people – and the speech made a clear political statement in front of media representatives, including making demands on the government. There were critical moments. One was when a number of people who had the opportunity to speak emphasized that they were the grandchildren of those who had been killed and that they would not forget. Another critical moment was when they read a long list of the places across Turkey from which Armenians had been taken and killed. After these speeches, we were told that we were going to walk down to Sirkeci and Eminönü to take a hired boat to Haydarpaşa. As the event drew to a close, an elderly Armenian-French man was being interviewed by a TV crew. He was talking about his great uncle, Siamento-Atom Yercanyan. He said: 'When we were young, we were told that Kurds were from mountains and Turks were killers. But, of course, this has now changed, to see a few Turkish intellectuals here with us is very important and moving.' I thought that even though we were a self-selected group, his words might be a little dangerous, particularly as they were delivered in a foreign language, and that they might trigger the ever-present imaginary of the hostile diaspora. Before I could finish my thoughts, another man approached the TV crew and asked them to interview him as an Azeri citizen. He said: 'I also want to say something. I come from Azerbaijan, and I did not know this event, but can I say something?' The interviewer said that this was a specific event and they were not really interested in polemics. The Azeri man replied: 'No, no polemics. I just want to say that my family was killed, my mother was killed by the Armenians.' The elderly Armenian-French man became agitated, saying this was nothing to do with him. The interviewer, gently and with some courage, terminated the conversation. But it was becoming obvious that a group of people – mostly men in dark glasses – were milling about around the flowerbeds that surrounded the participants in the commemoration, and they had observed this whole conversation. There was a feeling that the request to be interviewed had not been entirely serendipitous and had possibly been intended to provoke an argument.

We were again told the route we would take to walk down to the port. We were also told that all the signs and posters had to be taken down and no banners could be carried while we walked, only flowers (carnations). It was clear that any glimpse of a poster or banner would give the authorities an excuse to stop the walk as an unauthorized protest. My immediate thought was that this was a really interesting sign of control and power. If we were marching without banners, how would anyone understand what the march was about? We marched from Sultanahmet through Cağaloğlu and down Cağaloğlu Hill (Cağaloğlu Yokuşu) towards Sirkeci and Eminönü. There were large numbers of foreigners among the marchers, and the direction of the walk was not always very clear; it seemed the organizers did not want to attract attention by making it more of a coherent march. Some bystanders nonetheless realized that a group was walking down the hill. I could hear from their conversations that they were pondering what it might be all about. Talking among themselves, some said: 'Look, there is a demonstration [*abi bak gösteri var*]', and some even mentioned Armenians (*Ermeniymiş bunlar galiba*). But in general most people did not understand what was going on. There was palpable tension in the air. Talking on his mobile in Turkish to his family, one person said, 'Things are fine so far, no problems, but if something happens I'll give you a call.' He added that because of anxiety he had not had time to eat, but he would eat after the event in Haydarpaşa.

I walked with the others all the way to Galata Bridge. It was an odd experience as we made our way through large tourist crowds in somewhat isolated smaller groups. Unless any of these tourists already knew the significance of 24 April, there was no indication that might lead them to think that something specific was happening, or that people were marching for a commemoration. There was obvious unease among our group, a sense of being watched and of the inability to publicly communicate the reasons why we were marching or walking. The carnations were the only outward sign that this was a group with an intention – but again, perhaps even this was only a sign to those who already knew.

Questions ran through my head. Who was this event for? Was it just for ourselves, for those who already knew about it and had turned up to participate? What was the effect of this event, a walk through the centre of the old city with no signs or posters? Who constituted the public in this instance? As my fellow marchers took the boat to Haydarpaşa, I walked over the bridge to Galatasaray to observe a demonstration organized by the Patriotic Party against the lies about the 'so-called genocide'.

A large crowd had gathered in front of Galatasaray High School to march along İstiklal Avenue (İstiklal Caddesi) to Taksim Square. As it is the centre of the city, demonstrations in Taksim Square have a special significance. İstiklal Avenue is the main artery through the historic district of Pera, and it too is a significant place: it was the heart of many non-Muslims' lives in Istanbul during the latter period of the Ottoman Empire and into the republican period, and many Armenian, Greek and Jewish people lived and worked there until the end of 1950s. The crowd in front of the school's historic gates on İstiklal Avenue carried an immense number of Turkish national and party political flags. There were also many Azeri national flags. Some people carried huge banners bearing many different slogans. The mostly widely repeated slogans included 'We Are Atatürk's Soldiers [*Atatürkün askerleriyiz*]', 'Turkish-Armenians Brothers, America Don't

Interfere [*Türk-Ermeni Kardeş, Amerika Karıştırma*]' and 'We Did Not Commit Genocide, We Saved the Country [*Soykırım yapmadık, Vatan kurdardık*]'. Most surprisingly for me, there were also some large posters bearing Hrant Dink's face and a statement about anti-imperialism. This was really perverse. There must have been at least 5,000 people, both men and women of different ages, led by politicians and some public intellectuals. As they started to march, I felt reluctant to march with them, given the sentiments they were communicating; for me, this was an immediate emotional reaction. After a while I stood to one side and watched them pass by from a shop front. Some shopkeepers came out and applauded the march. It was not easy to be a bystander: people on the march urged everyone to join them, shouting slogans, and it was hard to hear anything else. At times I was approached and urged to join. At one point, a woman in her sixties carrying a banner approached me and asked, 'Why don't you join, what is your problem?' This was repeated a number of times. To my mind, the difference between this march and the earlier one in the old city was stark. There was no hiding here: the posters and flags were carried openly and proudly, and the slogans were shouted very loudly. The security forces seemed to be facilitating the progress of the march towards the Republic Monument in Taksim Square. In this manner the march reached Taksim Square and laid a wreath at the monument. Although the square has general significance for demonstrations in Istanbul, it was exceptional for the authorities to allow the marchers to reach the monument, as in recent years such actions had been banned and access to the square had been very closely monitored, particularly since the Gezi Park protests of 2013 (Seckinelgin 2016).

I did not join them in Taksim Square. Instead, I returned to Galata to attend a panel discussion organized by the Istanbul Bar Association to mark the day. The event was entitled 'On the 100th Anniversary of Transfers [*Nakil*] and Resettlement [*İskan*]: From Historical Reality to Political Fiction [*Kurgu*]'. It was held in the Bar Association's own building and included five speakers, with the deputy head of the Bar Association chairing the event. The speakers were historians and a lawyer, while the audience was a mix of between forty-five and fifty people, including experts, students and members of the general public. I describe this event in detail in Chapter 6, but I will note here that as the event was small, its impact on the public was probably limited. Nevertheless, it brought together academics who had appeared on various TV channels both before 24 April and on the day itself to discuss their views. It was an interesting meeting that reaffirmed why 'we' thought there had been no genocide. It was also a challenging event to sit through. In addition to targeting the diaspora, the speakers repeatedly singled out Turkish researchers working on the genocide, categorizing them as traitors, degenerates and 'bad blood [*kanı bozuk*]'. It was a relief to leave the building at the end of the event. The next event that had been announced for the day was a centennial commemoration march, again beginning at Galatasaray and following the route of the earlier march to Taksim Square.

This time, however, on arriving in Galatasaray I observed a different environment. There was an obvious increased presence of security force personnel, some of them in anti-riot gear, and there were armoured anti-riot vehicles. Curiously, there was also a small group of young protesters from the earlier march who had been allowed to remain in the same place, right in front of Galatasaray High School's gates and just behind the security personnel. While people gathered to commemorate the genocide, this small group carried flags and banners, one of them with the provocative slogan 'We Did Not Commit Genocide, We Saved the Country'. Tension was certainly in the air. Just across from this small group, a huge crowd was waiting to march with banners and signs in various languages (Turkish, Armenian, Kurdish and English) to commemorate the genocide. Although they were in marching formation, the police had not yet allowed the march to go ahead. The crowd was getting impatient. Then news passed through the crowd that the police would not allow the march to go ahead with any signs or banners other than the one being carried at the head of the march. The crowd was constantly warned not to raise any banners or posters so that the march could begin. At the same time, it was clear that the march was not going to be allowed into Taksim Square but would finish at the end of İstiklal Avenue, in front of the French Cultural Centre.

It was already clear to me that this march was being treated differently from the one that had taken place earlier. There was more security, and more pressure on the marchers to act in a certain way as a condition of being allowed to march at all. In any case, they were not allowed to go into Taksim Square. As we waited, it was also clear that many in the large crowd were speaking many different languages, including various Kurdish dialects as well as Armenian, Turkish, English and French. I decided to join the crowd as the march was getting ready. A number of people turned to look at me to see who I was, clearly suspicious that I might be an undercover security officer. The suspicion and unease were palpable in the tight space where everyone was waiting. A girl in front of me in her late twenties suddenly handed me a sign, telling me with a smile to 'hold it and walk with it'. The sign bore Hrant Dink's photo. I thought this was really to check whether I was willing to do it or not. I could see that a number of people around me were still a little uneasy about a stranger standing alone in their midst.

When the march finally moved off, the crowd was chanting in number of languages. They also chanted 'the criminal state will answer' in Turkish. This was a direct attack on the state, not on a specific government. There was anger in the crowd that after 100 years they were still being ignored. This generated some unease, and the march stopped few times along the way and was told not to chant. By this time daylight was fading, yet it was not hard to see that on top of the buildings all along the route there were riot police, what appeared to be sharpshooters, and cameras apparently recording the march. İstiklal Avenue is a long and not very wide pedestrianized street, and the buildings along it are tall, making the area very easy to control. While I could feel the anger, and the tangible danger, I could also see that people were exhilarated by the opportunity to shout such slogans in the middle of the city and march to mark the centennial. I thought this was outside the normal run of things, as the people were allowed to pass through, even though I remained worried about a possible intervention. After all, this area had been one of the main scenes of the Istanbul pogrom of 6–7 September 1955, when minority businesses, religious spaces and homes had been attacked and damaged by a government-sponsored mob on the pretext of nationalist sentiment. I also could not help wondering: Even if the march was allowed to go through, who would hear these voices? Would it be broadcasted or discussed in the news? After the head of the march reached the designated point, everyone gradually filled the entrance to İstiklal Avenue. A moment of silence was observed to remember the victims, and there were speeches that directly called on the Turkish state to respond and acknowledge the genocide. Again, I wondered who would hear these voices. Indeed, I wondered how far the largely self-selected public that was participating in the centennial commemorations, the march and other events would be heard by the broader Turkish public at all.

After the speeches, the crowd slowly dispersed. It had been a moving event that combined the current reality of the situation in Istanbul with reflections on the past. I went to catch a *dolmuş* (minibus taxi) back to Suadiye on the Anatolian side of the city. Sitting at the front of the *dolmuş*, I found myself next to a man in his late fifties. During the journey he received a phone call. Very quietly, he said 'yes' in Armenian, then switched to Turkish to say, 'I am fine and on my way. It was crowded but also very moving.' After hanging up he sat in silence, a little wary because I was sitting so close. I was still holding the sign that had been given to me during the march, which was folded up in my hand with few other things. As we drove through Istanbul, I gradually turned the sign right side out so that Dink's photo was visible, and I left it open on my lap. I noticed at one point that the man sitting next to me had spotted the sign. As I got out of the *dolmuş*, I turned to close the door, and he faintly smiled and nodded his head to say good evening. I thought he was also acknowledging an affinity and an appreciation, based on our sharing something in common. This happened very fast and only as a communication between two people who were returning from the same event; it would have been hard for anyone else to notice. Through the photo we acknowledged each other, but we did not chat about the event as we sat side by side. I walked home and thought about what had just happened in the *dolmuş*. The man had been navigating two publics in which the normal language he used positioned him differently: at the commemoration event, he had been within a group where his language made him a part of that group; in the *dolmuş*, his language had marked him as Other, or so he had thought. He clearly had not been happy to use Armenian to converse on the phone in a *dolmuş* as he sat between the driver and another anonymous man. However, I had not been too comfortable either, I realized: I had wanted to carry the sign inside out so that the photo and writing on it would not be visible to other people as I travelled home.

At home, I immediately turned on the TV to see how the various news programmes would cover the events. Apart from one channel, CNN.Türk, many did not mention the commemorations at all. Those that did mention them focused on the Patriotic Party march as our response to Armenia, and then mentioned that members of the diaspora had also marched during the evening. The different events that had taken place, the speeches that had explained why the commemoration was happening and who the participants were – all of this was largely silenced. Even a speech by a young Armenian-Turkish woman was reported as a statement by a member of the diaspora demanding things from 'us'. I had been part of the day, and I had heard many voices expressing past and present experiences; but for those who had not been there, none of these events had happened, and no voices had been heard. This attitude was also apparent in the next day's media coverage.

Newspaper coverage the next day

On 25 April 2015, the coverage of the events of the previous day broadly replicated the coverage that had led up to 24 April, ignoring and silencing the questions raised by the commemorations. Common themes touched on in the reporting were the role of the diaspora and international actors in the public debate, historical arguments purporting to prove that the genocide claims did not make sense and the idea of our shared pain. The reports pondered on the question of how many Turkish people might recognize that pain if only the debate were not clouded by 'so-called genocide' claims from outside the country. Considering the intensity of this coverage, 'silencing' might sound like an inappropriate term. However, for me, the coverage silenced multiple sources of thinking differently about the events of 1915 and afterwards. By focusing on reference points that were acceptable within the boundaries of public memory, the coverage silenced the ways of thinking that had been voiced at the previous day's events, even while it talked constantly about the 'Armenian issue' (*Ermeni Meselesi*). In this way, it reinforced and implicitly reasserted the public memory through the repetition of its reference points, guiding the public to remember the events in question.

Most papers focused their reporting on the main formal event of the day, the Mass held by the Armenian patriarchate at Surp Kevork Church, which for the first time had been attended by a government official. In major dailies such as *Milliyet*, *Habertürk*, *Sabah* and *Hürriyet*, this reporting concentrated on facts and highlighted statements made by Bozkır and Erdoğan. As he had left the church, Bozkır had said he was honoured to have participated in the Mass, and he had expressed his wish to consider events between 1870 and 1920 rather than just focusing on 1915. He said: 'In this way, it will be possible to look at a shared history. A shared memory, but a just memory, will emerge. We respect the experiences of Armenian brothers and sisters [*kardeşlerimiz*].' Erdoğan's statement had been read out in church by one of the priests. It had emphasized how welcoming Turks were, regardless of past animosities, referring to the annual joint commemorations of the Battle of Çanakkale with 'the grandchildren of our past enemies'. It added: 'I once more want to reiterate that we know the tragic [*hüzünlü*] events the Armenian community experienced and we share your pain with sincerity' (Erdoğan 2015b). This was a clear attempt to decentre the centennial of the genocide, focusing on the Battle of Çanakkale to further negate the genocidal violence experienced by Armenians as part of the narrative of general war conditions (see Yıldız 2021: 130–4).

On the same page as this report, *Milliyet* also published three smaller items on commemoration events including the first event of the day at Şişli (Karakaş 2015a). They mentioned the march that had ended at the French Cultural Centre. The small headline was 'Sit-in Protest in Front of the Consulate', and the event was described as 'a protest in Taksim related to the events of 1915'

(Karakaş 2015b). There was no description of the crowd, other than an emphasis on the participation of the diaspora and Armenians from Armenia. The piece also described the slogans that had been seen on the march about the genocide and Hrant Dink ('We Are Hrant, We Are Armenian'). It ended by describing the march as a 'sit-in protest' that had included photos of people deported from Istanbul on 24 April 1915. Similarly, on a page that mainly dealt with the formal centennial Mass, *Hürriyet* reported the Taksim Square event under the headline 'In Taksim, Commemoration and Protest'. This short piece mostly reported on counter-protests by associations that had used slogans such as 'Armenian Genocide Claim Is Not Possible. Real Massacres Were Committed by Armenians in Turkish Villages' (Purtul and Alkaç 2015). The next piece in *Milliyet* talked about the morning's event in front of the Cumhuriyet pharmacy, which I described in Chapter 2. Again, what is interesting about this piece is the emphasis on the diaspora: it began with the sentence, 'The Armenian diaspora, in collaboration with the Turkish human rights organisation Dur De, was in Istanbul for the 100th anniversary of the 1915 events' (Karakaş 2015a). The last, much smaller piece was about the memorial held for Sevag Balıkçı at the Armenian cemetery, although the photo accompanying the piece showed an event on the steps of Haydarpaşa railway station. The same page also included a report on the commemoration in Diyarbakır in Surp Sarkis Armenian Church; the report in this case focused on the statement by Selahattin Demirtaş, the joint leader of the People's Democratic Party (Halklarin Demokratik Partisi).

The pieces I highlight above, and some others like them, might appear to be factual reports by comparison with the opinion pieces written by the newspapers' columnists. There was no commentary attached to them. However, what was chosen for reporting, and the choice of words to describe the events, suggests something different. The choice of events and the language used guided the public communication and focused the public's attention on particular aspects of the commemoration events. The wider context of each reported event, and the questions raised within each event in relation to describing and thinking differently about the implications of 1915, was all silenced. For instance, the language broadly designated the events as diaspora-led and reframed the commemorations as protests (*eylem*). Similarly, the reporting of church services for the victims of 1915 made the issue appear to be others' 'pain and suffering' and our decency in showing our understanding of that pain. This implicitly established an 'us and them' logic that implied foreign interests and questions about 'our' security, at both individual and national levels. In this binary logic, it is not clear what understanding 'their' pain means or what the implications of this understanding are for acting and thinking differently. Thus, this communication erased the substantive questions raised by the centennial process. What was communicated to the public about the centennial further limited the public's ability to think how and what to do. The communication seemed to reiterate that neither the events of 1915 nor the centennial commemorations had anything to do with 'us'. They were mostly matters for the Armenian diaspora. This reinforced the centrality of the public memory repertoire as a way to contain thinking and communication within the language of the 'Armenian issue'.

While these reports silenced what exactly had happened during the centennial events in Istanbul, columnists in these media sources tended to further reinforce the public memory repertoire. For instance, in his column for *Milliyet* on 25 April, Güneri Cıvaoğlu chose to talk about historical conditions, calling on everyone to 'open their archives and see whether it was a genocide' (Cıvaoğlu 2015). Then he argued that Kaçznuni's report was enough to settle the issue against the claims of genocide: the report indicated that 'Turks knew what they were doing in 1915' and that they had been correct to take the action they took. The use of the language of 'Turks' is interesting in itself, as it allowed the communication to reinforce an ahistorical understanding of 'us' and 'them'. In the same issue of *Milliyet*, Hasan Pulur followed a similar line to justify the deportations and disagree with the claims of genocide. He ended by arguing that 'at the time, not only Armenians but many others also suffered' (Pulur 2015). In *Habertürk*, Nihal Bengisu Karaca began her column by reflecting on the other event of 24 April, the international peace conference in Çanakkale. She talked about the impact of the diaspora on the prestige of Turkey and reflected on Erdoğan's centennial message, pointing out that by taking such a positive approach rather than fretting about whether the US president would or would not say 'genocide' every year, Turkey should start raising questions about Europe's memory of events between 1821 and 1922, through Greek independence, the Balkan Wars and the First World War, in relation to Muslim populations (on 26 April, the daily *Yeni Akit* allocated an entire page to this particular issue) (Karaca 2015).

In *Sözcü*, Emin Çölaşan argued that 'we did not manage to put our case to the world properly compared with palm-sized Armenia'. He then repeated the historical narrative that Armenians had attacked Turks in 1915, and he criticized the Turkish government for not making an effective case against all these claims of genocide (2015b). Two columnists in the daily *Takvim* were even more direct in their arguments. Mehmet Akarca's piece used the familiar reference points of betrayal, ASALA and the diaspora. He wrote that there was no point sending these softer messages, as all these claims about genocide were 'Armenian historical ingratitude against a state that considered Armenians a loyal nation [*millet-i sadıka*]' (2015). He ends his piece with an implicit threat. His argument was that we should approach the issue in such a way as to put the Armenian diaspora on the defensive. Kurtuluş Tayiz writing in Akşam was interested in why the claim of genocide was supported today and painted a picture of a concerted attempt to undermine the integrity of the Turkish nation. The attempt involved the diaspora, anti-Turkish lobbies including the 'genocide lobby' and Turkish liberals who were working on these issues. He also praised Erdoğan's initiative to counter this attack on Turkey by organizing the international peace conference in Çanakkale (2015). *Aydınlık* published a photo of Obama superimposed on a photo of the march by the Patriotic Party, with the headline 'You Are the Great Disaster' (Aydınlık 2015b). The aim was to challenge Obama's use of the phrase 'great disaster' (*meds yeghern*), the Armenian term for the genocide, using the photo of the march as evidence of the 'great' opposition to his position. Inside the paper, in addition to the standard reporting, there was a small report on centennial commemorations in Armenia under the headline 'Fake Ceremony in Yerevan' (Aydınlık 2015b). Another page was devoted to Patriotic Party leader Perinçek's march to Taksim Square and his speech. A small headline on the same page said: 'Yesterday the Armenian Bandits, Today the PKK' (Aydınlık 2015b). This piece reported on the work of Uluç Gürkan, a former deputy speaker of the Turkish parliament, who had pointed out that the West had armed Armenians to fight the Turkish state during the First World War, arguing that the Kurdistan Workers' Party (Partiya Karkeren Kurdistan, PKK) was today being armed in a similar way.

The media reporting created a relationship between the arguments propagated by newspaper columnists and the equivocally factual accounts of the previous day's events. The media thus not only asserted the public memory repertoire but also undermined the possibility of thinking differently about the centennial commemorations. The comparison to the PKK (Kurdistan Workers' Party that is a militant, armed guerrilla group, political movement, considered as a terrorist group) and the use of the word 'terror' in general were attempts to negate Armenian experiences by turning the issue into 'our' security problem, in line with narratives in the repertoire. The media thereby asserted a national position for engagement with both the centennial and the questions raised by the commemoration events. A homogenous national understanding of and emotion about 1915 and its aftermath were asserted in order to dismiss those questions. By reinforcing each other, factual reports and opinion pieces in the media clearly communicated an understanding that confirmed for the public that 'we' bore no responsibility for the claims about 1915 developed by the Armenian diaspora and international interests. This further reinforced the public's defensive attitude towards questions about 1915. Before I conclude this chapter, I would also like to highlight that on 25 April 2015 there were a few voices in the media that provided different ways to think about the genocide centennial. Various columnists in *Hürriyet* engaged with the issue, and their approach was more nuanced than that taken by the pieces discussed above.

Ertuğrul Özkök, for instance, devoted the main part of his column to his opposition to one of the posters used in Yerevan during the centennial commemorations. The poster showed cartoons of two heads: one was recognizable as an Ottoman, with the date '1915' written between the fez and the moustache; the other had '1939' written between a flop of hair and a moustache that was easily recognizable as Hitler. The aim of the poster was evident. Özkök argued that while the poster attributed the Holocaust to one individual, the 1915 tragedy was attributed to all Turks, as the head in the poster could not be identified with a specific individual. He wrote: 'Look, my brother, I am not denying "Medz Yeghern", the "Great Disaster", but as someone who is proud to be Turkish, I reject this poster.' The piece ended with another call: 'Dear brother, if you remove that poster you will see among Turks living in this country, even if it's late, there are millions who feel the pain of the tragedy of 1915.' In the other part of his column, he presented an imagined scenario under the title 'I Had a Dream, the PM [prime minister] Was Standing in Silence [*saygı duruşu*] in Yerevan' (Özkök 2015). The piece imagined a situation where Turkish government officials would participate in the centennial commemorations and the Armenian president would participate in the Çanakkale commemorations. Özkök ended this piece with a reflection: 'Yesterday was 24 April 2015. That morning I woke up from a dream, it was a very beautiful dream. Afterwards, I returned to the reality of hate as sorrowful as 1915' (Özkök 2015). Verda Özer's column reported on an interview she had conducted with Emin Mahir Balcıoğlu, the son of Beşir Balcıoğlu, a Turkish diplomat assassinated by ASALA in Madrid in 1978. While the interview was broadly about his experience and how he had dealt with the impact of the assassination, he also talked about moving away from hate and the importance of empathy. He spoke about the diaspora, saying that hate had become part of their identity and how difficult it was to solve this problem. He supported more dialogue between Armenians and Turks to build relations through empathy (Özer 2015).

These examples were attempting to communicate different ways to discuss and think about Armenians and the events of 1915. However, by comparison with the rest of the media coverage, they did not present a strong position reinforced by other sources that provided knowledge to the public. They were limited in their ability to make a profound impact on what was being communicated. Furthermore, their appeal to reasonableness and empathy perhaps did not unpack the conditions under which the public would be able to think in reasonable ways to understand the situation. These interventions attempted to intervene in an environment where the mass media, by reporting the facts selectively, did not allow the public to see ongoing problems. For instance, very few media sources at the time reported that on the morning of 24 April 2015, the Nationalist Turkish Party (Milliyetçi Türkiye Partisi) and its youth wing Turan Ocakları laid a black wreath in front of *Agos*. The small-circulation paper *Yurt* reported this action on 25 April 2015 under the front-page headline 'Again Racist Provocation', with a photo of two people holding the wreath and giving fascist salutes.

Ahmet Hakan's piece in *Hürriyet* stood out in this regard. A journalist and TV personality, he had become a public figure, and his column on 25 April 2015 carried the headline 'Seven Theses on the Armenian Issue [*Meselesi*]' (Hakan 2015). He articulated his seven theses as a series of questions rather than in narrative form. His questions directly targeted the common reference points of the public memory repertoire. He wondered 'if it was really true that Armenian gangs were attacking and all the problems emerged from this . . . Why were all the Armenians deported, and why did the Armenian massacres happen? Why were the sins of the gangs taken out on sinless Armenians? (Hakan 2015)' Then he asked:

> Why are we remembering the CUP, the creators of the deportations, . . . instead of those people who protected Armenians and opposed the deportations, such as governors Reşit Bey and Mehmet Celal Bey or Mutasarrıf Faik Ali Bey. . . . Why aren't we shouting these names as our real forefathers? (Hakan 2015)

Next, he challenged those who said nothing had happened: 'Then what happened to the Armenians, who are one of the autochthonous nations of these lands? Where did they go? What happened to their property? Who appropriated those properties?' The next question he asked referred to the alleged peacefulness of the Turkish character:

> When we still use the word 'Armenian' as an insult, and before we say 'Armenians' we say 'excuse me', and we leave a black wreath on a day like this in front of *Agos*, where Hrant Dink was assassinated, how can we explain to the world that we are the most humanistic people and convince the world of our innocence that we would not even harm an ant? (Hakan 2015)

Finally, he moved on to the issue of genocide:

> Let's say it was not a genocide. . . . Does this save us from addressing the problems? Will we be spotless? Are we going to be cleansed of all the sins of our history? What are we going to do with those who signed the atrocious deportation orders? What are we going to do with all those who participated when they heard 'Armenians were massacred'? What are we going to do with the blood that was spilled? What are we going to do with the homes destroyed? (Hakan 2015)

These questions go to the heart of the problem with the public memory repertoire. They challenge the common wisdom established by that repertoire in public discussions. But while Hakan communicated them very effectively, one might ask who the addressees of these questions should be. It is clear from Hakan's writing that he was primarily targeting the public, and those in positions of authority as part of that public, to think about the justifications used in everyday life to dispute the events of 1915. Hakan's challenge was no doubt one of the boldest statements in the media, alongside the coverage in the daily *Taraf*, which reported the events under the headline 'See and Hear My Brother and Sister [*Kardeşim*]' and directly used the word 'genocide' in its reporting. *Taraf* also contained various columns dealing with the genocide: Ümit Kardaş wrote about Raphael Lemkin and the concept of genocide, while Hayko Bağdat discussed the public's inability to speak about what had happened and how the reproduction of public memory on this date stunted their emotions.

Amid all the intensely anti-Armenian and self-defensive mass media communication, these rare instances had a limited effect, as their messages did not relate to the public memory but rather challenged it. The debates that took place on many TV programmes also propagated the public memory repertoire. For instance, on the evening of 24 April, CNN broadcasted two episodes of Taha Akyol's documentary on the Ottoman Empire during 1914–18 (I will consider these episodes closely later in the book). The episodes focused on the eastern provinces and the 'Armenian issue' to explain why the deportations had been seen as necessary and why there had been a security risk, in effect reproducing the public memory repertoire. As such, they provided a knowledge base for the public to counter Hakan's questions.

The media's onslaught against challenging views was epitomized in other newspapers' attacks on *Cumhuriyet*'s front page of 24 April. The overall aim of these attacks when they appeared on 25 April 2015 was to undermine the credibility of *Cumhuriyet*'s approach in the eyes of the public. Writing in the daily *Sabah*, Hilal Kaplan began her column by accusing *Cumhuriyet* of hypocrisy, pointing out that in its early days the paper had used the Matosyan printing house, which had been confiscated from its Armenian owner in 1915. In *Aydınlık*, in a column headed '"Genocide" Brotherhood', Murat Şimşek criticized *Cumhuriyet*'s front page of 24 April and its publication of Rakel Dink's letter by linking it explicitly to the position of *Özgür Gündem*, which he called a PKK publication (Aydınlık 2015b). The immediate link thus established between Kurdish terrorism and the use of the word 'genocide' communicated that both publications were trying to undermine 'our' integrity, thereby producing a sense of insecurity. In *Sabah*, Melih Altınok wondered what had happened to the old nationalist, CUP-friendly *Cumhuriyet*, which was now virtually accommodating nationalist Armenian discourse (Altınok 2015). He also told the story of how in 1924 *Cumhuriyet* had used Matosyan, the printing house whose owner had had to 'leave' Turkey. What is remarkable in all these discussions is the absence of any voices from the centennial events, either to raise different questions or to explain how the public might understand those questions. The case of *Cumhuriyet* demonstrates that the debate was taking place within a closed system of self-reference and self-defence that established and confirmed 'our' position to seek compliance from those who belonged to 'us'.

Conclusion

While most of the mass media coverage reproduced the familiar and normalized public memory repertoire in the face of the 2015 commemoration events, Hakan's questions revealed the national threshold of public memory (Han 2018: 34). At this threshold, the public faces the unfamiliar and the anxiety it creates. It is important to unpack the relationship between Hakan's approach and that of the rest of the media. As Byung-Chul Han (2018: 34) argues, 'the threshold is a transition to the unknown'; beyond it, 'a completely different state of being begins'. Perhaps the general media coverage acted as a mechanism to inform the public about itself, to distance the public from the threshold created by the centennial of the genocide.

The overwhelming coverage repeatedly deployed narratives from the repertoire that either were based on our victimhood or silenced the questions raised by the genocide. The aim of the coverage was to ward off the potential transformation that crossing the threshold would produce. By not reporting in full on the 2015 commemoration events, the media created a distance from the threshold those events created. The coverage achieved this by re-emphasizing the familiar and normalized tropes about Armenians that were underwritten by the public memory. In this way, anxiety and transformative ways of thinking about Armenians were averted. The coverage only allowed what Han (2018: 28) calls the 'differences that conform to the system' to emerge. Thus, Armenians emerged as different from and opposite to what was represented by Turkish national subjectivity. They also emerged as a uniform Otherness. This erased Armenians' independent voices and their ability to appear and express themselves in public in diverse ways. The public received an image of generic Armenians, without seeing or hearing what was being voiced at different events by different people. According to Han (2018), not hearing and not seeing means that individuals within the public cannot perceive the Other in relation to themselves, hearing the voice of the Other 'allows the entirely Other to irrupt into the self' (Han 2018: 39).

Regardless of the claims that the commemorations and the questions about the Armenian genocide had nothing substantially to do with 'us', the coverage I have considered in this chapter suggested that the commemorations were not simply ignored as irrelevant. On the contrary, the mass media seems to have participated deeply in the commemorations, signifying that all this had a lot to do with 'us'. One can see the mass media and its reproduction of the public memory repertoire as an intervention to stop us from hearing the Other, since hearing might lead to listening: 'First I must welcome the Other, which means affirming the Other in their otherness. Then I give them an ear' (Han 2018: 70). It is possible that the ferocity of the coverage and its heavy use of different narratives from the repertoire indicated that the public's understanding was considered to be fragile and unstable. Thus, there was a need to turn on the repertoire to remind people of our memorialized history as citizens.

The next three chapters look closely at three interrelated parts of the mechanism through which this memorialized repertoire creates a baseline for the majority of the public to be comprehensible to one another, as citizens and members of an imagined community.

4

Public memory and the mass media

The previous chapter showed how the mass media intervenes in public discussions of the Armenian genocide in Turkey by reproducing narratives from the public memory repertoire. Each reproduction of the public memory repertoire's language strengthens the memorialization of those narratives as the content of the history that should be remembered. In this chapter, I focus on the role of the mass media (newspapers and TV) as not only a transmitter of information but also one of the main sources of knowledge in these debates. By focusing on the media in this way here, I position the centennial coverage discussed in the last chapter within its broader narrative context and analyse the media's role in gradually normalizing a particular way of knowing about the events of 1915.

In his recent work, Joachim J. Savelsberg (2021: 79) points out that 'Armenian ethnic organizations are potent contributors to genocide knowledge' insofar as they are a 'carrier group' and 'carriers of collective memory'. Turning this lens onto Turkey, I argue that the mass media constitutes a carrier group for the public memory repertoire. Over time, the mass media's repeated interventions establish what it communicates as the baseline knowledge for the public in Turkey. This is not the kind of knowledge that grows 'out of lived experience of social groups, including the experience of violence' (Savelsberg 2021: 55). Nonetheless, it seems to me that the knowledge the media communicates through its repetition becomes part of lived experience. But 'lived experience' here refers to repeated exposure to the media's communication of specific knowledge in Turkey. In some ways, this lived experience means that this knowledge becomes the only thing the public remembers intergenerationally.

Thus, I argue in this chapter first that by using specific reference points (such as the language of the 'Armenian issue') the mass media guides the public's recall of narratives from the public memory repertoire, and second, by directly using these narratives in its communications, the mass media turns itself into a domain of knowledge. While appearing to be a different, perhaps even independent domain of knowledge, the mass media strengthens the impact of these narratives as it appears to confirm their veracity. In this chapter, I look at some media coverage from the 2000s, before the centennial of the Armenian genocide, to highlight that what was communicated in April 2015 was meaningful as knowledge within the broader communicative space reproduced by the media. The content provided by the media is one of the central domains of knowledge through which Armenians and questions about the Armenian genocide are apprehended.

Why focus on the mass media? On 7 February 2019, Kadir Has University's Centre for Turkish Studies released its annual report for 2018, *Research on Social and Political Trends in Turkey*. The research was based on a large survey conducted in twenty-six urban centres across the country. It found: 'Gay people are the least preferred group as a neighbour, with 53.8% . . . "Armenians", with 33.5%, and "*Rums*" [Greek Turks], with 31%, are the least preferred neighbours in terms of ethnic identities' (Aydin 2019). These findings were neither new nor very surprising in light of previous such reports and other research in this area. However, the finding regarding ethnic identities is interesting. The numbers of Armenian-Turkish and Greek-Turkish/*Rum* citizens are very low, and most of these citizens are concentrated in Istanbul. Therefore, when the research participants expressed views about the unacceptability of Armenians or *Rums* as neighbours, they were basing their judgements on something other than everyday interactions with those groups. I suggest that they were drawing on the public memory of these ethnic groups to form their judgements about neighbourliness, and that the prompts in the questionnaires functioned as a guide to recall particular narratives from the public memory repertoire in relation to those groups. This is important. The possibility of such reaching out to the public memory repertoire while answering questions is also facilitated by the knowledge provided by the mass media. That knowledge becomes material for recall or remembering. Niklas Luhmann (2000: 1) captures this in the opening lines to his book on the mass media: 'Whatever we know about our society, or indeed about the world in which we live, we know through the mass media.'

There are various debates about the definition of the mass media. Some focus on its technical aspects, the production and dissemination of information. Others focus on the nature of the target groups, as suggested by the term 'mass'. My intention here is not to take part in these definitional discussions. I will simply use W. James Potter's (2013: 17) definition, which frames the mass media in relation to four aspects: '(1) a complex organization (2) that uses standardized practices to disseminate content (3) while actively promoting itself in order to attract as many audience members as possible and (4) condition those audience members for habitual repeated exposure'. This also reflects some of the concerns Luhmann raises in his work on the mass media. However, my interest diverges from Luhmann's (2000: 7) question, 'How do mass media construct reality?' His question is about the internal dynamics of the mass media in constructing a reality. This is helpful, as it focuses on the mass media as a productive domain of reality for the public, rather than as merely 'conveying information from those who know to those who do not know' (Luhmann 2000: 66). But I am more interested in the content of the reality the mass media constructs and uses to inform the public's views and behaviour. Luhmann emphasizes that the mass media creates its own reality as a social system, but I think this construction is still based on some shared knowledge embedded in an existing memory repertoire. I am suggesting a close link between that repertoire and 'the memory generated by' the mass media (Luhmann 2000: 65). This link is important not only because the reality constructed by the mass media is what gets communicated to the public, but also because that reality becomes the knowledge base of what is taken for granted in society. As Luhmann (2000: 66) suggests: 'They are media to the extent that they make available background knowledge and carry on writing it as a starting point for communication.' This recognizes the mass media's agency – or in Luhmann's terms, its social function – to facilitate public communication. Beyond being watched, listened to and read, the media provides that which can be further communicated, 'a description of reality' (Luhmann 2000: 76). The mass media in Turkey can therefore be considered an actor that intervenes in public discussions by providing knowledge that grounds how individuals communicate on the topic of the Armenian genocide. Luhmann's approach is helpful to locate the need to study the media in Turkey as it reproduces a particular kind of knowledge about the Armenian genocide. It is in this role of knowledge producer, and as establishing the grounds for a way of thinking, that the mass media becomes an important reproduction mechanism for the memory repertoire regarding the Armenian genocide.

This memory process is repeated in media communications, thereby becoming more sedimented. This in turn allows the public to use that knowledge as 'normal' knowledge in further communications, without the veracity of the knowledge becoming an issue. The media establishes 'certain assumptions about reality as given and known' on a particular topic (Luhmann 2000: 65). For instance, the language of the 'so-called Armenian genocide claim' is commonly used in the media to signify a knowledge base that demonstrates the untruth of such claims by building on the memory repertoire. The repeated use of this language makes the claimed 'untruth' of the genocide a given, normalized known, for all public discussions. This untruth as memory, in Luhmann's (2000: 65) words, 'checks on consistency by keeping one eye on the known world, and it excludes as unlikely any information that is too risky' given what people already know. The givenness the mass media establishes by repeating the same language in various forums on a particular issue – in this case, the 'so-called Armenian genocide' – makes it 'possible to judge whether it is considered acceptable or provocative to stand apart and reveal one's own opinion' (Luhmann 2000: 65). Thus, the media's repetitive usage of the language of 'so-called genocide' links the public to the memory repertoire, normalizing a way of thinking that also becomes a way of controlling the boundaries of the public's knowing. People judge their own views during a discussion against this normalized knowledge and within the assumptions given by it. In the rest of this chapter, I look closely at the ways in which Turkish mass media sources normalize the public memory and create the ground for people's recall of specific narratives from the memory repertoire as the basis of their public discussions.

I will consider four episodes that reveal how media discussions of the Armenians and the genocide gradually establish what needs to be known. The content used by the media over time in these cases becomes *the* knowledge on the issues. Two of these episodes manifested themselves as responses to external events, particularly in the United States; the other two were discussions about the Turkish experience of Armenians within Turkey.

Will he, won't he say 'genocide'?

Every year around the month of April, the Turkish media begins to discuss whether the US president will use the word 'genocide' in his annual statement to mark the 24 April commemorations. This discussion is more heated in some years than others, and there is always speculation about what a newly elected president will do. I will look at one such episode to highlight the intensity of the discussion, which dominated the media.

In April 2009, Turkish media speculations about what the newly elected Barack Obama would say were intense. Tensions were running high because during his 2008 presidential campaign, Obama had explicitly acknowledged the Armenian genocide and had even said that he would formally recognize it if elected. In a speech to the Turkish parliament in Ankara on 4 April 2009, during his state visit to Turkey, Obama talked about the importance of dealing with the difficult past: 'I know there's strong view in this chamber about the terrible events of 1915. And while there's been a good deal of commentary about my views, it's really about how the Turkish and Armenian people deal with the past.' He went on to talk about the importance of good relations between Turkey and Armenia (Obama 2009). While he did not use the word 'genocide' during the speech, simply reminding members of parliament that they needed to deal with a tragic historical event was enough to increase the anxiety. Most newspapers and TV channels reported the speech. On 8 April 2009, the daily *Milliyet* reported the views of Devlet Bahçeli, the leader of the Nationalist Movement Party. He had reportedly said that he 'considered the call to face the past an unacceptable impoliteness' and that 'we refuse his demand for us to accept the lies' (Bahçeli 2009). On 9 April 2009, in her column in the daily *Sabah*, Nazlı Ilıcak (2009) wrote:

> By not using the word 'genocide', Obama made us happy. While underlining his intention not to disrupt but to support the ongoing discussions between Turkey and Armenia, he did not satisfy the 24 April expectations of the Armenian diaspora. It is clear that in his speech on that day, Obama will talk about tragic and horrible events but will not say 'genocide'.

Although Obama's speech to the Turkish parliament was considered to have signalled his decision not to use the word 'genocide' on 24 April, tensions remained. Writing in the daily *Zaman* on 22 April, Atacan Cuma reported that the head of the Association of Turkish-American Businessmen had said, 'I am 100% sure that US president Obama will not say "genocide"' (Cuma 2009: 22). On 24 April, the daily *Radikal*'s Washington correspondent reported on the anxiety around Obama's statement. Stating that according to Robert Wood, the spokesperson for the US State Department, 'there is nothing to add to the president's statement made in Turkey'; *Radikal* report reminded the reader that 'Obama did not say "genocide" in Turkey' (Radikal 2009a: 9). The rest of *Radikal*'s report connected the discussion to the United States' geopolitical interest in the ongoing negotiations between Turkey and Armenia, which implicitly restrained the US president's approach to his statement. On the same day, in his column in the daily *Zaman*, Mehmet Yılmaz covered similar ground, stating that Turkey was besieged by 'the genocide thesis claimed by the Armenian diaspora' (2009: 22).

In all these discussions, the persistent image was of Turkey as a country being bullied by the Armenian diaspora and doing its best to defend itself by using its geopolitical power. However, this kind of reporting implicitly presented the Armenian genocide as an irrelevant issue for the Turkish public beyond the geopolitical threat it posed. The language used in the reporting limited the possibility of thinking about the genocide by placing the word 'genocide' (*soykırım*) in scare quotes or using the term 'so-called genocide'. By marking out the word 'genocide', these linguistic forms reminded readers of the incorrectness of the genocide claims on the basis of what we knew through our public memory. Such reporting was dramatically different from how the Istanbul-based Armenian-Turkish weekly *Agos* reported the topic on 24 April 2009. Under the front-page headline 'We Haven't Even Reached 1919', the paper stated: 'Turkey has always tried to forget, and made others forget, 1915 and the experience of returnees who in 1919 declared 24 April a day of commemoration' (Agos 2009). This paper also carried a number of pieces in its inside pages that considered various experiences of deportation and massacre in 1915. These pieces described in detail many aspects of the 1915 process. They often used the words 'suffering', 'deportations', 'killings', 'massacres', 'sadness', 'denials' and 'disappearance of people'. *Agos*'s coverage provided a way of remembering that was an alternative to the mainstream media. There was clearly a wide divergence between the memories recalled in *Agos* and those recalled in the mass media. The latter occupied the public's attention more than the former.

Finally, on 24 April 2009, Obama issued his presidential statement. He did not use the word 'genocide'. Instead, he described the events and used the term *Mets Yeghern*, which is used by many Armenians to refer to the Armenian genocide of 1915 and is commonly understood to mean 'Great Disaster' or 'Great Crime':

> Today we solemnly reflect on the first mass atrocity of the 20th century – the Armenian *Meds Yeghern* – when one and a half million Armenian people were deported, massacred and marched to their deaths in the final of days of the Ottoman Empire. (Obama 2009)

While the statement did not use the word 'genocide', both the description of the events and the use of *Meds Yeghern* clearly indicated the president's position. On 26 April 2009, Oktay Ekşi, lead columnist in the popular daily *Hürriyet*, argued in his column that Obama had played with words to balance US geopolitical interests but in the end had been unable to satisfy either Turks or diasporic Armenians. Ekşi stated that 'Turkey is angry', citing statements by the then Turkish president Abdullah Gül and the Turkish foreign minister as evidence of that anger (Babacan 2009a). Both statements had described Obama's words as unacceptable and pointed to the importance of 'remembering the hundreds of thousands of Turks killed in 1915 in the same region'. An inside page of *Hürriyet* on the same day referred to Gül's statement with the headline 'You Should Have Remembered Hundreds of Thousands of Turks Too' (Gül 2009). The dailies *Zaman* (2009: 18) and *Milliyet* (2009: 22) also reported Gül's statement and highlighted that all party political leaders were very angry about Obama's words (see Radikal 2009b: 10).

One of the central reactions to such statements by Obama and other US presidents is to argue that it is not for politicians to decide whether 1915 was a genocide or not – the issue should be considered and studied by historians. The same was also said of the Turkish-Armenian dialogue that was taking place at this time. Underwriting this approach is the sense of being victimized by the deployment of inaccurate – that is, inconsistent with the Turkish view – historical evidence and analysis regarding the events of 1915. From this perspective, either the use of the word 'genocide' or the description of events given in Obama's statement would immediately indicate that inaccuracy. In opposition to any such statements, the deployment of the view that 'it is not possible for us to accept the interpretation of 1915 events' (Babacan 2009b: 27) directs the public's attention to the repertoire I discussed earlier. In this particular instance, the language used signalled a utilization of the repertoire that raised questions about the claims that Armenians had been specifically targeted in 1915 by pointing out that many others had died too under wartime conditions, creating an analytical equivalence in order to dismiss the genocide claims. In the daily *Radikal* on 26 April 2009, Avni Özgürel (2009: 15) wrote that 'on the question of what happened in 1915, of course there is no one answer', arguing that Armenians' views and 'our' views differed. He then reported the experiences of Käthe Ehrhold, a nurse working in Van during April 1915, based on her memoirs, which had been studied by Mete Soytürk. The focus of Özgürel's report was the killings perpetuated by Armenian gangs in conjunction with the Russian army. While this particular report initially suggested a balanced approach, its account of events in Van was presented as a riposte against the claims of genocide. The report thus provided support for the more general media coverage of Gül's statement.

By presenting these views without critical analysis, the mainstream media further reproduced the public sentiment that 'we don't know what happened, many people were killed, why blame us?' The reporting emphasized that the 'so-called genocide' had no historical grounds and that 'we', the Turkish people, were being put under pressure due to foreign interests once again. This position was also implicit in the then foreign minister Ali Babacan's (2009a) response to Obama: 'History can only be written and discussed on the basis of incontrovertible evidence and documents. The joint history of the Turkish and Armenian nations can only be analysed on the basis of independent and scientific data.' While the language used in these media pieces allowed the historical veracity of the Obama statement to be publicly questioned, the pieces were less concerned about the veracity of the claims they themselves made to challenge the Obama statement's evidential basis. Statements issued by Turkish politicians that used the language of the 'Armenian issue' were not analysed in the mainstream media with the same historical scepticism, but rather were accepted as truth claims confirmed by what we already knew. By regularly presenting this defensive position, the content of media reporting reproduces the public memory every April. The focus on the US presidential statements is itself a performance of national identity. Each annual presidential statement becomes a marker to recall the repertoires of this memory in order to solidify a national position on the Armenian genocide. Even when the new US president Joe Biden finally used the word 'genocide' in his statement on 24 April 2021, debate over the issue remained a central focus in the Turkish media. Next, I will look at a less regular event that also generates media attention and through that attention becomes another opportunity to reproduce the public memory. This too is an event related to a decision in a foreign country that generates a domestic response in Turkey.

Will they accept it? Can we lobby against it?

Every few years, during the period leading up to 24 April, there is an attempt to introduce the Armenian Genocide Resolution in the US House of Representatives (see Başar 1978). If this resolution were to be adopted, it would grant formal recognition to the genocide and call on the president to use the word 'genocide' in his annual statement. In 2007 Nancy Pelosi, the speaker of the House of Representatives, supported the move along with other members of the house. The Bush administration did not support the resolution, and enough representatives were against it to ensure that it did not reach the floor of the house for a decision (Hulse 2007). However, the attempt caused much anxiety in Turkey, and the Turkish media closely followed the process.

The mass media focused on the Turkish government's work to influence the process through various lobbying efforts in the United States. This focus presented the issue as a major threat to Turkey's traditional relationship of security and friendship with the United States. The opposition of a number of well-known US politicians to the resolution formed part of the media coverage. Most of the coverage reminded readers how damaging acceptance of the resolution would be to strategic military and trade relations between the United States and Turkey (Demirel 2007; Yeni Şafak 2007). Some of the coverage also presented arguments to question the genocide claim that underwrote the resolution. In his column in the daily *Sabah* on 11 February 2007, the well-known popular journalist Hıncal Uluç tackled the question by reflecting on a discussion he had had with an Armenian in the United States in 1977. He aimed to show that the other side could be convinced that the 'Armenian issue' did not relate to the Republic of Turkey and that the Ottomans had been acting in self-defence. According to Uluç, the discussion in 1977 had been prompted by a radio news report that a Turkish diplomat had been assassinated by the ASALA. On that day, Uluç had been attending a picnic, and an Armenian-American professor who was also attending had said: 'Some of our fanatical youngsters want to take revenge for 1915.' Uluç had asked the professor: 'What happened in 1915?' The professor had replied: 'Turks massacred Armenians. . . . They killed 1.5 million Armenians' (2007). Uluç's column continued his account of the conversation:

> 'Look', I said. . . . 'Let's think rationally, without myths. First, 1915 is the history of the Ottomans, not the Turkish republic, whose ambassadors are being killed at the moment. . . . Within the Ottoman Empire, it had 72 nations from different religions and races. There is no claim about massacring any of these.' (2007)

After talking about how the Ottomans had tolerated religious and ethnic difference and had even helped Jews who were being persecuted in Europe, Uluç asked: 'Why would they [Ottomans] have massacred Armenians?' He then answered his own question:

> Because they didn't massacre. . . . Around the time they talk about Armenian genocide, Armenians were important bureaucrats, important artists were living with dignity and respect in this country. . . .
>
> 'Look', I said, 'I tell you what happened in 1915. The Russian army invaded from our eastern borders. They arrived in Erzurum after raiding, demolishing and burning Turkish villages. In the meantime, some fanatical Armenian gangs in eastern Anatolia, in cooperation with the Russians, attacked the Ottoman army from the rear. Beyond attacking, they raided unprotected, defenceless Turkish villages and killed everyone without sparing women and children. The Ottomans had to intervene.' (2007)

After setting out these justifications, Uluç's column talked about the deportations and emphasized their importance for the security of the empire, adding: 'Given all this, you can imagine how these really unpleasant things happened.' He then talked about how the United States had interned citizens of Japanese descent in 1942 during the Second World War, drawing an analogy with 1915. He reflected on the use of Turkey as a common enemy for a dispersed people to maintain its sociocultural identity while living in different places as a diaspora, and he tried to link this with the rationale behind groups such as ASALA (Uluç 2007). He assumed that he and the professor had arrived at a common view during their conversation. He thought this was because he had made a convincing comparison between 1942 and 1915. He thought that in 2007, on the brink of the Armenian Genocide Resolution, US politicians needed to be reminded of their own past. While his aim was to give advice to US officials, his article invoked three narratives from the memory repertoire around the issues of betrayal, wartime security and victimization. His words prompted readers to reach out to those repertoires. Given that the bulk of the content reported a discussion that had taken place in 1977, this column by Uluç is a good example to show the implicitly ahistorical nature of the knowledge that is communicated and shared in the media. The ahistoricism gives the impression that the content of the knowledge must be true on a general level.

On 25 February 2007, the daily *Radikal* newspaper published a column by Hasan Celal Güzel, who was not only a journalist but also a politician who had been a government minister from 1987 until 1989. Güzel intended his column to tackle 'the lies in the Armenian Genocide Resolution' by challenging the historical veracity of the genocide as presented in the resolution. He raised a number of issues on the basis of research conducted by 'his friend Professor Dr Kemal Çiçek, head of the Armenian desk at the Turkish Historical Society'. The discussion focused on two central issues: (1) the incorrectness of the number of Armenians massacred (1.5 million) as stated in the resolution, and (2) problems with the international warnings allegedly issued to the Ottoman government in 1915 and with the 1918 Constantinople trials. Contesting the numbers suggested by the resolution, Güzel (2007) argued:

> Firstly, the resolution seems deliberately to talk about the 1915 deportations as if they had been extended until 1923, to implicate the Republic of Turkey. To date, neither statistical studies nor the deliberately inflated numbers used by others have shown the Armenian population in Turkey to have been two million. Both the American consul in Harput and the anti-Turkish Leslie Davis's report state that 'it is impossible to estimate how many Armenians died, but it can be said that the number is not less than 1 million'. Even the Armenian theoretician Dadrian in many publications presents the number of losses as 1.1 million and talks about those left alive as one million. At the 1919 Paris conference,

Bogos Nubar Pasha talks about 600,000 to 700,000 deportees [*tehcir edilen*]. In addition, the patriarch in Istanbul gives the number of Armenians in Anatolia at the end of the war as 644,000.

The discussion of numbers is curious, as it does not really say much beyond aiming to challenge the number cited in the resolution. It says little about the actual targeting of communities or mass murder. Then it moves on to look at a few other areas, including the 1918 Constantinople trials and the declaration issued by the governments of the Allied countries on 24 March 1915, which had warned the Ottoman government against ethnic cleansing:

> At the time, the views of the powers that made agreements to split the Ottoman Empire relied on the views of the Armenian groups that were terrorising people. At the time of the declaration on 20–24 May, the Russians invaded Van and Armenians massacred 35,000 Turkish and Kurdish Muslims without sparing the elderly, women or children. Among those who issued the declaration, at the time the Russians were massacring their own Jewish population, and Britain was deporting people of German descent or putting them in concentration camps. (Güzel 2007)

Güzel also mentioned the role of the Armenian Revolutionary Federation (Dashnaktsutyun) in disseminating misinformation across Europe about events in Anatolia. His discussion then moved on to discredit the Constantinople trials as 'kangaroo courts'. Here Güzel drew on arguments developed by Justin McCarthy to present the trials as having been used by the victors and locals controlled by the occupying forces to take revenge on those who had been put on trial. Again, it is not clear what this argument is about, other than to suggest that Çiçek's research contested the historical reference points used in the US resolution. Çiçek's research was thus presented as a way to counter and challenge the resolution. Güzel used facts from Çiçek's research to develop an alternative historicity that invoked the memory repertoire. Once again, wartime security, the enemy within and the victimization of the Ottomans at the end of the First World War were the backbone of this newspaper column. Insofar as it marshalled alternative historical 'facts', Güzel's argument fits well into Stan Cohen's (2001: 12) category of literal denial, as the column was constructed to argue that 'it did not happen'. It not only created a link with the memory repertoire but also reproduced the view that Turkey was still under attack. The column asserted facts in such a way as to present the preferred historiography underpinned by the public memory, which in turn supported the public sentiment of being victimized by external forces manipulated by the Armenian diaspora.

Both of the examples I have considered so far in this chapter were reactions to events outside Turkey, and the agents of those events were broadly depicted as foreign actors with a strategic interest in Turkey. Therefore, the media language used in these examples is based on the position of defending Turkey's national dignity and interests (see Bayraktar 2015). The media's language implicitly claims all those who are Turkish citizens as belonging to the truth of this position. The media asserts the justness of the position by using narratives from the public memory repertoire, especially the narrative of the distinction between the Ottoman Empire and the modern Turkish republic. Looking at the media as a reader, one recalls the knowledge provided by the repertoire that supports this distinction, which establishes the perceived innocence of the republic in these debates. In addition, the language used ensures that the public in Turkey recalls the repertoire. The expectation seems to be that this recall will engender a sentiment of surprise, given what we know to be true, in the face of these outside events, which are seen as attacks against 'us'. This will *normally* guide the reader to wonder why Turkey is being targeted when 'we' have no responsibility for the Armenian issue.

This approach externalizes the 'Armenian issue' as a concern only for Turkish foreign policy, and thus as an issue against which citizens are united regardless of their political leanings. In this way, by taking this view of how 'we' should all respond to these foreign claims, the media asserts a homogenous Turkishness. In other words, the refusal to recognize other positions supports the reproduction of a national subjectivity that is antagonistic to Armenians' questions. This mechanism of propagating a national position through a set of knowledge claims that are used to delineate what is appropriate is also used domestically in Turkey. I will now look at two instances of this in the media. My aim is to highlight how over time the media becomes the source of claimed true knowledge by delineating what needs to be remembered.

A role model for modern Turkish women or an Armenian? Does it matter?

On 6 February 2004, the Istanbul-based Armenian weekly *Agos* published an article on Sabiha Gökçen, an adopted daughter of Mustafa Kemal Atatürk and the Turkish republic's first female fighter pilot. The article reported a claim that Gökçen – after whom Istanbul's new airport had been named in 1998 – had been from an Armenian family. This had the makings of a perfect storm: a piece on the ethnic origin of someone close to Atatürk, published by the Armenian press to highlight a possibly divergent view of her origins. 'Hripsime Hanım', a member of the Sebilciyan family who now lived in Armenia, had claimed in an interview that Gökçen was her maternal aunt and had been adopted after the deportations of 1915. She had claimed that Gökçen's real name was Hatun, but this had been changed after the adoption. *Agos* also reported her as saying that this had been known in the family for a long time (Agos 2004). The *Agos* piece did not present these claims as definitive facts. It ended by reflecting that a similar story about Gökçen had appeared in 1972 in a book by Simon Simonyan. Given the similarity between the 1972 publication and what was being claimed in 2004, the journalist said, 'we don't know whether Hripsime Hanım was inspired by this story or not' (Agos 2004). Nevertheless, the new claim was regarded as sufficiently newsworthy to be published. By publishing the claim as a speculative possibility, *Agos* also seemed to be seeking to approach 1915 from a different angle in order to raise implicit questions about what had happened to the many survivors of the genocide, particularly women and girls, who had been assimilated into Muslim communities in Anatolia, in most cases by conversion. My interest here is not in the veracity of the claim about Gökçen. I am more interested in the media reactions to the claim. *Agos* was a weekly with a limited circulation, and its reporting only became wide public knowledge on Saturday 21 February 2004, when the front page of the daily *Hürriyet* reported the story under the headline 'Sabiha Gökçen's 80-Year-Old Secret'.

The media reaction to this story cannot be separated from an official statement issued by the General Staff of the Republic of Turkey (TC Genelkurmay Başkanlığı). The statement warned against opening up a discussion about a national figure such as Gökçen, who (it pointed out) had occupied an important honorary position as the first female fighter pilot in the Turkish armed forces. It went on to highlight her position within the republican imaginary as embodying an image of Turkish women for the wider society as 'desired by Atatürk'. The statement warned: 'Opening such a figure up for discussion, regardless of the aim of such a move, is an approach that contributes neither to national unity nor to peace in society' (General Staff 2004). The statement argued that it was not clear what the aim of the publication had been, and it sought to remind the public that defending the values of the republic and the unity and togetherness of the Turkish nation was the responsibility of each and every Turkish citizen no less than of the Turkish armed forces. This was an abrupt intervention that generated questions about why this topic was a matter for a formal statement by the military: Did it really matter whether a person had an Armenian background, so long as they were Turkish?

Oktay Ekşi, then the lead columnist in the daily *Hürriyet*, wrote on 24 February 2004 that the General Staff's intervention was unclear, as ethnic background was irrelevant to evaluate people's belonging. He added: 'It does not really matter whether Gökçen was of Armenian or Zoroastrian descent, what is required is to be a true Turkish nationalist, to prove one is ready to give one's life for this nation on the battlefield.' He asks why it would be a problem to 'talk about her ethnic background, nothing changes if she is one thing or another, as her importance is because she embodied the model Atatürk considered appropriate for Turkish women' (Ekşi 2004). Similarly, the popular columnist Hıncal Uluç began his piece in the daily *Sabah* on 24 February 2004 by asking: 'Sabiha Gökçen is of Armenian descent . . . so what [*Eee*]?' He went on: 'She is the citizen of a country whose constitution says that "everyone who has a link of citizenship with the Turkish republic is Turkish".' Uluç (2004) argued that it was wrong to talk about someone's being Armenian as if it were a denigration, and that 'our brains rather than genetic codes determine my and everyone else's Turkishness'. Writing in the daily *Vatan* on 23 February 2004, columnist Güngör Mengi followed a similar line to question the rationale behind the General Staff's statement. He also questioned *Hürriyet*'s motives for reporting on the interview, which had originally been published by *Agos*. He went on:

> In Turkey there is a strong enough civil consciousness to defend both Atatürk and Turkishness. It is easily possible to disprove this claim by relying on archives. Besides, with a one in a million chance that this claim will prove to be true, if even one Armenian orphan was adopted, it can only be considered as further extoling both Atatürk and the nationalist principles he represented. (Mengi 2004)

In the daily *Cumhuriyet* on 24 February 2004, Ali Sirmen asked: 'If Gökçen were of Armenian descent, what would happen?' He described how the argument had emerged to point out that it had invoked the question of ethnicity in an irrelevant way. He questioned the General Staff's rationale by asking why a discussion of 'Gökçen's background should be seen as threatening national unity', and asked: 'If Gökçen were a Turkish citizen of Armenian descent, would this remove her status as the symbol of liberated Turkish women?' (Sirmen 2004). He also discussed the importance of the irrelevance of ethnic evaluations, arguing that the nature of Turkish citizenship did not permit such divisive considerations. On the same day in the same newspaper, the respected veteran columnist İlhan

Selçuk took a different line and argued that the situation had been created by external actors to sow ethnic divisions within Turkey. What is interesting here is the unclarity regarding who those external actors might be: both *Agos* itself and the journalist who had written the original report were evidently Turkish, albeit from Armenian backgrounds. Selçuk was not the only one to take this line in the media, but before I look at my second example, I would like to turn to the nature of this media coverage.

Following Luhmann, I argue that this media coverage provided a way to recall the baseline knowledge located in the public memory regarding being Turkish and its relationship with being Armenian. The knowledge provided through that recall reiterated society's self-understanding. This then established the basis of further public communications on the topic. It is also clear that the media outlets cited above provided a sense of 'differentiated provision' (Luhmann 2000: 71), creating the view that individuals among the public could pick and choose what to read and think. I argue that in this particular case this diversity was not real, as the basic message communicated across diverse outlets seems to have replicated a common understanding produced through narratives from the public memory repertoire. There were several knowledge claims repeated in various discussions. This highlights the repetition of limited numbers of such claims embedded in the narratives of public memory. These narratives provided the public with a way to judge the (knowledge) content of an acceptable way of thinking about the matter. Most of this media coverage engaged the public through two broad registers. The first was a reaction to the military statement from a civil democratic perspective; the second was a consideration of ethnicity underwritten by the sociopolitical nature of Turkishness as defined through citizenship. On the face of it, most of the coverage might appear to have been defending a position that was interested in discussing ethnicity neither to evaluate social status nor to determine an individual's status as Turkish. Thus, the coverage seemed to be defending the possibility of a multicultural society underpinned by the idea of Turkish citizenship as defined by Atatürk and the Turkish Constitution. The media set out a framework that located being Armenian within the context of being a Turkish citizen, that is, as a social status that was not in contradiction with being part of society. In this way, the media discussion used reference points to guide the public to recall various memory repertoires regarding the foundation of the republic and its formation of citizenship, which had included a number of groups by formally recognizing them as minorities. Nonetheless, there are significant issues with this approach, which seems to suggest that ethnic 'blindness' is one of the central conditions of membership in Turkish society. This blindness is only blind to ethnicity and race if people act within an assumed nature of Turkishness that is broadly (as I discussed earlier) founded on a commitment to national history and a single national language as identity markers.

This media coverage is produced by repeating the narratives of public memory regarding the foundation of the republic, Atatürk, the values that were established for the new nation to live by and how the foundation of the republic accommodated minorities as citizens. These reference points locate thinking about Gökçen and the issue of being Armenian within the language of the new republic. This language allows the public to recall narratives that are about the War of Independence, waged against both internal and external enemies. In this way, media discussions based on the inherent inclusiveness of Turkish citizenship indicate that the issue of being of Armenian descent is considered from within being Turkish according to a given public memory. Ethnic blindness is only relevant if minorities (and others, such as Kurdish and Alevi people, who are not formally or legally considered to be minority groups) agree with founding imaginary of the republic. This approach limits the possibility of different memories and different ways of being part of society. Given that such different memories would present a challenge to the assumed coherence of the public memory, the media coverage, with its 'us and them' logic, ensures that 'the system produces itself' (Baecker 2001: 63). The mass media selects the knowledge that is communicated, thereby motivating the public to further communicate that selection (Luhmann 2000). This approach solicits compliance from Armenians (and others such as Kurds) with the public memory repertoire in their self-understanding as a part of being Turkish. This solicitation seeks to guarantee the acceptance of the public memory repertoire as the threshold for belonging to society.

From a different viewpoint, independent of its immediate focus on Gökçen, the piece in *Agos* recalled memories of orphaned children (especially girls), how they had been converted and adopted, and importantly why they might have been orphaned in the first place. In this sense, for me, the piece was an attempt to open up a debate that would recall and think through different memories that were not available within the public memory repertoire. But the media's decision to approach the discussion as the defence of a view about Turkishness silenced the general issues raised by the *Agos* piece. More centrally, this process communicated what questions and answers were relevant for the public in this matter: Gökçen's Turkishness was relevant, while other potential issues were not. The media coverage built its approach in such a way as to foreclose for the public the possibility of asking different questions or remembering 1915 and its aftermath through different knowledge in a different manner.

Mengi's remarks about orphans, discussed above, are a revealing example of this. Rather than asking why the children had been orphaned, he focused on how the adoption (he did not mention religious conversion) of these orphans was a good confirmation of Turkish values. As this example shows, the media approach reinforced the public memory repertoire as the only source of remembering. This was operationalized by linking the possibility of remembering to Turkish citizenship, legally defined as not based on race, religion or ethnicity. The public was reminded of its duty to remember in this way (Michel 2018). Implicitly, this also asserted that for belonging to this citizenship, there could be no alternative memories. This is because, as Alexander Görke and Armine Scholl (2006: 649) argue, 'the common function of the mass media is to enable and direct society's self-perception'. The positive attitude of the media coverage I have analysed maintained a certain self-perception while enabling the public to communicate, but only through the socially understandable codes of being Turkish embedded in the public memory.

This process is also observable in Emin Çölaşan's coverage of the Gökçen affair in *Hürriyet*. Writing on 22 February 2004 – the day the newspaper first reported on the *Agos* story – he began by presenting facts about Gökçen and why she was important. Then he stated: 'An Istanbul-based Armenian [*Ermeni*] newspaper has published about Sabiha Gökçen. She was Armenian [*Ermeni imiş*]!' He asked: 'Who is claiming this? An Armenian [*Ermeni*] lady. As if Sabiha Gökçen was her aunt's daughter' (Çölaşan 2004a). The word 'Armenian' (*Ermeni*) was deployed to create distrust in the reader, or at least to give a sense of otherness. The reader was first told that the reported claim had been made by an Armenian and printed in an Armenian newspaper. Then Çölaşan moved on to object that Gökçen's 'records are available, and her past is known', emphasizing that Gökçen was known to 'us'. He also wrote: 'What happens even if she was Armenian, is it shameful to be Armenian? What matters is the inside of her brain, her life and what she left behind' (Çölaşan 2004a). Even though Çölaşan's question 'what happens even if she was Armenian?' gave the initial impression that he had a positive attitude, the overall effect of the piece was to designate Armenians as an existential enemy. This was implicitly raised again in his piece on 24 February 2004. After talking about Gökçen's autobiography, Çölaşan (2004b) asked in light of the history of her family, 'Whose interests are served by this claim?' Construed in this way, the claim reported in *Agos* appeared to be an attack against both Gökçen and, through her, Turks in general. Against this attack, 'we' had to defend Gökçen as a symbol of modern Turkey as well as 'ourselves'. There was an implied sense of the enemy within. The move to establish Turkishness as the main grounds to think about the issues raised is a common moved based on emotions that recall ahistorical memories of being victimized since the end of the Ottoman Empire. Çölaşan's discussion developed in an apparently simple manner to link 'us' and 'them' within a particular social imaginary that directed readers to the public memory of the 'internal enemy' and their 'external links'.

In order to underline this designation, the piece went on to create further reference points for people to reach out to a narrative within the public memory repertoire by talking about the events of 1915 as a necessity of war and security due to 'the Armenian gangs still fighting with our armies in the closing period of the war in 1918' (Çölaşan 2004b). But the piece did not only remind people about the past through a specific lens; it also formed their thinking in the present to link what they knew about 1915 with the discussion of Gökçen. As it went on to state, 'After long years, some of the Armenians around the world are still hostile even today to Turks and Turkey' (Çölaşan 2004b). It is noteworthy that the usage of the word 'Armenian' in the piece foreclosed the possibility of 'their' having anything to say about the past or the present that mattered to Turkey. As a result, there was no contribution they could make to define Turkishness. The expectation was that Armenians should accept whatever was already described as Turkishness in order to register their belonging to society.

Was he a hero, or was he part of the violence against Armenians?

A similar silencing that is operationalized by shifting the discussion to Turkishness rather than unpacking questions about Armenian orphans can be seen in a news story about Kazim Karabekir. The story was initially reported by Şükran Özçakmak on 16 May 2000 in the daily *Milliyet* under the headline 'Karabekir's Children'. This report aimed to present little-known aspects of Karabekir's contributions during the War of Independence, not only as a strong military leader but also as a civil leader concerned about the future of the orphans he had encountered. Drawing on archival material from the Kazim Karabekir Museum, it highlighted 'Karabekir's Army of Robust Boys', the military group he had created at the end of the First World War in eastern Anatolia, particularly around Erzurum. The report stated that this group had comprised 6,000 war orphans, 4,000 boys and 2,000 girls. Many of these orphans had received training in various skills in the technical schools of the day. The report concluded by describing Karabekir's affection for these children, in whose lives he had remained interested and with whom he had communicated until his death in 1948. The media has returned to this story several times since 2000, and it has generated interest over time, receiving more media focus than the Gökçen story discussed above. Therefore, I will look at it closely to analyse the main reference points it has generated for thinking about Armenians and the Armenian genocide.

Many publications on this topic since 2000 have cited the report published in *Milliyet*. They also cite the article 'Sarikamiş, a "Children's Village"', written by researcher Makbule Sarıkaya and published in the *Atatürk University Institute of Turkish Studies Journal* in 2004. Sarıkaya's article made two interesting observations: first, Karabekir 'was concerned with and took care of the education of thousands of children left behind due to World War I and the Armenian cruelty [*zulüm*]' from 1919 onwards; second, after the liberation of Kars, Karabekir 'observed the American committees taking care of 18,000 Armenian children in Tiflis, Gümrü and Erivan, and influenced by his observations, he also focused on this issue' (Sarıkaya 2004: 238–9). Sarıkaya's emphasis here highlighted the benevolence of a military leader, and by association of his nation the Turks, in the face of the cruelty of the Armenians, without explaining how that Armenian cruelty had led to the existence of thousands of Armenian orphans in eastern Anatolia. The argument thus used reference points about Armenians as the enemy and Turks as saviours.

The issue of the children's army was picked up by the historian Ayşe Hür in her column in the daily *Taraf* in 2009 (and again in 2011, in *Radikal*). Discussing the role of children in political activism and militancy, she looked at how children had been incorporated into scout-inspired militia groups during the late Ottoman period. Her analysis of Karabekir's actions pointed to the multiple causes behind the children being orphaned, beyond the general conditions of the First World War. She talked about the 1915 deportations and the massacres (*kıyım*) that Armenian populations had experienced (Hür 2009). Hür also suggested that according to some sources, some orphans, including the Armenians who became Karabekir's children in 1922, had been 'placed in military school in Bursa on the pretence that they were the children of Turkish families' (Hür 2009).

A response to this came in an interview with Karabekir's daughter, published by the daily *Hürriyet* on 8 October 2010. In the interview, Timsal Karabekir stated that she was searching for living members of her father's children's army or their descendants in order to bring them together. She said that '5000 Armenian orphans who were saved by Karabekir and sent to Trabzon also considered him their father', and added that while he had not discriminated against children of different ethnic backgrounds, 'thinking about the future, he never mixed Armenian children with Turkish orphans'. She argued that one author's claims that 'in the children's army they had Armenian children [and] that some of them afterwards were sent to military school' were entirely untrue (Hürriyet 2010).

Most of the reporting on this case in subsequent years, including online, has focused on the benevolence of Karabekir as the 'father of the orphans' and his care for the children (see Fikriyat 2019). Some of these reports entirely ignore the question of why there were such numbers of Armenian orphans in the first place, only talking about them as a group rescued by the benevolent soldier. For instance, a piece by Mustafa Aytar (2016) on the website *Retired Officers* treats it as a story about benevolence: 'Wherever he went, he became a father to those orphans who had lost their families due the attacks of the Armenian gangs and saved them from squalor.' The juxtaposition of benevolence and Armenian cruelty is a common reference that links readers to narratives from the memory repertoire about victimhood, the enemy within and self-defence. In the same piece, Aytar (2016) uses material from the interview with Karabekir's daughter described above to reaffirm that there was no mixing between Turkish and Armenian children that would have clouded the ideal Turkishness. Both in Aytar's report and in the interview, the idea of Turkishness is represented in reference to the purity of the military officers, for whom being of Armenian descent would create a problem.

The issue of Karabekir's children and Armenians came to the media's attention again in a TV commemoration of the seventy-first anniversary of his death, broadcast live on the 24TV channel on 27 January 2019 in the history programme *Moment and Time with Koray Şerbetçi* (*Koray Şerbetçi ile An ve Zaman*) (Şerbetçi 2019). The live format changed the usual one-way communication and made it more interactive, engaging with the audience by providing answers to questions posed by individuals throughout the programme. The programme's presenter, a historian, interviewed the above-mentioned Timsal Karabekir Yıldıran over 2 hours to discuss his life, achievements and engagement in the politics of the late Ottoman and early republican period. The presenter clearly admired Karabekir, and Timsal Karabekir (Yıldıran) brought her father's life into perspective with the help of archival photos and many detailed anecdotes. Their discussion emphasized both Karabekir's importance for the Turkish War of Independence in 1919–23 and his close interest in eastern Turkey, where (we were told) he was regarded as the hero who had liberated Kars twice and saved Erzurum and other cities in the region, defending them against Russians and Armenians.

The remarkable aspect of this programme is how it wove in reference points about Armenians throughout the discussion to reiterate the idea of the enemy within and Armenian cruelty. It pointed out that Karabekir had been brought up in a milieu where he had encountered Armenians either as people working for his family or as friends in Van. According to the discussion, the young Karabekir had first encountered problems in trying to understand a disturbance related to Armenians in Istanbul around 1896. The audience was told that as a young military student, he had asked his brother about the disturbance. When the situation had been explained to him, according to his daughter, he had asked: 'Are they *our* Armenians?' Timsal Karabekir Yıldıran said: 'He clearly could not believe these people, with whom they lived like brothers, could be doing this' (Şerbetçi 2019). His brother, the audience was told, had said: 'If you create discord between people, they become enemies.' The same emphasis – '*our* Armenians' – was used a few more times during the discussion, and it was linked to the idea of discord leading to betrayal (*ihanet*). This strategy repeatedly deployed the pronouns 'us' and 'them', signifying for the audience both a break-up in the social fabric and a move to emotionally distance 'us' from 'them' by using Karabekir's experience of estrangement from Armenians after he had seen their cruelty. For thinking about Armenians and the Armenian genocide, this further established the language and ideas of victimhood and the enemy within as 'automatic' reactions (Halbwachs 2015: 176).

Karabekir's experiences after his return to the East dominated the discussion, mixed with comments that on a number of occasions he had witnessed Armenian cruelty, which had motivated his desire to save 'our brothers' and his benevolence towards the orphans. For instance, the audience was told that he had been keen to visit his childhood home in Van but had been unable to find it, as Van had been pillaged and burned. Timsal Karabekir Yıldıran added: 'Even if you go to Van today, you still feel that pain' (Şerbetçi 2019). During the discussion there was a constant evocation of the emotions of sadness and anger, juxtaposing Armenians against the suffering of Turks. When the discussion turned to Karabekir's entry into Erzurum, his daughter said that 'in Erzurum there was a particularly painful experience' and wondered whether she 'should talk about it or not'. She was encouraged to talk about it by the presenter, who pointed out that when Karabekir had arrived in Erzurum as commander, he had witnessed history with his own eyes; there had been terrible cruelty, the presenter said, and 'we should talk about this because today we are besmirched across the world, we are trying to make our voice heard' (Şerbetçi 2019). Timsal Karabekir Yıldıran then described the scene in horrific detail: on entering the city, he had encountered 'people who were impaled alive and died in pain' due to the cruelty of 'Armenian gangs' (Şerbetçi 2019).

The programme linked the orphans to Karabekir's arrival in Sarıkamış. This part of the discussion revolved around his 6,000 children: how they had been treated, how they had been educated and how some of them had eventually become high-ranking army officers in the new republic. As various photos of the 'Robust Boys' were shown, the presenter said, 'Please pay attention to these children' and asked, 'They are orphans, no?' The answer was, 'They are orphans, no mothers or fathers, they were all martyred' (Şerbetçi 2019). The presenter reiterated this: 'They were killed brutally by the Armenian gangs.' Timsal Karabekir Yıldıran added: 'Yes, they were killed by impaling' (Şerbetçi 2019). On one hand, the subsequent discussion highlighted Karabekir's care for and attentiveness to these children; on the other hand, it strongly emphasized that no Armenian orphans had been included in the group. The conversation was interspersed with references to Armenian cruelty. Again, the topic turned around Armenian cruelty, which had been documented by Karabekir in a small pamphlet that was also sent to Istanbul. Timsal Karabekir Yıldıran recalled his discussions about the pamphlet with high-ranking officers in Istanbul in 1918, during which he had said: 'I sent you this document, why didn't you publish this? In the future, Armenians will accuse us of the opposite of this' (Şerbetçi 2019).

The presenter at this point was impressed by Karabekir's foresight: 'This is interesting, this is exactly what is happening now.' In a similar vein, the programme argued that the cruelties observed by Karabekir had also been documented by Russian sources, and the presenter reminded the audience of one particular source that had observed that many Turks in Van had been burned and that the 'streets were covered with burned human fat'. In response to some of the questions from the audience, the discussion moved on to the situation of the Armenian orphans, and once again it was emphasized that they had been kept separate from Turks, as Karabekir had thought that 'it was not reasonable to put groups who fought each other in the same environment, as this might lead to animosity, and that if they are Armenians they should be brought up in their own culture' (Şerbetçi 2019). The presenter thanked Timsal Karabekir Yıldıran for these insights, saying that 'they answer accusations from some circles that the Armenian orphans were forcefully converted' (Şerbetçi 2019). She replied that of course they had not been, and she mentioned a letter and a drawing that some of the Armenian orphans in Trabzon had made and sent to Karabekir as a thank you. With great emotion, she and the presenter argued that this was an important '"slap" in answer to attempts to besmirch Turks with degenerate lies' (Şerbetçi 2019). In response to a question about whether her family over the years had maintained links with these orphans similar to their other close relationships, she said that they did not have any links with these children. She added that they did not know what had happened to them; while in Trabzon they had tried many times to trace them, but they had not found anything. Here again, benevolence regardless of religion or ethnic group was emphasized.

Independent of this discussion of Karabekir's life, the TV programme systematically othered Armenians by homogenizing all the discussion through the language of Armenian gangs and their cruelty. This language was woven into the narrative in such a way as to provoke particular emotions among the audience, allowing them to reach out constantly throughout the programme to the narratives of public memory along with specific knowledge about the issues. The differences between Hür's reporting, discussed above, and the views expressed in the TV interview are stark. Hür's piece spoke directly about the deportation and massacre of Armenians in 1915 as the context within which the orphan situation had been created. Thus, it prompted the reader to think about 1915 through a nuanced lens that went some way to explain why there had been Armenian orphans in the first place. This perspective was entirely missing both from the TV programme and from the above-discussed newspaper coverage over time. While this media coverage linked the existence of orphans with Armenian cruelty, the experiences and fates of Armenian and other orphans remained unexplained. For instance, it was not clear whether the existence of Armenian gangs also explained the existence of Armenian orphans. This obfuscation silenced and ultimately erased questions about Armenians and what had happened to them. Armenians were represented homogenously as agents of the cruel gangs and their alliance with the Russian army.

This is not surprising. As in the Gökçen case, this TV discussion and the other media coverage of Karabekir discussed above considered the problem from the vantage point of nationalism, that is, what mattered to 'us' Turks. By choosing to represent the orphan question and other issues related to Armenians in this manner, they 'self-described' (in Luhmann's terms) what mattered for society. Their having done so meant 'it [was] barely possible to opt for any side other than "where the action is"' (Luhmann 2000: 78). The action – that is, the question we had to deal with – then became less about orphans and more about our self-defence and benevolence. The media did not engage with obvious questions about the orphans' position: Why had they become orphans, what had happened to their parents and communities? This obfuscation was a function of the repositioning of questions about the orphans as questions of national integrity or of the personal integrity of people who mattered to the national historiography. As demonstrated by the media coverage of 'Karabekir's children' since 2000, the media regularly communicates reference points to operationalize the public memory repertoire. The communication of the same knowledge through different media turns the repertoire into the only ground from which to know about Armenians.

The content of the news communicated in the media on this issue creates a link between the present and the repertoire. In this process, events in the present establish the veracity of the claims made by narratives in the public memory repertoire. This informs further communications within society on Armenians and the Armenian genocide. Arguably, this reproduction of public memory also establishes the victimization of Turks as the only grounds on which any sensible position about the Armenians and the Armenian genocide can be articulated. This of course removes any possibility of thinking about Armenians beyond the stereotypes established in the media and linked with the public memory. Furthermore, by relying on first-hand discussions with a historical figure's daughter and her access to his personal archives, the TV interview made an implicit truth claim about the content of what was being broadcasted. With each reference to Armenian orphans and Armenian cruelty, the broadcast created 'an appearance of a compact relationship to facts which can no longer be unpicked' (Luhmann 2000: 77). The mass media approach simplified the discussion of the orphans: by focusing on Turkish orphans, it made an immediate link to Armenian gangs on one hand, while removing questions about the existence of Armenian orphans on the other. The latter's treatment by Karabekir was used as evidence of his benevolence. Earlier in this chapter, I observed similar simplifications in the mass media coverage of and responses to international discussions about the Armenian genocide, including in relation to US presidents' statements. As Luhmann (2000: 77) suggests, such simplifications inform the public at different levels to 'generate judgements, emotions, calls, protests'. These are produced on the basis of the denialist public memory. They emotionally inform people about how they should act in public when they encounter questions about the Armenian genocide. In addition, this kind of TV programme provides evidence for other mass media outlets to use in their reporting on Armenians – and on orphans in this case – in order to deal with conflicting views, thus providing stability in the denialist knowledge about the issue that is available to the public.

Conclusion

In this chapter I have considered the overall context of the public discussion that has been created over time and perhaps even intergenerationally by the mass media. My concern has been with how the mass media works as a carrier of knowledge about the 'fact' that 1915 was not a genocide. As a carrier of knowledge, the mass media is also a mechanism to diffuse and sediment a certain knowledge as normalized knowledge. By using linguistic reference points, it pushes the public to recall and reach out to certain narratives as the content of knowledge to remember that the Ottoman Armenians' experiences of 1915 did not constitute a genocide. I have analysed four episodes that generated public discussions about questions related to Armenians. In each of these, the media constructed a reality that projected 'our' (Turkish) unity against 'them' (Armenians), and it confirmed that unity by reaching out to narratives that projected a common destiny in the face of past calamities. Repeated reports of the same views about Armenians affirm for the public the reality of the respective positions of Armenians and Turks. I argue that this repetitive use of certain narratives turns the mass media into a knowledge domain. Through the repetition of restricted denialist knowledge, generations of people experience questions about Armenians and the Armenian genocide in this media space.

As Luhmann (2000: 70) suggests, this is due not to simple repetition but to a process in which something is 'construed and confirmed again and again as social reality'. This is observable in the media coverage of Armenians and the Armenian genocide. The media provides a view on how to think about Armenians, and then, by confirming this view time and again while discussing different issues connected to Armenians, it establishes that view as the knowledge base to use for understanding questions about Armenians and the genocide. This becomes a functional reality that frames the public's experience and thinking and guides the public's position. I would suggest that this functional reality provides justifications for the public to inhabit the reality of being Turkish, in most cases regardless of any encounters with real Armenians in everyday life.

Another aspect of this repetitive communication is the way it gradually erases the relevance of any alternatives with which the public might think. With the disappearance of other domains of knowledge, the mass media content becomes the reality. According to Luhmann (2000: 70), this process of 'construing and confirming' adjusts people's interest in particular truth claims by 'using simplifying explanations, enabling perceived reality to be reduced to a schema of power and victims'. To paraphrase Paul Ricoeur (2004), in reaching out to remember, the public memory repertoire acts as a verification of the truth of the reality presented by the media in its simplified knowledge claims. This affirms the descriptive reality produced by the mass media about the binary us–them schema around the themes of enemy–victim and insecurity–self-defence, among others. The media as carrier of knowledge facilitates the public's memory praxis by suggesting a responsibility to remember on the basis of the repertoire's historical truth claims. These claims are underwritten by the binary oppositions, which create the responsibility for us as self-defence. These processes are not only about reproducing and confirming the reality, but also about attributing and allocating value to the choices that members of the public can make about whether to be one or the other in these binaries. In this way, as Ricoeur points out, they are processes of 'unification, *of totalization*' of the truth (emphasis in original 2004). They assert value attributions that are communicated – implicitly and sometimes explicitly – in each repetition of the reality in the mass media, implicitly soliciting compliance by the public. As a result, talking about Turks as benevolent and Armenians as cruel gradually creates stabilized conditions that reflect a specific relationship between self-referencing and other-referencing that is not open to alternative articulations (Luhmann 2000: 75). It is within this context that the mass media produces and reproduces the 'knowledge of the world' that the public uses in new discussions or questions about the genocide (Luhmann 2000: 76).

I argued above that the mass media as a carrier of knowledge and public memory functions in at least two general ways. But these functions are grounded in making the public recall through a limited number of narratives to remember. This means that what needs to be remembered is already given to the public. As I have argued, the mass media is one domain that creates this givenness. However, it relies on the content of the public memory repertoire to create this givenness, which emerges from the repetitive nature of the media production of knowledge. In order to remember, the public still needs to recall something given from within this repertoire. The next chapter turns to the mechanism that creates this 'already givenness' of the narratives, focusing on the education system.

5

Formal education

Creating citizens

The last two chapters focused on how the mass media repeats, and thereby reproduces and strengthens, a set of narratives that I call the public memory repertoire. I observed that by using the language that underpins these narratives, the mass media guides public attention towards the narratives' content. In other words, it creates the possibility of recalling and remembering the past that is contained in the public memory. Over time, the knowledge embedded in these narratives becomes constitutive of collective knowledge. The knowledge shared in this way denies not only the veracity of the Armenian genocide but also knowledge about the genocide provided by sources other than the public memory. I argued that this knowledge – which is embedded in the narratives of the public memory repertoire and the language it creates, a language that is used by the media – signifies the limits of what to know about 'our' history (or how 'we' become Turkish by knowing in a specific way) and the rules of apprehending each other in public. In this sense, the language the public encounters on these issues in various ways, including through the mass media, constitutes a grammar of social comprehensibility – norms and rules of speaking for individuals to take part in public discussions as members of the non-Armenian majority in Turkey. In this chapter, I focus on how 'we' encounter these narratives in the first place. Where do members of the public learn about them in such a way that the narratives become cognitively given descriptions that frame the public's understanding and can be recalled in everyday life, facilitated by linguistic cues and reference points? I argue that one of the central mechanisms that create the givenness or naturalness of this knowledge base is the education system. The education system creates a baseline knowledge for all members of the public, and it does so intergenerationally (see Gökçek 2014: 285–95). Again, the intergenerational transmission of knowledge about 'our' past, constructed in contradistinction to others' histories, helps to normalize what new generations claim to know.

It is worthwhile remembering that this normalization of knowledge is not simply about the availability of the same material across generations; it is also about the normalization of its content as truth claims regarding an identity that is embedded in and committed to those knowledge claims. So, when the public are guided to recall the narratives of public memory, they are guided to remember what they already know from their educational encounters. This process also reveals the construction of deep denialism and its intergenerational normalization. Thus, in this chapter, I focus on the education system in order to understand the process by which the knowledge base of the narratives of public memory is encountered as part of formal history instruction.

On 9 March 2010 on the Habertürk TV channel, Fatih Altaylı's discussion programme One to One (*Teke Tek*) featured two guests. One was Yusuf Halaçoğlu, then head of the Turkish Historical Society, who later became a member of parliament from 2011 until 2017. The other was Sevan Nişanyan, an Armenian-Turkish journalist, historian and linguist. They had been invited onto the programme to discuss the issues at stake in the Armenian Genocide Resolution, which at that time was passing through various stages in the US House of Representatives. Altaylı put the first question to Nişanyan, asking what the passing of the resolution would do for Armenians. Nişanyan said it would be a symbolic win. He added, 'I am always asked what Armenians want', and then he said, 'they want, I think, just like all human beings in the world, they want to be held in esteem and dignity [*adam yerine konmak istiyorlar*]' (Altaylı 2010). Altaylı asked, 'But are Armenians not held in esteem?' The response was 'no', and Nişanyan's answer was direct:

> The Turkish republic, from the days of the genocide until today, has followed state policies that have assumed that Armenians do not exist, that insult and degrade Armenians by saying as people you don't exist, your history doesn't exist, you don't have your historical monuments, your memories are fake, your demands are fake. They are faced with the policy of denial and non-existence. I am not sure you can imagine how this touches a community's spirit. (Altaylı 2010)

Altaylı said: 'Well, if what you are saying were true, it would indeed be tough, but does this situation really exist in Turkey? Now, but if you go to the east [eastern Anatolia], there are examples of Armenian art' (Altaylı 2010). Nişanyan gave a detailed analysis of how in many cases the historical narratives that were circulated both in schools and by local authorities did not speak about Armenians; in fact, most of these narratives aimed to show that Armenians had never lived in many areas. He argued that when these narratives did talk about them, Armenians appeared as the instruments of late-nineteenth-century global imperialism; the narratives then said, 'thank God they were cleared out'. Altaylı was surprised and asked, 'Are you sure?' He also said: 'We also read the same history in schools, but I have never perceived it this way.' Nişanyan replied: 'At least, all Armenians across the world perceive it this way' (Altaylı 2010).

At the centre of this discussion was the education system, which intergenerationally reproduces and reinforces the knowledge base that is retained as the public memory repertoire. It was on the basis of what he knew from school that Altaylı, the programme's presenter, doubted the position of one of his interviewees. The other interviewee's intervention as a senior historian added to these doubts, as his position supported what had been learned in school to reinforce the grammar of being Turkish and how to think about 'our' past. The question raised by this interaction is critical: How can 'we' think differently, beyond the knowledge we have been given by the public memory repertoire? How can we engage with the alternative knowledge provided by Nişanyan, without regarding his views as implausible in light of the knowledge 'we' have received throughout 'our' education?

In this chapter, I argue that the education system is central to the reproduction of the knowledge that is retained as the public memory repertoire. The education system introduces a way of thinking through a set of truth claims – in this case, claims about being Turkish and the history of that identity. That knowledge is then normalized through repetition. This learning process allows the public, when prompted by events or issues, to remember aspects of this knowledge as a part of the public memory repertoire. In this central role, the education system maintains the relevance of the knowledge that informs the public memory repertoire. The public recall or remember what they were taught about Armenians or Armenian lives during the Ottoman Empire, as demonstrated above in Altaylı's immediate response. It is clear that the education system reproduces and maintains a particular view of Armenians (and other groups) as a function of its construction and embedment of a particular idea of being Turkish.

The implications of this are amplified in Turkey, where the end of secondary school is the end of formal education for many students. Therefore, the education system, as a matter of policy, needs to provide students with knowledge that will be important for their everyday lives, as they will be exposed to international discussions and claims about 'Armenian issues' (Metin 2015). Significantly, Erhan Metin (2015) emphasizes the importance of the language used in history teaching. He suggests that 'students who encounter particular concepts and language in this way will use them in their everyday lives once they leave school', and he adds that in the building of a consciousness of history and culture, 'no doubt the most important medium is language' (Metin 2015: 10). In the next section, I focus on how the education system produces knowledge about Armenians that can be seen as engaging with the Armenian genocide. This will help to understand what students are expected to learn as knowledge about Armenians, and also the language of that knowledge, which grounds students' understanding of their own history in relation to and against Armenians. In the subsequent section I consider how the education system evaluates its own approach to teaching this knowledge by considering a set of education policy reviews. This provides important insights regarding the embeddedness of the knowledge that grounds the public memory repertoire. My choice of textbooks for discussion also takes account of the critical roles and concerns of teaching staff, who use the available material to educate their students in these narratives. I look at this issue briefly at the end of the chapter.

Educating Turkey

The role of education in building citizenship, and in many cases national identity, is well recognized (Anderson 2006; Ersanlı 2011; Ozan and Kuş 2021; Üstel 2021). Given the extensive literature on this topic, I am not going to rehearse the debate here, and I will instead accept this role of education as a given. Instead, I will focus on the content of education materials and the way they frame the view of Armenians within the Turkish education system. According to Füsun Üstel, the Turkish system is similar to education systems elsewhere in that it aims to create an 'acceptable citizen [*makbul vatandaş*]' (2021). The origin of this approach goes back to the late 1920s and 1930s and the reforms around language and history that I discussed in Chapter 3. For my purpose in this chapter, the important aspect of the aim to create acceptable citizens is the intergenerational reproduction of a national identity based on a national ideology of 'shared ideas and beliefs' (Giddens 1997: 583). While these shared ideas and beliefs underwrite the conditions of belonging to the larger community – 'us' – they also produce ideas and beliefs about others. The acceptable citizens created through the education system thus broadly share a sense of belonging. At the same time, as a condition of that belonging, these citizens also become sensitized to what differentiates 'us' from 'them', who by definition become unacceptable – in other words, unlike 'us'. As I discussed earlier, one of the pathways for this bifurcation is to forge an exclusive identity around national language and history. Discussing the concept of hegemony in Antonio Gramsci's writings, Carl Boggs (1976: 39) reflects on hegemony as a way of diffusing particular ways of life into society so that those ways of being and thinking become internalized and normalized. As Üstel (2021) discusses, this requires a centralized education system that can produce centralized narratives which instil certain ways of thinking, across the population and intergenerationally.

With regard to this centralization of its imaginary, the Turkish education system is a good example of the sociocultural engineering that produces acceptable citizens. After considering the content of foundational citizenship and the teaching materials used in history teaching, I agree with Elif Gençkal Eroler's (2019: 205) observation that the approach to understanding history and citizenship found in today's textbooks reproduces the nation-building ethos of the 1930s. This does not mean that there has been no change in how school textbooks present history. Throughout various political periods, the education system in Turkey has changed many times. However, the change in this process is observable in the style of the presentation, rather than in the content of what gets presented as knowledge to instil the nature of being Turkish.

During my formal education, I did not encounter any material on Armenians or any other minorities until I was in secondary school. I have memories of hearing or reading in the media about the assassinations of Turkish diplomats in the late 1970s; nor do I have any memory of spending time on the topic in primary school classes. However, young students already encounter an exclusive national identity through the knowledge they are given at primary school level about the foundation of the Republic of Turkey. Some of this instruction follows the national annual holidays that commemorate various events around the Turkish War of Independence (*Kurtuluş Savaşı*), which started in 1919, and the foundation of the republic in 1923. In this sense, primary schoolchildren are already set on a path of learning that emphasizes a Turkish identity formed explicitly against other identities, which in most cases appear as foundational enemies.

This gradually changed as I started secondary school in September 1980, the same month as the military coup. My main formal introduction to the topic came in classes taught under the title of 'History of the Revolution of the Turkish Republic [*Türkiye Cumhuriyeti İnkılâp Tarihi*]'. At the time, of course, we students were not aware that this particular course would be part of our educational life right through to the end of our university years. On reflection, I can see that we were taught the same content in the early 1990s as we had been in the early 1980s, albeit with some changes and additions. The aim of the teaching about this part of history remained the same: to create acceptable Turkish citizens who could participate in and contribute to the social life of the nation. Here the critical issue is the way in which one becomes comprehensible as acceptable by the language one uses, which demonstrates one's agreement with the givenness of 'our' knowledge of the past, that is, knowledge about the origins of the nation. However, looking back at the textbook we used time and again in the 1980s, I can now see that what we were taught highlights the problems of the system and the kind of citizen it aimed to produce for the benefit of society.

The textbook in question was written by Mükerrem K. Su and Professor Ahmet Mumcu. The title of the book was *History of the Revolution of the Turkish Republic*. It was produced and published by the Ministry of Education (Milli Eğitim Bakanlığı, MEB) in 1982 and reissued repeatedly thereafter. I still have my copy of the second edition, with my annotations inside. In line with most history teaching, it presents a chronological narrative to explain late Ottoman political turmoil and conflict in the lead-up to the Turkish War of Independence and the foundation of the republic. Then it focuses on the immediate republican period to look at the formation of the state and society under Atatürk, and at his republican principles as the pillars of the republican revolution, as indicated by the title of the book. After a general introduction, in which the Eastern Front is mentioned but Armenians do not appear, the book begins with the 1918 Mudros Armistice (*Mondros Mütarekesi*), signed between Great Britain (representing the Allied powers) and the Ottoman Empire at the end of the First World War.

'The Armenian issue' first emerges in the section on the War of Independence. It is covered when the book focuses on revolts against the newly established Government of the Grand National Assembly in Ankara. On page 104, in two short paragraphs, the authors talk about revolts by minorities together with 'those uninformed Turks, Armenians and Greeks, who derived great benefit from the break-up of the country'. The book then points out that on '10 July 1920, the Armenian Revenge Brigade [*Ermeni İntikam Alayı*] entered Adana and inflicted great cruelty' (Su 1982: 104). In this short passage, students are given an image of cruel and scheming minorities. There is no clarification about the name of the Armenian brigade: For what were they seeking revenge? The second time 'the Armenian issue' is considered is in a part of the book that examines the battles leading up to the final battle of the War of Independence. The section headed 'The Armenian Problem [*Ermeni Sorunu*] and War with

Armenians' is divided into three subsections: 'The Armenian Problem Until World War I', 'The Armenian Problem During World War I' and 'The Armenian Problem During the War of Independence and the Treaty of Alexandropol [*Gümrü Antlaşması*]' (Su 1982: 117–20). The first subsection presents Armenians as Ottoman citizens living broadly 'in eastern Anatolia, who due to the tolerance [*hoşgörü*] policy were rarely seen anywhere else [*az rastlanan*] and lived happily until the end of the 19th century' (Su 1982: 117). This subsection points out that in time Armenians moved out of this area, and some settled elsewhere in the empire. The Ottoman governments tolerated this, and 'as loyal Ottoman subjects they were in fact employed in many levels of government'. The book then makes a comparison with the Russian Empire and the pressures Armenians experienced under the Russians to conclude that the Ottoman Armenians were free to use their own language and exercise their own religion: 'Even the real owners of the country, the Turks, were not as comfortable and free as them [Armenians]' (Su 1982: 117).

The rest of this subsection tries to explain why these free and comfortable people became a problem. The explanations given include the spread of nationalism in the nineteenth century and the manipulation of Armenians in the twentieth century by foreign powers – including Russia, Britain and France – that were acting their own interests. The next subsection looks at 'the Armenian problem' during the First World War. Here the focus is on how the Russians manipulated Armenian gangs to invade eastern Anatolia and on the gangs' cruelty towards the people of the region: 'They raided many cities, towns and villages. Tens of thousands of Turks were killed, including children, the elderly and women' (Su 1982: 118). Students are then told why the Ottoman government decided to move the Ottoman Armenian population out of the region:

> This attitude [i.e. raids and killings to support the Russians] of the Ottoman Armenians was making the war with Russia difficult. As a result, the Ottoman government decided to initiate the migration [*göç*] of Armenians living in eastern Anatolia to Syria, which was not a theatre of war [in 1915]. This was the right decision. The Ottoman army did this to secure itself and the country. If Armenians had continued to live in these areas without creating problems [*rahat otursalardı*], the government would not have been forced to take this decision. During the migration, some of the Armenians died due to the natural conditions [*doğa şartları*] and security. But it should not be forgotten that the natural conditions and the lack of support also led to the deaths of nearly 100,000 Turkish soldiers in Sarıkamis. For the events during the Armenians' migration, the Turkish nation certainly [*kesinlikle*] was not responsible. As a matter of fact,

thousands of Armenians arrived alive and well [*sağ salim*] in Syria and lived there under the protection of the Turkish state [*Türk Devletinin*]. (Su 1982: 118)

The historical knowledge here locates Armenians as troublemakers who were manipulated by foreign powers, forcing the government to implement a deportation policy. While the textbook thus recognizes the deportation policy, the Armenians are considered to have brought it on themselves, and it is not given its specific name – '*tehcir* [deportations]' – instead being presented as 'migration [*göç*]'. There is nothing in this account to answer the following questions: What were the security problems that caused some of the migrants to die? If these migrants were under state protection, what happened to them? Given that the government eventually reclaimed this territory, which was occupied by Russian troops under the new Soviet administration, why did these migrants not return to their homes? Perhaps this subsection on Armenians was not written to answer such questions. The subsection ends with Russia's withdrawal from the war after the revolution, and with how eastern Anatolia was finally returned to the Ottomans under the Treaty of Brest-Litovsk. The authors state: 'As a result, this region of ours found its real owners' (Su 1982: 118). This statement requires unpacking. It clearly presents a political view as fact thanks to the phrase 'real owners'. According to this view, the Armenians deported from the region were foreigners, enemies, who had been cleared out of the region. This ignores the fact that the region was one of the Armenians' homelands where they constituted autochthonous communities. It not only depicts Armenians as the enemy but also erases their belonging.

The next and last subsection then deals with the events leading up to agreements with the new Soviet government. Here we meet the Armenians again, this time under a subheading about the battles in southern Anatolia. The Armenians are now considered in relation to the occupying French forces, alongside whom some Armenian volunteers fought. These Armenians are discussed not in the main text, but in extracts from two local stories from the period that are provided as further reading. The first extract concerns Sütçü İmam and his involvement in a well-known episode in Maraş. He was one of the people who fired the first bullets on Friday, 31 October 1919, before the War of Independence was fully underway. The extract recounts this event, beginning with an emotional narrative about its significance:

> The day after the French occupation of the city, the people of Maraş realised they could not tolerate the French and Armenian ebullience and impertinence. The first person to announce this with his gun was Sütçü İmam. He showed the

enemy that the hand that touches Turkish virtue and honour will be broken, the tongue will be pulled out. (Su 1982: 122–4)

Then the event itself is narrated, focusing on how the local Armenians behaved particularly badly in relation to Turks with the arrival of the French and Armenian troops: 'The insane [*deli*] Armenians of Maraş were leading these soldiers to see the city, demonstrating with them and insulting the Turks they encountered on the streets' (Su 1982: 122). The story reaches its climax when the French soldiers encounter women who are 'coming out of a hamam in Uzunoluk Street, and approaching one of them [a soldier] pulls off her full veil, saying, "This is not Turkey any more. In a French country, no one goes out in a veil [*peçe*]"' (Su 1982: 123). The woman faints while others scream and cry. Men sitting in a nearby coffee house tell the soldiers to mind their own business and go away, and a gunfight ensues in which a local is shot by a soldier. At this moment Sütçü İmam comes out of his shop with his gun and shoots the soldier who bothered the woman and killed the local. The story ends with Sütçü İmam disappearing and the French and Armenians trying to find him, to no avail. The story is clearly narrated to engage students emotionally with the implicit 'us and them' framework in which 'we' students need to identify (including in light of the earlier historical narrative) with Sütçü İmam and develop feelings that are close to animosity when we think about Armenians. The depiction of local Armenians (and Greeks) as having been excited about the occupying forces is a common one that also appears in historical accounts of the occupation of other cities at this time, such as Istanbul and Izmir. However, in this case as well as in many others, the story is presented in a way that does not make clear why there was such local excitement, nor does the story in this case explain why Armenians were volunteering for the French army in 1919. The only implicit explanation is based on the depiction of local Armenians and Greeks as the enemy within. This does not provide an analysis of who these Armenians were or consider their possible reasons for joining the occupying French forces. Students are left to think about their actions as existential animosity.

Reflecting on this situation over the years, I wondered what we had learned during those classroom discussions. I realize now that we were not supposed to learn how to think about history. Instead, we were supposed to absorb the discussions didactically in order to ground our understanding of who we were as Turkish citizens. The textbook described above ends with Atatürk's death. According to Refik Turan (2015), the orientation of this particular book can be explained by comparing it with the period before 1980, when 'the Armenian issue' was not systematically included in teaching beyond brief comments. Before 1980, Armenians were presented as one of the groups that had lived in Anatolia during the eleventh century, which is traditionally considered to mark the entry of Turkic groups into the region as political entities. Turan (2015: 1480) points out that 'in response to the emergence of Armenian Secret Army for the Liberation of Armenia [ASALA] terrorism targeting Turkish diplomats from the 1970s onwards, in order to give the right consciousness to young Turkish generations on the Armenian issue' – including information about Armenian problems and deportations – specific teaching materials were chosen. As a result, the MEB 'approved the "History of the Revolution of the Turkish Republic" teaching programme and its associated texts', which included the above-mentioned topics for the first time (Turan 2015: 1480; see also Metin 2015). It is clear that the book I studied was part of this new approach to make 'us' aware of the inaccuracy of the Armenian historical claims, and we were expected to use this knowledge whenever we needed it in our everyday lives.

This simplistic, one-dimensional historiography was the backbone of teaching on this topic. In the narrative arc of this historiography, Armenians were one-dimensional, self-interested villains who had emerged from a homogenous Armenian population and culture and had stabbed Muslim-Turkish Ottomans in the back. There was nothing on the social, cultural or economic dynamics or diversity within Armenian communities across the region. Nor was there anything about the dynamic and differentiated political discussions and views within the Ottoman Empire's Armenian population. As time passed, I began to wonder how this story was being communicated today. I could not help speculating as to whether what I had been taught had changed in the twenty-first century, given the significant deficiencies of the teaching material in question. Through my research I discovered that the situation had remained largely the same, with some adjustments. Turan (2015: 1480–1) reports that although the education system has been through various changes, the material I presented above still constituted the bulk of what was being taught in newly configured history courses across the education system during the 1990s. He observes that at the beginning of the 2000s, as the events of 1915 became increasingly linked to the idea of genocide in global forums due to work by Armenia and the Armenian diaspora,

> Turkey felt the need to take more extensive and effective precautions. The work of the newly created [on 25 May 2001] Committee to Coordinate the Struggle with the Baseless Genocide Claims [Asılsız Soykırım İddiaları ile Mücadele

Koordinasyon Kurulu, later replaced by a new body in 2011] is reflected in the materials used in schoolbooks. (Turan 2015: 1482)

The main aim of this reorientation was to provide more extensive knowledge to students on the issue of the deportations and to counter the 'so-called genocide claims'. In other words, the new approach did not change the denialist orientation that I had observed in the 1982 book. Instead, it expanded that orientation, presenting it at greater length and in more detail, in order to equip students with the ability to directly challenge the depiction of the events of 1915 as a genocide. The MEB explained its new aims:

> [To make students] better comprehend the role played by European powers against the suppression of the Armenian revolts, comprehend the measures that were taken against the atrocities committed by Armenians, comprehend the reasons behind the deportation policy, comprehend the principles of implementation of the deportation policy, comprehend the situation of Armenians after the deportation decision, comprehend the situation of Armenians in Turkey under the Treaty of Lausanne, and comprehend the Armenians' so-called genocide claims since 1945. These new aims are added as skills to analyse the invalidity of Armenians' genocide claims. (MEB 2002/2: 531–41)

The new aims were entirely in line with the aims expressed in Basic National Education Law (*Milli Eğitim Temel Kanunu*) number 1739 (1973). This law lists a set of general aims in terms of how to educate Turkish students according to 'Atatürk's principles and revolution [*inkilap*] as citizens aware of their responsibilities for Turkish nationalism, who love their country and nation and are loyal to the Turkish republic' (MEB 1973). Within this overall education policy, the new aims for the teaching of republican history thus defined good Turkish citizens as those who were able to defend the Turkish republic against Armenian claims about the 'so-called genocide' by mastering the analytical skills to present the Turkish position. The aims covered a number of questions linked to the Armenian genocide. But before I look at these closely, I want to emphasize that the content of teaching according to these aims – the knowledge communicated – utilized narratives that underwrote the public memory repertoire. What one had learned within the education system became what one would remember to take part in discussions of the events of 1915 outside the education system.

One outcome of this approach was the production of a new textbook entitled *Atatürk's Principles and History of the Revolution*. Published in 2006, this book was produced by a commission of six historians: Refik Turan, Mustafa Safran,

Necdet Hayta, Muhammet Şahin, M. Ali Çakmak and Cengiz Dönmez. The book is immediately distinguishable from its predecessor by virtue of its apparently less emotional language and the footnotes it provides to back up some of its claims. Otherwise, its structure and didactic narrative style are familiar. It unfolds from the causes of the collapse of the Ottoman Empire to the foundation of the new republic and its distinctive principles and structures. In between, we have the First World War and the War of Independence. Armenians are first mentioned in relation to the Eastern Front and the Caucasus during the First World War, but they are discussed more broadly within the context of the Russian withdrawal in 1918 after the Treaty of Brest-Litovsk: 'Due to the Armenian atrocities in eastern Anatolia, as the Russian forces were withdrawing, the Turkish forces decided to act to stop this situation' (Turan et al. 2006: 72). An extended discussion of Armenians is delivered in the second part of the book, in a section about the state of the country after the 1918 Mudros Armistice, in a subsection about minorities and their activities (Turan et al. 2006: 92–103).

Compared to sections on various other minorities, the book spends longer, nearly ten pages, to analyse the situation of the Armenians. It aims to provide students with an understanding of the situation of Armenians in three sections. First, there is a general view of Armenians, broadly based on a short generic discussion of their status as a loyal nation (*Millet-i Sadıka*) under the Ottoman Empire. The focus shifts to 'the Armenian issue' before the First World War, and then to the events of the First World War and their consequences. The section on the period before the First World War presents a common story of how foreign powers launched various plans to break up the Ottoman Empire, and in particular how Russia manipulated Armenians for its own interests in order to gain access to the Mediterranean by supporting the creation of an Armenian state in eastern Anatolia. The book argues these manipulations were successful when combined with the general influence of nationalist ideas at the time, and there were Armenian revolts in '1862 in Zeytun, in 1863 in Van' (Turan et al. 2006: 94). Then students are given detailed information about how these manipulations worked, and how the ideas underpinning them were incorporated into various treaties the Ottoman government signed with foreign powers in the late nineteenth century to end various wars. This section also informs students about the foundation of various Armenian associations and political parties advocating political freedom. The section presents some of these groups as having been founded outside the country by foreign influences in order to manipulate the 'Armenians of Turkey [*Türkiye Ermenileri*]' (Turan et al. 2006: 96). This process, according to the book, led to 'the Ottoman Bank raid in 1896, the second Sasun revolt in 1904, and the attempt to assassinate Abdülhamit II on 25 July 1905'. In conclusion, students are told that after the declaration of the Second Constitutional Era in 1908, Armenians did not find satisfaction, and this culminated in the 1909 Adana revolt (Turan et al. 2006: 97–8). The processes narrated here give a sense of the natural progression of violent events over a long period of time, which seems to infuse Armenian animosity within the Ottoman Empire with an ahistorical and homogenous inevitability. While students learn that Armenians have been 'the enemy within' for a long time, there is a total lack of knowledge about the social, economic and political contexts of Ottoman Armenians' lives. The presentation is didactic, and it is not structured to make students curious or to raise critical questions that would explore the issues further. The aim is to get students to absorb these discussions as facts that can be recalled in everyday life, without feeling the need to think or learn beyond them.

In the last section to talk about Armenians, the presentation focuses on events during the First World War. The section begins by arguing that the Ottoman Empire's entry into the war provided the justification for the Armenian committees (*komiteleri*) to initiate long-planned revolts, starting with Zeytun and spreading to the area around Maraş; at the same time, the authorities realized that 'members of the committees, who got in touch with Armenian Americans to get their help and support, aimed to turn Kayseri into the logistical centre for protests they had planned for later'. The text then talks about an 'Armenian named Kevork' who had 'trained in America as an expert in bomb-making' and turned his 'house into arsenal' (Turan et al. 2006: 100). It is not clear who this person actually was; other than his name, no details are available in the text. The text is structured to outline the 'heinous' attempts to revolt and the Ottoman government's futile attempts to stop them during 1914 and 1915. Students are told that the government realized it would not be able to stop the revolts and would have to take other measures. The government therefore warned notable Armenians, 'who considered these warnings as a weakness of the government and increased their treacherous activities' (Turan et al. 2006: 101). In the end, according to this narrative:

> The government decided to issue a new law on 14 May 1915. According to this law, known as the 'deportation law', if those acting against government orders and the defence and security of the country could not be controlled by other measures, they would be subject to forced migration, either individually or in groups, to other regions of the country. . . . During the migration, many events took place. Armenian armed bandits hiding in the mountains attacked the migrant convoys to stop the process, and those who were in the convoys also

misbehaved. The people responsible for the convoys [i.e. Ottoman officers and soldiers] were obliged to act to stop these events and achieve their goals. Under these conditions, fighting between the two sides was inevitable. As a natural consequence of this, many people died. In order to use Armenians for their own purposes, the British presented these events internationally as a genocide, an Armenian massacre committed by Turks. Yet during these events, the number of Turks who lost their lives was much higher than the number of Armenians who lost their lives. But no one was interested in the cruelties and massacres that Turks experienced. (Turan et al. 2006: 101)

The section ends with a discussion of agreements reached with Russia after 1917. The narrative here is certainly more detailed compared with the 1982 text. While the text portrays the Armenians as having been responsible for what happened to them, this is captured in the idea of 'forced migration', the ultimate responsibility for which lies with the foreign powers that had manipulated the Armenians against the Ottoman government over a long period of time. Again, the outcome of this situation is given an air of inevitability. However, a new angle is also introduced: the text seems to recognize that many people died during the forced migration. Nonetheless, broadly speaking this is considered to be due to tactical attacks by Armenian armed groups, or *perhaps*, in some cases, acts of self-defence by Ottoman soldiers during those attacks. The narrative thus establishes that both the Ottoman government and the Ottoman soldiers who were responsible for the migrating Armenians were the victims of the process. The text achieves this through its writing style. The section aims to provide history, but it is written as if it were a story, without any of the precise demarcations or details that would provide an understanding of the reasons behind the events narrated on either side. While it outlines a detailed chronology of Armenian activities, there are no explanations other than general statements about foreign manipulation. It is not clear who was manipulated, how those being manipulated related to the general population, whether the Armenian armed groups were attacking the other Armenians who were being deported or why those people were still deported all the same. Rather than providing historical knowledge, the text builds emotional states that work by portraying the story as being once again about 'us' as victims and 'them' as perpetrators of crimes against 'us'. Given that Armenians only appear as people who perpetrate crimes, the text can only convey a strong sense of resentment, as highlighted by the statement that the much larger Turkish casualties were (and are) ignored internationally. The text is no doubt an attempt to solidify students' sense of belonging to the specific historiography they are being taught, according to which a new nation was created in the face of all these heinous acts committed by the enemy within, who indeed were so vicious that they even attacked their own neighbours. It is interesting that while the text offers clear discussions of the violent actions taken in self-defence by both Turkish-Ottoman subjects and the Ottoman government itself as a matter of survival, the same analytical lens is not used to think about other Ottoman groups' actions in the same period. One effect of this is evident in the above extract. It normalizes the perception of mass violence against Armenians in general as justified due to the victimization of Ottoman Muslims.

The self-evaluation of the education system

It is evident that there was a change in the textual presentation of the events of 1915 between the 1982 book and the 2006 book. The change was due to newly established learning outcomes that had been created to support the overall education policy. On the basis of the Turkish government's desire to resist the international pressure arising from the 'so-called genocide claims', the new approach aimed to provide younger generations with narratives they could use to counter such unfounded claims. In this section, I will focus on how the education experts who participated in this process have evaluated these changes to the education system. I will do so in order to understand what the system is structurally concerned about in its approach to teaching history. Furthermore, my analysis also allows me to understand how the education system monitors itself.

The changes I noted in the previous section of this chapter are considered to be important, as they highlight a change in history teaching in Turkey. In his comparative analysis of the changing nature of the curriculum on the history of the Republic of Turkey, Mehmet Serhat Yılmaz (2014) identifies clear differences between textbooks used in the 1980s and the 2000s. His analysis shows that while similar topics are covered in both periods, the new approach reorganizes the links between some of these issues and the new curriculum. He states that it is encouraging to see that the new texts discuss the period after Atatürk's death by considering various topics including 'natural resources, Turkish energy issues, minority schools, the European Union process, Armenian and Cypriot issues, the Korean war, separatism, religious fundamentalism and foreign missionaries' work' (Yılmaz 2014: 4). He points out that this new curriculum is designed to give students the skills to understand current issues. Then he reviews the unsatisfactory way in which the old approach covered the 'Armenian issue and deportations' and 'developments on the so-called Armenian genocide claims' (Yılmaz 2014: 4).

Yılmaz (2014: 4) observes several specific deficiencies here. The old approach suffered a lack of both 'visual materials' and 'convincing population statistics', which are accepted as the right tools to present persuasive arguments. He sees the new approach as better addressing the issues under new titles such as 'National Awakening: Reactions to the Occupation of Our Country', 'Either Freedom or Death' and 'Turkey After Atatürk', and also in some designated subsections, such as 'Forced Migration, Why?' (Yılmaz 2014: 5). He regards these new sections as superior because they use more population statistics, present the activities of Armenian political parties and gangs against the Ottoman Empire in more detail and provide more detail about the Russian occupation of eastern Anatolia and how Armenians volunteered in the French army to support the occupation of Antep, Maraş and Urfa. The sections also recount heroic stories of resistance by local Muslim Turks. Another improvement, according to Yılmaz (2014: 9), is the clear coverage of how from 'the 1970s onwards, Turkish diplomats were targeted by Armenian terrorists', particularly under 'the subheading of "Threats Against Turkey"'. It is also in this section that the book covers the claims about the 'so-called genocide' by arguing that 'there has not been any documentary evidence to prove this. Their [Armenians'] arguments are based on fake documentation and the work of partial historians' (Yılmaz 2014: 10). Ultimately, Yılmaz (2014: 9) argues that these changes provide better content that is central to the development of future 'Turkish citizens who will know and be able to discuss the reality of the deportation event [*sic*]'.

A similar study by Deniz Tonga (2015), looking at secondary education history textbooks and how they cover 'the Armenian issue', makes similar observations about the content of the teaching material. Tonga acknowledges the increased space devoted to the many phases of 'the Armenian issue', including the atrocities Armenians committed in eastern Anatolia, the Armenian insurgency leading up to the deportation process and the ASALA assassinations of the 1970s. Interestingly, however, he finds it problematic that this very important content is delivered in a condensed manner. His recommendation is to allow students to better absorb this material by being introduced to it gradually from the beginning of their secondary education, and by spending more time on each of these topics individually as students move through the education system.

Studying the same issue, Refik Turan (2015) looks at roughly the same period and textbooks. He observes changes over time similar to those identified by the scholars discussed above. Gradually during the 2000s, and particularly after 2007, he says, 'the coverage of the Armenia issue, deportations, together with Pontic Greek and Assyrian-related issues' increased compared with the previous period (Turan 2015: 1497). Interestingly, he points out:

> The subjects of the Armenian question and deportation gradually increased in history textbooks after 1981, when they were included in the curricula in parallel to the increase in the efforts of the Armenians to introduce the events of 1915 as genocide.... [T]he language, and the manner in which it is used in textbooks on relevant subjects, is stronger at present in parallel to the expansion of the information given regarding the subject. (Turan 2015: 1475–6)

His analysis finds that in more recent years the textbooks have explained correctly and in detail how 'the Ottoman government protected and took measures to address the economic needs of citizens exposed to deportation, both during and after the process' (Turan 2015: 1497). It is interesting that Turan chooses this point as worth highlighting to demonstrate the improvement in the textbooks, given the previous literature on the systematic dispossession of the deported Armenians through different legal mechanisms during this period (see Akçam and Kurt 2017). Moreover, when pointing out the expanding coverage, he states that the 'baselessness of the genocide claims is presented in textbooks not only in the context of historical realities, but also in terms of international relations and legal aspects' (Turan 2015: 1497). His review includes an extensive presentation of one of the most recent history books, which he clearly sees as the state of the art for Year 10 secondary school students. However, Turan has a major complaint concerning the timing of some of this teaching. He argues that the most important issues around 'Armenian atrocities, Armenians' status in the Treaty of Lausanne, baseless Armenian claims about genocide since 1945, ASALA [and] the views of Turkish Armenians on the Armenian problem' are the last topics this particular book covers. 'Being the last topics to be covered, and being covered towards the last weeks of the teaching year, could become a handicap for sufficiently and effectively teaching these [topics] to students' (Turan 2015: 1497).

In the extensively researched report *'Armenians' in Turkish Textbooks: From the Republic to Today*, Erhan Metin (2015) also considers textbooks and Armenians. Over 180 pages, he provides a detailed analysis of Armenians' inclusion in or exclusion from textbooks since the foundation of the republic to trace certain continuities and trends. When looking at recent decades, he considers books similar to those mentioned above, and he more or less shares those scholars' view that the coverage has become gradually more detailed and in-depth in relation to 'the Armenian issue' and deportations to include more 'pressing' issues around ASALA terrorism. However, Metin's approach is different: he analyses the use of language in reference to Armenians, examining what he calls unscientific and subjective language that implicitly or explicitly creates a general 'us and them' narrative. His overall assessment is that history textbooks have become more scientific and objective, with a change in the language used, and with the introduction of more original material to provide a more detailed historical analysis of the facts rather than relying on emotional language.

For instance, he points out that a 1933 history book reveals an anti-Armenian bias when it uses the phrase 'the new Turkish army took the Armenians down a peg or two [*haddini bildirdikten sonra*]' (Metin 2015: 56). Metin's sensitivity to emotional and partial language is clear when he analyses the use of 'abstract and relative terms' to talk about Armenians. He argues that describing 'all Armenians as "very happy" without establishing historically that this was really the case for all', and the use of 'all kinds of freedoms' as an undefined description of freedom, constructs narratives that move away from a 'scientific and objective position' (Metin 2015: 85). At the same time, the language of one narrative on 'the role of missionary activity and minority schools in manipulating Armenians against the Ottomans' is taken as evidence of 'the attempt to use language that is not anti-Armenian in Turkish textbooks', as it shows that 'Armenians were not primarily responsible for the revolts against the government at the time' (Metin 2015: 86, see also 88). While recognizing that the use of words such as 'savagely [*vahşice*]' and 'mercilessly [*acimazsızca*]' to define the atrocities committed by Armenians is unscientific, he argues that such usages in Turkish history books have gradually been reduced, indicating a change in publication policies to 'move away from painful and emotional language' (Metin 2015: 87).

Using a similar interpretive logic to analyse Kemal Kara's 1996 book, Metin (2015: 92, see also 94) points out that the book discusses the deportations by arguing that 'Armenians who were collaborating with the enemy had to be migrated [by the government] to different regions'. This, says Metin, recognizes that the deportations – which are considered to be the backbone of the genocide claims – in fact did not include all Armenians. In his search for 'objective' descriptions of the facts, he compares two extracts from two different books to show that the more recent book focuses on facts and has moved away from emotional language such as 'innocent [*günahsız*]' and 'crazed [*gözü dönmüş*]' as qualifiers to indicate 'us' and 'them' (Metin 2015: 117). This also seems to clarify what he means by 'objective': it is about not using emotional language to present facts, rather than about where those facts come from. For example, he uses an extract from a book published in 2005 that describes the relationship between Russian policies and Armenian political parties in the 1880s to present the Armenian revolts. It is indeed written very factually. However, at the end of the extract, the authors state: 'The first [Armenian] revolt happened in Erzurum. . . . There was an attempt to kill the governor of Van. In skirmishes in Merzifon, 25 Turkish soldiers were martyred' (Metin 2015: 117). While Metin points to the 'objective', factual language of this extract, he seems to accept the concept of martyrdom – particularly in relation to 'our' dead – as also indicating such objectivity. His analysis praises this text for its objectivity even though it depicts some soldiers' deaths as martyrdoms while others are mentioned as 'mere' deaths, as dead enemies. The text thus communicates in an emotional language that strongly resonates with the Turkish public, given the spiritual connotations and value attributed to martyrdom in Turkey. Here, then, the text continues to assert a logic of 'us and them'.

Metin also discusses the textbook *History 10* (*Tarih 10*), written by a commission that included Vicdan Turan, İlhan Genç, Mehmet Çelik, Celal Genç and Şenol Türedi. *History 10* was published 2011. It includes a subsection headed 'Forced Migration, Why? [*Zorunlu Göç, Neden?*]', and Metin (2015: 119) argues that this choice of subheading is further evidence of the positive change in history textbooks, since it is intended to motivate 'students to wonder and question rather than learn the facts didactically'. This interpretation seems to stretch the assumed critical intentionality too far. The long extract provided from the book does not provide any alternative pathways that might lead students to think differently. Instead, it communicates the now normalized view that what happened to the Armenians in 1915 was due to Armenian revolts and banditry. Admittedly, it provides more details about these events, but nothing else. Remarkably, after providing extensive extracts from this textbook, Metin quotes verbatim twelve pages that relate to the Armenian issue, without offering any specific analysis. It is not clear why calling a movement based on a policy of forced deportation 'migration [*göç*]' is more objective or factual in terms of what happened in 1915.

According to Metin, the 2011 book does not only consider the events that occurred in eastern Anatolia due to the conflict with Russia during the First World War, in which both Armenian-Russian soldiers and Armenian gangs perpetrated atrocities; it also talks extensively about more recent events since the 1970s. While the earlier history is presented within the familiar framework of the Ottoman government's security concerns and the Turkish population's victimization by Armenian violence, the latter discussion is presented under the chapter subheading 'Armenian Claims and ASALA [*Ermeni İddialari ve ASALA*]'. Metin focuses on this text to highlight the improvement to the narrative, which he argues now gains more detailed content to clearly establish a language that informs the facticity of a particular view. For instance, he points out that the book clearly presents the events of 24 April 1915 as 'the Ottoman interior ministry deciding to take measures against the increasing Armenian rebellion and deciding on 24 April 1915 to close down all Armenian parties [*komiteleri*]', and 'due to this decision, in Istanbul leaders of the Armenian Hıncak [Hunchakian] and Taşhnak [Dashnakyastoun] parties were arrested' (Metin 2015: 130). He considers the book to further elaborate on the 'true' nature of the deportations as protective and defensive. Here, he says, the book argues authoritatively that there was a wide-ranging rebellion that could have damaged the Ottoman state, and that all the people arrested in Istanbul, whom Armenians often present as martyrs, were in fact leaders of the rebellion (Metin 2015: 130–1). In this way, he portrays the book as aiming to remove any ambiguity for the next generations of students about Armenian claims regarding 24 April 1915, and therefore about the 'so-called genocide'. Thus, the aspects of the text he praises here are also the ways in which it successfully removes or erases the very possibility of considering that these events might have been genocidal.

Metin's review of this book next considers its sections on the Treaty of Lausanne, Turkey's membership of the North Atlantic Treaty Organization, its relations with Armenia and the emergence of Armenian terrorism with ASALA in the 1970s. Again, he mostly quotes the text verbatim and without any analysis. This strategy seems to be designed to show that much more relevant information is provided by this book, particularly on recent history. One verbatim extract is a two-page list of the Turkish diplomats assassinated by ASALA (Metin 2015: 135–7). At the end of the extract, the book links ASALA terrorism with the Kurdish terrorism initiated by the Kurdistan Workers' Party (Partiya Karkeren Kurdistan) (Metin 2015: 138). Both the book itself and Metin's review of it seem to present Armenians as an ahistorical threat to Turkish existence, in an unbroken narrative arc from the 1890s until the present day. Armenians are presented as constantly attempting to undermine the Turkish existence in Anatolia. Both texts then present Armenians as targeting Turkey through their ongoing attempt to gain recognition for the 'so-called genocide claim'. The textbook talks about various processes around these discussions, after broadly considering the issue: 'Armenians are constantly trying to present themselves as a community that suffered from cruelty [*zulüm*] and injustice [*haksızlık*] to be able to amplify their claims for the recognition of the so-called genocide' (Metin 2015: 138).

It seems that Metin considers this textbook as representing progress because it covers the period up to the 2000s and is explicitly constructed to counter genocide claims, in line with the Turkish Government's Committee to Coordinate the Struggle with the Baseless Genocide Claims. According to Metin, the content presented in this book provides students with the clearest and broadest contemporary information on 'Armenian issues'. He adds that the book treats the ideas of 'genocide' and 'deportation' conceptually, in order to overcome the conceptual confusion presented by Armenians (Metin 2015: 140). In the conclusion of his report, Metin (2015: 147) considers this book to be the best available, arguing that 'the reality of the situation is that today the "Armenian issue" is presented in a more objective and scientific manner'. But he still finds it unsatisfactory that 'the issue is presented in a shallow manner without visual materials, without activities to make students more active in learning, and without using local historical resources' (Metin 2015: 147). As Metin suggests, no explicitly emotional terms indicating an 'us and them' logic are used in the construction of Armenian identity, either in the way in which Armenians' history in Anatolia is narrated in the 2011 textbook or in Metin's own review. But the overall structure of the narrative can be seen as inherently one-dimensional and derogatory.

The books reviewed and the reviews themselves normalize a denialist knowledge that comprehensively resists any consideration of its own epistemological limits. What the reviewers I have discussed here consider to constitute the textbooks' success is their ability to establish and diffuse in-depth denialist knowledge as the only base from which to know about these issues. The reviews by the three education specialists considered above make it clear that they decided to analyse the change in history teaching over time according to two different registers: language use, that is, the impact of using emotional/derogatory terms, and the scientific accuracy of the knowledge claims presented in the various textbooks. These reviews come across as attempts to see how 'we' can better educate students in 'our' understanding to support 'our' national narrative. All of these analyses miss the central critical point – the unchanging content of the historical narrative across the textbooks considered. The position represented in the reviews does not pose any questions about the factual veracity of the content that is being expanded, elaborated and deployed. By focusing on the language used, the reviewers' interpretive strategy sidelines the question of veracity. Most importantly, the contestability of the content is negated, as the reviewers present the problems with the textbooks as technical issues of presentation and the availability of more in-depth material to support the content, rather than identifying problems with the content per se. Thus, the interest in reviewing existing books and producing new ones is confined to concerns about how the same content can be amplified to allow students to absorb the narratives and then reproduce them when needed in their everyday lives. Neither the history books nor the reviews of them discussed above provide a critical orientation to knowledge by considering wide-ranging research to rethink the historical frames they use. As the bibliographies of the texts make clear, they do not include any alternative resources to provide different views of these events that might raise questions for students. The texts are produced through a rather narrow national historiography in a self-referential manner that excludes all research that does not agree with the national position.

Today, students are perhaps exposed to less direct emotional language. At the same time, the history they study desensitizes them with regard to certain issues, as they do not encounter different ways to think. The textbooks replicate an 'us and them', 'victim and perpetrator' logic that presents Armenians as the perpetual enemy within: then, against the Ottoman government; today, through their unfounded genocide claims against the Republic of Turkey. In this way, these historical narratives use the word 'Armenian' to signal an existential otherness, an existential insecurity, for the Turkish student. The texts are structured to replace the possibility of any critical analysis with a focus on a *longue durée* perspective on being Turkish. This relies on narratives that displace questions about specific events to deflect students from a nuanced understanding of those events. For instance, in this historiography, it is not important to ask specifically what is meant by the Armenian rebellion(s), why people rebelled, who those people were or why people who are now labelled as terrorists were arrested in Istanbul on 24 April 1915. It seems that what matters is to use specific language to instantiate the long-term animosity that is supposed to underlie Armenian actions. The argument thus establishes the ahistorical truth of the otherness of the Armenians, without using any explicitly emotional language to do so. That absence of emotional language certainly does not make any of these narratives objective, despite the claims of some of the education specialists discussed above. Although the reader is given a long history, the character of the Other – as Armenian – is fixed as the villain of the narrative. 'The Armenians' only appear in 'our' history to inflict some self-interested harm on 'us'. Consequently, these texts normalize a specific interpretive strategy that creates a space where readers – who are mostly students – feel comfortable and unchallenged within this particular system of thinking.

So, when these narratives are later recalled in everyday life as part of the public memory repertoire – when people use what they have been taught during their formal education – it all feels reasonable and right. This narrative is underpinned by a distinction between the Armenians who remained loyal and those who revolted against the Ottomans (as presented in the textbook *History 10*), and Armenians' ability to belong to Turkish society is tied to their acceptance of this narrative and that distinction, an acceptance that would negate their own voices. This simplistic historiography depoliticizes Armenians in such a way that they appear timeless, outside politics, with no relevance for young Turkish people's thinking today. In more general terms, given that teaching in this area typically starts with the Turks' entry onto the world stage and the establishment of various Turkish political authorities and states (particularly the Ottoman Empire and the Republic of Turkey), other actors, including Armenians, are only discussed as long as they are relevant in some form to this processional historiography of 'ours'. For instance, Armenians are mentioned as one of the groups the early Turks encountered in Anatolia. They appear again midway through the nineteenth century as the villains of the story. This way of teaching history – through wars, state formation and state succession – aims to ground a homogenous national identity. As the publications reviewed above highlight, this process of teaching fails entirely to provide any understanding of the social, cultural, political or economic histories through which different people interact with and encounter each other to build relations and societies. As a result, students learn history as the politics of becoming Turkish and acceptable citizens, without understanding the politics of living together with difference.

I mentioned in Chapter 1 that the focus of this book is the non-Armenian majority in Turkey. However, in light of the way in which the education system is structured, I will comment briefly on how what I have discussed here impacts on the experience of Armenian-Turkish students. The current relationship between the MEB and the minority schools in Turkey creates a difficult situation for students in those schools. As the ministry maintains control over how the sections of the curriculum on citizenship and history are delivered, it is clear that – at least as a formal expectation – Armenian-Turkish students in these schools are supposed to be educated through this historiography. They are also required to think about the Other – that is, themselves – in the register of the enemy within and outsiders. Thus, they are supposed to think about themselves and the past through the lens of 'our ancestors, the Turks' (Barış 2021: 240).

Perhaps the expectation is that this will allow them to become acceptable Turkish citizens or at least to perform what is expected of them as Turkish citizens. Linda Barış (2021) considers some of these issues in her recent book on the topic. She critically points out that as spaces where national identities are built, schools impact on minority students – in this case, Armenian students in Turkey – in challenging ways, since they are taught a national history that is built on undermining their own identities. She highlights two important aspects: 'First, their identity is presented as the enemy; second, they are brought up with a history that teaches about the other ethnic group rather than their own' (Barış 2021: 128). The implication of this situation is very important. As Barış argues, these students are very aware that students in other schools are also educated in this discourse of animosity against Armenians. This no doubt influences their sociability in public. The policy aims to instil a way of thinking that expects students to resolve differences by subsuming them under being Turkish. Yet it sets out the majoritarian view of the past as the compulsory way for everyone to perform their belonging by engaging in public discussions, regardless of different groups' experiences and knowledge of the past.

Conclusion

In this chapter, I first analysed the content of two textbooks that have been used as the main knowledge base to teach secondary school students in Turkey. Then I looked at the changes in teaching content as the education policy changed over time with regard to the teaching of foundational knowledge about the history of the Turkish republic. To consider the latter, I studied reviews of these changes written by education specialists. This was helpful, as it revealed how the education system maintains its main ideological epistemology, which is directly built on ontological Turkishness. The reviews were detailed and found problems with the implementation of some of the changes in teaching. But none of the reviews were critical of the ideological framing of the content of the knowledge taught.

As discussed above, the knowledge that the education system sees as relevant is content that is in line with Basic National Education Law number 1739, which states that the aim of the education system is to create acceptable citizens based on the founding principles of the Republic of Turkey. While this underlines how history textbooks present Armenians as the constitutive Other, augmenting the nature of Turkishness as 'us', the changes in the textbooks discussed above introduce an additional approach. As I observed in the case of *History 10*, students are now presented with more detailed content that links the past to the present. The texts are written more explicitly, albeit in less emotional language, to provide material for students to counter the 'so-called genocide claims'. Here, the arguments are developed not by critical historical analysis but by the assertive deployment of a 'nationalist language' that conveys the positions of 'us and them' (Eroler 2019: 228). This approach is not accidental; nor is it objective, notwithstanding some experts' assertions. Rather, it reflects how the knowledge is structured. It builds on the additional national educational aims stated by the MEB in 2002, which introduced the idea that students as Turkish citizens should be provided with the skills to understand 'the invalidity of the Armenian claims' and 'to counter those claims' (MEB 2002/2: 531–41). The knowledge that is taught is structured so as to achieve these aims, framing what can be known from a denialist position. In this way, the education policy and the textbooks that deliver on its aims reproduce the logic of the acceptable citizen as a denialist identity, which, as Üstel (2004: 322–4) observes, is created at the intersection of 'a cultural and ethnic sensitivity, an obligations-based rights system and a perception of threat that aims to create a sense of social vigilance against the designated Other'. This approach aims to limit students' understanding, and it provides them with no opportunity to engage with different ideas once they leave the education system. It also indicates students' long-term responsibilization to defend the positions they are taught as Turkish citizens against the Other. The limited knowledge students encounter in their education comes to underwrite the narratives of public memory they will encounter in everyday life to recall what they remember.

The education system had undergone changes to ensure that it provides students with the tools to think when they leave school as part of the Turkish public, as representatives of ontological Turkishness. These skills include the required knowledge to perform being Turkish and the language that underwrites their ability to 'speak denialism', allowing them to relate to the knowledge they were given, even for those whose formal education ended at the end of secondary school.

The education system is therefore the central mechanism that normalizes a set of linguistic tropes as the condition of talking about Armenians and history while also performing being a good citizen. This normalization process educates students in the grammar of denialism by inculcating the rules and norms for speaking of 'our' past, which are then performed in everyday life to be comprehensible to other citizens. Even the mass media, as a carrier of denialist knowledge, still relies on the learned, normalized language of Turkishness to perform its role as communicator of that knowledge. The relationship between the appropriate language and what it allows to be recalled underwrites the stability of the public memory repertoire and its denialist knowledge. The knowledge constructed to propagate a certain imaginary of nationhood and citizenship is the only thinking the public can remember. While the mass media keeps this knowledge fresh as it reproduces it time and again, the veracity of what it repeats is limited to what people can recall from their own engagement with the public memory repertoire, which in turn is centred by what they recall from their past education. The educational approach analysed here in general leaves space for nothing other than the replication of the foundational myths of national republican public memory. What students learn and the attitudes they reproduce as appropriate Turkish citizens become a cyclical verification mechanism for the national ideology, to which students may already have been exposed before school, whether in the family or through public discussions they have observed in the media. In this central role, the education system produces specific narratives about Armenians, both in the present and intergenerationally.

While this discussion has focused on textbooks for secondary education, it also relates to two other directly relevant areas: the training of the teaching staff who use these books to teach broadly denialist knowledge, and the role of the higher education system. Teacher training is related to the way in which the higher education system produces knowledge, as are all the textbooks I have considered here. All the textbooks discussed in this chapter were produced by professional historians with academic positions. In this sense, my analysis – especially my analysis of the reviews of these textbooks – also reveals the limitations of academic historical research on these issues in Turkey. Commenting on the role of universities in Turkey, Ethem Eldem (2018) considers their work to be a part of the development of an introverted national understanding of historiography and the social sciences. In setting out the aims of the education system, Basic National Educational Law number 1739 regulates academic research too. Thus, academic research developed under the requirements of this law aims to produce knowledge to undermine the other knowledge about the genocide that has been available since 1915. In addition to building the national history that underpins secondary education through their research, academic historians also educate students, both as the next generation of researchers and as public intellectuals who can take part in media discussions on issues such as the Armenian genocide to inform the public about 'the truths of such unfounded claims'. Thus, historians play an important role in the reproduction and deepening of the knowledge base that reinforces what people learn during their school education by telling them about that knowledge again and again in the media. They participate not only in the structuring of students' thinking through formal education about Armenians and 'our' history, but also in public education through their various media appearances and public speaking engagements.

6

Educating the public

In the previous chapter, I argued that the education system in Turkey works as the mechanism that distils the nature of both being and becoming Turkish in that it establishes the conventions regarding how to think about Armenians and the Armenian genocide. While I focused in that chapter on secondary education, I also highlighted that higher education and research play central roles in this process. They are central not only because of their impact on the secondary school curriculum and teachers but also because they inform the public through the dissemination of the narratives that constitute the public memory. In this chapter, I will focus on this public communication of academic research in both academic conferences and documentaries developed for TV audiences in Turkey. The chapter also highlights how the knowledge disseminated through different mediums becomes a mechanism to confirm the veracity of that knowledge – a triangulation mechanism, so to speak. The direct quotations presented in this chapter are from the notes I took while attending academic events and watching TV programmes based on academic research.

Encounters with academic research

The year 2015 began with a large international symposium that took place in Istanbul on 5–7 January. The symposium was led by Istanbul University and supported by a number of other organizations, including Istanbul Turkish Hearth (İstanbul Türk Ocağı), a nationalist civil society organization originally founded in 1932, and the cultural department of Istanbul Metropolitan Municipality (İstanbul Büyükşehir Belediyesi). It was entitled 'Turkish–Armenian Relations in the 19th and 20th Centuries: Cohesion [*Kaynaşma*], Resentment [*Kırgınlık*], Division [*Ayrılık*], New Directions [*Yeni Arayışlar*]'. When I saw the programme, I thought I should certainly attend the symposium. The programme was very extensive, with two parallel sessions running through four time slots; each session had three research presentations. With more than seventy presentations over three days, the symposium promised to be wide ranging.

On the day, I arrived at the university and tried to find out where to go for the symposium by asking some students. At first they did not know what I was asking about, but then one of them said, 'Are you looking for the Armenian meeting [*Ermeni toplantısı*]?' Thereafter they directed me to the right place. No one asked me anything as I sat down; this was a public academic event. The public engagement angle was underlined by a concert that formed part of the programme to mark Armenian composers' contributions to Ottoman music. The symposium was clearly designed to present a historical analysis focusing on the first three processes referenced in symposium subtitle: cohesion, resentment and division. The fourth process named in the subtitle, 'new directions', was mostly confined to the expression of sentiments about 'working together' during the opening and closing sessions. During these sessions, some presenters remembered that 'two communities', the Armenians and the Muslim-Turkish Ottomans, had lived together before 1915 and wondered what had happened to change that state of affairs.

While the first session began by looking at Armenian-Turkish relations to highlight their historical cohesion in broadly sociocultural terms, by the last two sessions of the first day of the symposium the focus had shifted to the period leading up to the First World War and highlighted the emergence of resentment. This focus orientated the rest of the symposium, in three stages: (1) examining the causes of division by unpacking Ottoman political relations with Russia and other powers during the period; (2) considering the emergence of the Armenian problem from the late nineteenth century onwards; (3) considering relations between various European powers, missionaries and Armenians. The symposium further explored these issues by looking at events during the First World War through French and British documents, in addition to considering the legal issues around the Armenian property that had remained in Turkey during the war years. The last day then considered relations between Armenians and Turkey after the end of the Second World War, including within the European Union. I noted that this three-stage structure seemed to be analogous to the way 'Armenian issues' were taught in secondary schools (discussed in Chapter 5). The underlying strategy was to present a kind of incredulity that a national community that had been well respected should have behaved so badly over time, behaviour that had then led to the decision to deport them during the First World War. The presentations focused on a number of topics, including the status of Armenians as the most loyal nation (*millet-i-sadıka*) in the nineteenth-century Ottoman polity and the tolerant and benevolent nature of the Ottoman political attitude towards Armenians. This logic provided the analytical scaffolding for the symposium. But it also revealed the nature of academic research on these issues in Turkey: for the researchers, what needed to be explained was why a nation (i.e. the Armenians) that the Ottomans had considered to be loyal, and which they had therefore treated well, had decided to act against both Ottomans and their own interests within that sociopolitical space. The research presented thus focused on the Armenians' betrayal of the Ottomans. This concern centred Muslim-Turkish Ottomans as the wronged party, a centring that formed the starting point for the logic of the research. The research presented during the symposium aimed to offer various answers to this question. In many different versions, the narratives of 'the enemy within' and 'manipulation by European powers' were both explicitly and implicitly used to explain Armenians' behaviour, that is, their betrayal. In this way, the argument that the Armenians' own culpability had resulted in security concerns was used to explain the Ottoman government's decision in favour of their deportation (*tehcir*) in 1915. Many of the researchers recognized that many lives had been lost due to the deportations, but the question of the responsibility for those losses was broadly for Armenians to answer, as they had 'rebelled' against their own government.

For instance, one professor of history focused on the nature of 'rebellion against the state' by discussing 'the 1893 Armenian rebellion'. He began by directly appealing to the logic described above, arguing that 800 years of neighbourly relations had been impacted by 'the influence of Russia and England'. He then outlined chronologically how, thanks to that influence, Armenian subjects of the Ottoman Empire had acted badly. This led into his discussion of the events of 1893. Here, his focus was on links between, for instance, American missionary schools such as the American College of Merzovan (Merzifon Amerikan Koleji) and the emergence of organized Armenian political committees (*komiteleri*) in Anatolia. His presentation provided detailed information about the formation of these political committees and their activities, listing them as a series of uprisings leading up to 1885, when 'within 66 days there were 23 Armenian uprisings in the area from Kayseri to Van'. The presentation concluded with the reflection that 'the Anatolian population, who had lived in neighbourly relations, did not deserved such treatment' and that 'even in the smallest things, neighbours can help each other [*komşu komşunun külüne muhtaçtır*]'. These statements expressed both incredulity and sadness at what the professor described as betrayal.

Another presentation, entitled 'The 1897 Bâbıâli Incident [*Olayi*]', focused on a specific event: 'the bombing of the centre of Ottoman government by Armenian terrorists' who initiated parallel attacks on the Ottoman Bank and Galatasaray police station in Istanbul. The speaker located this event within the broader process of 'demonstrations and riots that took place in 1880–1905 in Istanbul to demand concessions from the palace'. The presentation identified 'three Armenians who had arrived from Russia a year before' as the culprits. It then focused on the measures taken against Armenians in Istanbul by Sultan Abdülhamit II for security reasons, presenting the situation as the outcome of an international manipulation that had been opposed by loyal Armenian public figures in Istanbul. The presentation concluded that Abdülhamit II had been clear that the innocent Armenians who had opposed these events should be treated differently from those who had been responsible for them. While the particular incident in question was presented in some detail, it was contextualized only by a discussion of how some Armenians had been manipulated by foreign influences and agents – thus further highlighting the victimization of the Ottoman government. Curiously, the discussion entirely omitted to mention the broader political and economic context created by what had become known as the 1894–6 Hamidian massacres, which the Ottoman government had initiated against Armenians across the country. Without this contextualization, one was immediately and inevitably led to think that our neighbours had attacked an unsuspecting, benevolent government and people.

In a similar vein, a presentation on the Zeytun uprising argued that the uprising had encouraged other Armenian groups across Anatolia. The presentation focused on the period 1890–5 and concluded with a look at the events of 1921. There was no clear contextualization of the events to understand why there had been an uprising in the region. It began with an interesting demarcation: 'In Turkey, the Armenian issue started with Zeytun and ended in Zeytun. With the 1921 intervention, this issue finished for Turkey.' The presenter provided an overview of relations between Armenians and Turks in the region through a wide historical lens, stating that 'in 1895, 9000 Armenians and 7500 Muslims' had lived in the area, figures that had risen in 1914 to '10,500 Armenians and 8068 Muslims'. The presentation then depicted the history of Armenian unrest in the region throughout the nineteenth century and the Ottoman attempts to control that unrest. It went on to point out that after local Armenians had attempted to rebel during the summer of 1914, and after the Ottoman government had entered the First World War at the end of October 1914, the area had become a destination for many Armenian deserters from the Ottoman army. The reason for the deportation of Armenians from Zeytun in July 1915 was presented as the constant conflicts between Armenian bandits and political groups demanding independence, as well as all the Ottoman military operations to deal with those conflicts. Of the Zeytun deportations, the presenter said: 'This is the first banishment [*sürgün*]; 1500 of them returned.' But with regard to what had happened to those 1,500, the audience was told there had been a problem.

According to the presenter, after the end of the First World War in 1918, these returnees had associated with the occupying French forces and disturbed the local population. Occupying the local military barracks as a defensive position, they had attacked Turkish forces in the midst of the War of Independence, and they had also attacked local people. This had made the military action taken against them in 1921 inevitable. After the military operation in the summer of 1921, 'the area was cleared of Armenians'. While presenter's account listed the numbers of Turkish soldiers killed by rank and regiment, there was no explanation of what had happened to the 1,500 or 2,000 Armenians who had returned from the deportations of 1915. Who were they? Were they all male militia? Were there women and girls? The argument suggested that these people had simply been removed to calm the region and allow the local Muslim population to live in security. The presentation engaged with the Armenians only from the perspective of removing barriers to the ongoing Turkish War of Independence. Questions about what had happened to the Armenians who had not returned were not part of the discussion. Why these Armenians had been armed, what they had been trying to do and why, given their very small numbers, the Turkish army had seen them as a major threat – all of this remained unexplained. In addition, it was not clear what had happened to this group of 1,500 Armenians in the end. The presentation gave the impression that they had simply been casualties of war due to their own fault. The silences in these presentations, and in the symposium in general, allowed the audience to hear detailed narratives from an already well-established public memory repertoire that reiterated the victimization of Turks and the resulting imperative to secure their place in Anatolia.

This large symposium, which looked at 'the Armenian issue' from various perspectives, was not only an academic event. It was also a public relations activity to establish the Turkish position on 'the Armenian issue' during the centennial year of the genocide. The presentations of historical research framed a representation of the relationship between Turks and Armenians from the perspective of the Turkish national thesis. The presenters' historical analyses further embedded the victim–enemy modality within this logic by providing detailed accounts of the victimization of the Turkish population by Armenians, who were broadly presented as a generic category. These representations were both grounded in and reiterated by the narratives that constitute the public memory as the only knowledge with which 'we' can think about these issues. In this way, each presentation provided an academic justification and research evidence to reiterate the relevance of the knowledge base that grounds the public memory repertoire.

Academic research as public communication plays an important role as one of the mechanisms that produces the conditions under which the Turkish public comes to think about 'the Armenian issue'. This symposium was not only performing science by presenting the results of scientific endeavours. It was also reconstructing various historical events. The representations of the deportations, the 'Zeytun uprising' and the 'Bâbıâli incident' further normalized an anti-Armenian attitude that became part of knowledge and what that knowledge claimed to evidence. Such historical narratives were used and repeated across the symposium to reference points that underwrote the Turkish national thesis as the ontological frame for the audience to think about Armenians and 'the Armenian issue'. The narratives unfolded through a causal chain in which the agency of various actors – such as the Ottoman government and its officials, Armenians and foreign powers – was positioned within a framework that provided explanations of how the 1915 events had been reached. These causal narratives provided reasons why the Ottoman government's security measures in 1915 had been justified. The possibility of developing these narratives was embedded in the representation of Armenians as a homogenous group and in the disregard of the questions I posed above. These causal narratives, as didactic tools, implicitly led the audience to think that given the logic presented, the events could not be considered a genocide. Therefore, these academic narratives engendered a way of understanding that allowed the audience to apprehend the events within a limited field of vision.

These presentations amounted to an elaboration of the past with what appeared to be more detailed case studies by current historians for a present-day use that fitted in with recent political interests, in the same way as I observed with regard to the textbooks discussed in the previous chapter. The symposium presentations aimed to motivate the public and students to actively challenge Armenians' arguments by amplifying the status of Armenians as the generic villains of Turkish history (a similar conference took place in Van in May 2015, see Battal 2015). This mechanism – legitimating a particular national thesis on the basis of academic research – reproduced the public memory repertoire as an incontrovertible truth claim. For me, as a general member of the audience, what I recalled about Armenians through the public memory repertoire was reiterated by the academic research, and this gave me more confidence about the position I might take up by using those narratives regarding the untruth of Armenians' positions on the events of 1915 and knowledge about the genocide.

While there were many critical questions to ask about the construction of these historical narratives, many of the questions from the audience in fact sought further elaborations regarding why Armenians had turned against their neighbours, how Muslim Turks had defended themselves and other similar topics. The aim of these questions appeared to be to seek confirmation from the researchers of what 'we' already knew. Many of the academic researchers who participate in academic meetings such as this symposium also publicly communicate their views in discussion programmes on TV, repeating their positions for a larger audience. For example, smaller versions of this symposium communicated the same material across the country later that year, and many historians also took part in various TV discussions, delivering the same narratives to larger audiences in the run-up to 24 April 2015.

Much smaller than the symposium discussed above, but important nonetheless, was a panel discussion organized and hosted by the Istanbul Bar Association on 24 April 2015 (mentioned in Chapter 3). The event was entitled 'On the 100th Anniversary of Transfers [*Nakil*] and Resettlement [*İskan*]: From Historical Reality to Political Fiction [*Kurgu*]'. The panel was chaired by the deputy director of the Bar Association and included historians and a lawyer. The authority and public credibility of the Istanbul Bar Association underlined the importance of the panel and its message, hours before the main centennial commemoration march was to take place nearby. A number of panellists would have been familiar to the audience from their frequent appearances on TV discussion programmes during the period leading up to 24 April 2015. It was immediately clear from the panel chair's opening statement that each panellist was there to discredit a particular aspect of the Armenian claims. The line of argument each panellist presented reiterated the main lines of the public memory repertoire. For instance, the panellist from the Bar Association repeated the legal status of the United Nations Convention on the Prevention and Punishment of the Crime of Genocide and the reasons why it was impossible for the Republic of Turkey to be an addressee of genocide claims. Another panel member provided historical insights into the period before 1915 by emphasizing the Ottoman government's generally tolerant approach to Armenians and the development of Armenian 'treachery' against the Turkish population, which had led to the deportations as a self-defence measure. As the title of the panel suggested, the overall narrative was an attempt to provide a corrective, based on 'our' historical research, to the 'so-called Armenian genocide claims', which were treated as a fiction based on knowledge provided by the Other.

In his opening remarks, the deputy head of the Bar Association said: 'Many pages have been written to create problems for Turkey. Through these political discussions, the debate is moving away from historical realities. . . . Without any legal basis, a claim of genocide has become widespread.' Another speaker also argued that 'a legal issue [i.e. genocide] is being made part of a political debate'. Again, the presentations were based on academic historical research and presented by the researchers to reiterate the Turkish thesis. The title of the panel is interesting in this regard, as it talked about 'transfer' and 'resettlement' rather than deportation. As a labelling exercise, this choice of words directly signalled a way of thinking and speaking about the events of 1915: it underwrote the aim to present the violence experienced by Armenians during these events as a self-defence policy on the part of the Ottoman government. The policy was presented as inevitable in the face of atrocities, despite the government's tolerant attitude towards Armenians, who – as the idea of resettlement implies – were given helpful new opportunities. This recasting did not simply reiterate the public memory repertoire but presented a new stage in its reproduction as a proactive defensive posture. It turned a partial historical narrative into a resource for the public to actively use to refute the Armenian claims.

The discussion during this panel explicitly countered not only the Armenian claims but also the language of 'shared suffering' used by Turkish president Recep Tayyip Erdoğan and Turkish prime minister Davutoğlu in their 24 April messages (discussed in Chapter 2). According to the panellists, this emerging view was a weak, compromised position that pushed the country towards an unacceptable apology. The panellists expressed the view that what we know should not be diluted by politically driven expressions of sympathy – which of course was also the underlying theme of the Istanbul University symposium discussed above. Thus, the panel opposed any deflection from a strong nationalist and denialist position. According to one panellist, Turkey was facing a 'well-planned and orchestrated Armenian campaign'. He argued:

> [One of the starting points of this campaign was] the 2005 conference in Bilgi [i.e. Istanbul Bilgi University], to which no serious historians were invited. Only those agreeing with the Armenian position were invited. This campaign

has been going on with increasing intensity for 10 years. . . . The diaspora side [*tribünü*] looks more active than the Turkish side in this.

This statement is interesting. People who did not agree with the knowledge 'we' claimed to have were dismissed as not 'serious', implying that the knowledge they claimed to have was irrelevant. Picking up on a similar issue, another speaker argued: 'Armenians have their specific memorialisations that they use. These are based on false knowledge. They always make the same mistakes.' As a corrective to this false knowledge, the panellist's starting point was to present what he regarded as a good example of such mistakes: accounts of the arrests of 24 April 1915. According to him, the arrests had been of a limited number of Armenian activists who had been working against the Ottoman government. He contested the view that many had been arrested and put into prison in Ayaş, or that many had been killed. He added: 'Many of these were sent to Syria and outside the country. Gomidas was one of them.' As part of the audience at that moment, I found this presentation uncomfortable to sit through. This academic was communicating a denialist narrative that flew in the face of the facts, manipulating the stories of the victims to prove the innocence of the perpetrators – according to Stan Cohen's (2001) categorization, denying the existence of facts. But it seemed that the rest of the audience did not share my discomfort. Some asked incredulously how the diaspora could maintain their claims against such historically 'true' facts as those given by the presenter. The presenter went on: 'In the last three years, there has been this move towards apology. This is not a simple apology. This apology is part of a strategy . . . to penalise Turkey, to include these claims in schoolbooks and seek financial restitution.'

This discussion took a didactic approach to reiterate the importance of maintaining vigilance amid an environment where rather than 'defending our republic', we were moving 'towards an apology'. This didactic move turned the audience into students who were there to learn from the presenters as teachers. There was a circular process here: the public memory repertoire was reiterated, and the audience used existing reference points to link what they already knew with what they were being told. Because of the close correspondence between what the audience could recall and what they heard during the panel discussions, the content of the presentations became truth claims about Armenians. Within this relationship, the presentations strategically constructed the ongoing commemoration of the genocide centennial – the main event of which was yet to take place at the time of the panel discussion – as part of an Armenian strategy to undermine Turkish self-confidence by attributing unjustified collective guilt. They also communicated a sense of insecurity and called on the public to be vigilant. This worked within a truth regime built through the historical narratives that grounded the public memory, limiting the possibility of thinking otherwise and engendering a continued sense of insecurity for the public in the hope that they would be vigilant and take action against these alternative sources of knowledge. Within that regime, questions regarding what was being commemorated and what issues were raised by the commemorations remained outside what was cognitively available to the audience. One clear manifestation of this regime and its research output can be comprehensively seen in a five-volume publication by Yeni Türkiye: Stratejik Araştırma Merkezi on *Ermeni Meselesi: Özel Sayısı* (Armenian Issue: Special issue) in 2014. Another domain where this can be observed is the two periodicals, *Ermeni Araştırmaları* published in Turkish and *Review of Armenian Studies* published in English by AVİM – Centre for Eurasian Studies in Ankara since early 2000s (https://avim.org.tr/tr/Dergi/Review-Of-Armenian-Studies/46).

Documentaries as public education

The medium of documentary-making sits at the intersection of historical research and its public use. Documentaries are produced on specific topics and rely on academic and non-academic researchers as experts to construct their narratives and communicate their messages on-screen. While the material content they present aims to provide knowledge based on research, the way in which they are structured is based on the documentary maker's views. In regard to their structure, documentaries thus arguably share similarities with fiction in the sense that they construct their narrative according to the message they want to communicate. The construction of these messages draws on ideological and aesthetic frameworks to engender understanding and emotion. Documentaries construct their narrative by bringing together expert commentary, witness statements (when available) and images that often provide a way of seeing and hearing to amplify the impact of the message.

In this section, I look at two documentaries produced for and broadcasted on Turkish television channels: *The Blond Bride* (*Sarı Gelin*) and *1914/1915*. I have chosen to look at these two documentaries not only because of their content but also because they were used as part of a policy to reproduce the public memory repertoire. My interest is in how far their narratives reiterated the public memory repertoire by relying on the kind of national and nationalistic historical research presented at the academic events discussed above and in the textbooks I discussed in Chapter 5.

The Blond Bride: Inside the Armenian problem

This documentary series was produced by state authorities to present the Turkish case more comprehensively, drawing on historical research and discussions to the counter genocide claims, which had been on the rise throughout the 1990s. The production was undertaken by the General Staff of the Republic of Turkey (Genelkurmay Başkanlığı) and started in 1999. From 2001 onwards, the production was also overseen by the government's Committee to Coordinate the Struggle with the Baseless Genocide Claims (Asılsız Soykırım İddiaları ile Mücadele Komisyonu). Production was completed in 2003. Over 4 hours and six episodes, the series tried to highlight the nature of the issue. It was presented as a work that would objectively shed light on Turkish-Armenian relations. The clear aim of the documentary was to establish the unfoundedness of the Armenian genocide claims against Turkey. It aimed to challenge and discredit the knowledge base of these claims, and to focus instead on 'our' knowledge in order to demonstrate that the real guilty party was the Armenians themselves. This was an intentional effort by the state to produce a documentary that would present the public memory repertoire in a narrative form so as to communicate it more directly to the public and refresh the public's memory. School education evidently needed to be supplemented by this kind of public education work.

I remember watching the series when it was first broadcasted on TV (see YouTube 2022). I was puzzled by the title of the documentary: I knew 'Sarı Gelin' is an Armenian folk song, but it is also sung in various local languages and dialects in eastern Turkey, including in Armenian. So I thought that perhaps the title signalled an understanding of a joint history and heritage. 'Interesting', I thought, 'perhaps this is a documentary that will talk about Armenian lives in Anatolia and provide a positive story'. Unfortunately, as I watched the first episode, my immediate feeling was disbelief that so much time had been spent to produce such a badly structured and presented piece of work. I was not sure why the title had been chosen at all. To build its narrative, the series seemed to use the song to engender emotions of loss and longing, accompanied by flashing imagery supposedly showing Armenians killing Turks. This was supported by what appeared to be interviews with local villagers who were said to have seen Armenians killing Turks. In one unforgettable instance, the interviewee was an elderly man who wept and talked about the Armenian militia acting 'cannibalistically'. This statement was very shocking, not only in its content but also in the way it was used in the programme. Little attempt was made to verify these claims, and it was not clear who these interviewees were, where they had been interviewed and by whom and whether realistically they were old enough to have observed these killings and be able to talk about them some eighty years later as their own memories. Next, interestingly, the programme presented interviews with a number of Armenians who presented particularly ultra-nationalistic views. Again, I felt that the statements had been edited to structure the narrative so as to convey an ahistorical impression of Armenians' bad intentions towards Turkey and the victimization of Muslim Turks in Anatolia. These intentions were evidenced by the interviews mentioned above, repeated images of mass graves, skulls and bones and stories of rape and murder. At the time I thought there was no way this documentary, with its substandard production and narrative, could convince anyone that it was an objective presentation of the events of 1915. It directly blamed Armenians in a way that could be seen as inciting racial hatred among the public. There were obvious ethical problems in the way the narrative developed to frame Armenians as a group. For me, it was not fit for public broadcast in terms of the imagery and language used. Then I mostly forgot about it – except that every now and again, if I heard the song, I would ask myself one more time why on earth they had used it for the title of that documentary.

Some years later, in 2007, this documentary series suddenly re-emerged unexpectedly as a topic of public conversation. It is this re-emergence that is important for my concerns in this chapter. In its first incarnation, the TV broadcast of the series had clearly been trying to reproduce the public memory repertoire. In its second incarnation, the series was utilized within the formal education system as a part of public policy. On 4 December 2007, the Turkish Ministry of Education recommended the use of the series as supplementary educational material for teachers in all schools. In addition, it started to distribute DVDs of the series to all schools, including Armenian schools. There is also evidence that at the end of 2008, the ministry's local education offices requested all the schools in their respective areas to show the documentary series to all students and report the results of the exercise back to the ministry (Bianet 2009a). According to one report, 'there is clear evidence that from June 2008 onwards the documentary series was used in schools, including in Armenian schools' (Bianet 2009b). At this point there were complaints from some parents who objected to their children's exposure to this documentary series. The interesting public policy issue here is that the documentary series was prescribed formally on 4 December 2007 (Bianet 2009a) as an educational tool in the aftermath of the murder of the Armenian-Turkish journalist Hrant Dink on 19 January 2007 in Istanbul. The public outcry against his assassination and the solidarity that manifested itself at his funeral revealed a rupture in terms of the public memory repertoire. Arguably, the policy to use the documentary series sought to limit the extent of that rupture and its impact on the knowledge practices embedded in the public memory.

1914/1915

This documentary series (see Akyol 2015) was produced and presented by Taha Akyol, a journalist, newspaper columnist and researcher who was also one of the presenters at the January 2015 symposium discussed above. In Akyol's words, the series' focus was on 1914 and 1915 'because 1914 was perhaps the longest year of Turkish history, the year World War I started and the year we [Turks] entered the war, and because 1915 was perhaps the bloodiest year of Turkish history'. While the series was about the Ottoman Empire's entry into the First World War and the various battles of the war's first year, including the Gallipoli campaign and the Eastern Front conflicts with the Russians, more than three of its ten episodes discussed the Armenian deportations. Akyol looked at the reasons for the deportations, Armenian life in the Ottoman Empire before 1914 and the consequences of the 1915 deportations for the Armenians. This focus is interesting, as it gave the impression that the entire series was structured to present Armenian-Turkish relations to the public and to teach the public about the role Armenians had played in Ottoman society and what had *really* happened in 1915. (This impression was strengthened in November 2015 by the publication of a book by Akyol based on the series, with the same title, *1914/1915*, but with the addition of a subtitle: *The Years of Ottoman and Armenian Disaster*.) Both of these public education aims fitted very well with the content of the January symposium too. The series directly pointed out that Armenians had faced many disasters (*facialar*) in 1915. In discussing these disasters, Akyol went further than many other commentators, who had talked about 1915 as the shared suffering of many people across Anatolia during the First World War without commenting on the atrocities the Armenians had suffered.

Another interesting aspect of this documentary series is that its sixth and seventh episodes, which focused on aspects of the Armenians' experience, were both shown on CNN Türk on the evening of 24 April 2015. When I got home that evening after attending the genocide centennial events in Taksim Square, I watched the news and realized that the centennial commemoration events were barely being reported. Some TV channels did have discussion programmes, but it seemed that few channels wanted to discuss Armenians. Instead, there were a number of programmes that focused on 'the Armenian issue' by considering the situation of the Ottoman Empire in 1915. These programmes examined the events of 1915 from various perspectives, including the dynamics of the First World War, occupation and security. Against this media backdrop, CCN Türk decided to broadcast these two episodes together on the same evening. The immediate question was: Why?

The answer to this question relates to the narrative structure of the documentary series, which presented the development of events during the First World War across its ten episodes so as to gradually bring 'the Armenian issue' to the attention of the public. The whole series broadly repeated the same message. Armenian violence against other subjects of the empire, particularly Muslim Turks, was brought into sharp focus as one of the main challenges facing the Ottoman government of the day. The series started with a relatively close examination of the state of the Ottoman economy, the empire's military capacity, its capacity to maintain security within its borders and its challenging and declining relations with various European powers, both in the run-up to 1914 and in 1914 itself. The image created was critical of the state of the Ottoman Empire. The series pointed out that the empire had been weakened by various revolts and the economic difficulties caused by successive wars, most importantly the defeats of the 1912–13 Balkan Wars. On the whole, the narrative drew a picture of a political system that was at the end of its capacity to govern, particularly as it was under attack on different fronts. It first narrated the emergence of the new Ottoman political elite within the CUP, which had gradually taken power and ultimately governed the empire by 1908. There was also a focus on the CUP leadership, Talat, Enver and Cemal Pashas, who had become the leaders of the Ottoman government and been responsible for taking the empire into the First World War. The audience was taken through this dramatic but well-known situation of the Ottoman Empire. In its earlier episodes, the narrative arc of the series was built on expert opinions from academic researchers and the use of original footage and pictures of both the war and the Ottoman society of the time. The series provided a lot of detail about politics, political leaders and their concerns about the empire. It clearly outlined the economic deficits of the Ottoman government, the influx and logistical challenges of over a million internally displaced Muslims from the Balkans at the end of the Balkan Wars and the empire's lack of military preparedness to support soldiers in the field at the beginning of the First World War.

The sixth episode then focused on 1914 itself. The main focus was on how the Ottoman government under CUP direction had tried to build alliances with European powers. The audience was told that England, France and Russia had not been interested in this as they had considered the Ottoman army to be weak. From here the episode went on to present the emergence of the Ottoman–German alliance in 1914. It also discussed Russia's involvement in the training of Armenian militias against the Ottoman Empire, and how Russia had pressured the Ottoman government to sign an agreement on Armenian reforms in eastern Anatolia. The references to Armenians in the episode were few and mostly in passing. The main point of the episode was to portray the political and military difficulties that had enveloped the empire in the run-up to the First World War and the difficulties involved in its decision to enter the war at the end of October 1914. The audience then immediately watched the next episode.

The main part of this seventh episode focused on the Ottoman experience on three fronts: the Caucasus, Suez and Çanakkale. The presentation highlighted that while Çanakkale had been an important win for the Ottoman Empire, the Caucasus and Suez had been major disasters. But the episode began by considering the Sarıkamış disaster, in which up to 90,000 unprepared and unsupported Ottoman soldiers had died in atrocious weather conditions, without even encountering the Russian army they had been sent to fight. The episode presented the situation in Sarıkamış by using music and dramatic reconstructions to depict the soldiers' movements in heavy snow, clearly aiming to engender an emotional response from the audience. Then the narrative switched to the Russian offensive in eastern Turkey. The central message here was that the Russian army had not faced the Ottomans on its own: it had been joined and supported by six regiments of Armenian volunteers. This information was presented through the repeated use of group photographs of armed men. Then the focus shifted to Suez and Çanakkale.

The final segment of the episode, which lasted about 11 minutes, opened with a series of photos showing armed men in what appeared to be local costume, interspersed with photos of towns in eastern Turkey, including Van. These photos were shown without any commentary. Then the subtitle for the segment appeared: 'Towards Deportations [*Tehcire Doğru*]'. Akyol introduced the segment by stating that in 1915, in addition to the events considered above, 'there was a series of disasters: Armenian armed groups [*komitaları*] joining the Russian army, the Van rebellion, the massacre of the Muslim population around

Van and its surroundings, and the tragic Armenian deportations'. The audience was then told the story of the increasing clashes and animosity between Armenians and Muslims in the Ottoman Empire throughout the forty years leading up to 1914. The episode used several examples to bolster this narrative, particularly with regard to Russian interference and the Russians' manipulation of the Armenians. Karekin Pastermadjian was cited as an example of how individuals had been radicalized and begun to work against their own government under the nationalist ideals propagated by the Armenian Revolutionary Federation (Dashnaktsutyun), among others. These highlights prepared the audience for the main focus of the segment: the Van rebellion on 19 April to 9 May 1915. The episode presented pictures and original footage showing Van at the time while the narrator talked about the great massacre of Muslims in Van and Bitlis in addition to the deportation (*tehcir*). It also reiterated once again that the Ottoman government had not been in a position to deal with such military activity due to the war effort, and so there had been few internal security forces. Akyol argued that there had been a worry that the rebellion might spread to Erzurum, with reports of activities by Armenian groups in other cities in Anatolia and the discovery of large caches of weapons. The Ottoman government had therefore started the first Armenian deportation in Erzurum. By 24 April, all Armenian political activities had been stopped, all their documents had been confiscated and 2,345 Armenian public figures had been arrested. The infamous deportation law was passed on 27 May 1915.

The direct suggestion of the segment was that the policy to initiate deportations in the face of war and widespread rebellion had been a rational military decision, and the Ottoman government had had no other choice in light of the shortage of human resources created by the war. The documentary series had already presented the Ottoman Empire's ability to engage as a challenging affair. The opening episodes had prepared the audience to see the deportation policy as a reasonable decision, particularly given the portrayal of Armenians' viciousness towards local Muslim populations as well as their collaboration with the Russian army. This image of the victimization of Muslim-Turkish Ottomans constructed the context of the Ottoman government's decision by reiterating and justifying what the audience could recall from the public memory repertoire. In the context of the public memory, the audience was given no possibility to question what they were watching, as their vision was contained by the knowledge they had already absorbed. There was nothing in the knowledge communicated by the TV programme that might suggest a different way of thinking about Armenians or the Ottoman government's position in relation to them leading up to the genocide. Combining knowledge apparently based on academic research with visual material, the documentary series and these particular episodes allowed the audience to locate the deportations and the 'disastrous events for Armenians in 1915' within the processes of the war, and to attribute reasonableness to the violence experienced by the Armenians, who had acted against their own government. In this way, the broadcasting of these episodes on 24 April aimed to counter any concern that might have emerged within the public due to the centennial commemorations taking place on that day (Gillespie 2020; Cohen 2001). These two episodes were stepping stones in the narrative arc of the entire series, as they created a preliminary and foundational grounding in relation to Armenian behaviour. This narrative explicitly created an analytical and emotional baseline for the possibility of thinking about 1915 by arguing that at a time of existential struggle for the Ottoman Empire, the Armenians had betrayed their government, their neighbours and ultimately themselves.

This was important in guiding the understanding of the subsequent episodes in this series, where the narrative each week focused on specific periods. Once this baseline had been set, the eighth episode began by going back to consider Armenian lives in Anatolia from the time of their conversion to Christianity onwards. The 19-minute opening segment suggested that Turks and Armenians had lived harmoniously for 1,000 years after the rulers of the day had established peace in Anatolia and that they had also had a similar experience under the Ottoman Empire. This segment is interesting as it provided a sense of Armenian lives having been greatly politically, economically and culturally integrated within the empire, with many Armenians holding high-ranking civil service positions during the nineteenth century. The episode then moved to focus on the nineteenth century up to 1905. The main discussion concerned the emergence of Armenian nationalism and the different groups that had 'organised for terror' in coordination and cooperation with various Armenian church leaders. The tone of the presentation moved from tolerant multiculturalism to the nature of Armenians as a central threat to Turks, particularly following Greek independence in 1821. The focus here was broadly on the Zeytun and Adana massacres. The episode framed these events as attempts to undermine the authority of Abdülhamit II, who had been 'keen to help Armenians'. It portrayed the events as a betrayal that had been developed throughout the long nineteenth century by Armenian nationalist and armed groups, who had been trying to gain independence with the support of Armenian religious leaders. Abdülhamit II's creation of the Hamidiye corps to deal with various rebellions during the late nineteenth century was explained within this context. At the end of the episode, Akyol commented: 'They [Armenians] did not know perhaps that their actions up to 1905 were preparing the path to the events of 1915' (2015). This observation was interesting in that it implicitly placed the responsibility for 1915 squarely on the Armenians within the empire. According to this logic, the Ottoman government's agency had been limited by its imperative to protect itself, and its response to the Armenians' 'unexpected betrayal' had been informed by that imperative. The Ottoman government appeared as a benevolent, tolerant and somewhat reactive (rather than active) actor that could not have acted differently. This conveyed to the audience the difficult position in which the Ottoman government had found itself in 1914 and the inevitability of the violence against the Armenians in 1915, contrary to the government's good intentions.

The ninth episode of the series further underlined this position. It focused on events from 1905 to 1915. The concern here, as Akyol presented it, was to consider whether the obvious problems created by the Armenians could have been resolved during the Second Constitutional Era (*II. Meşrutiyet*), which had been ushered in by the Young Turk Revolution against Abdülhamit II in 1908. This process had led to a new constitution and an elected parliament that reflected the multicultural nature of the empire. Many politicians from different religious groups, including Armenians, had been elected to this new parliament. After looking closely at this era, Akyol answered his own question in the negative. He pointed out that again, unfortunately, Armenians had not fully engaged with the process to resolve their differences. Even some of the Armenians elected to parliament had been strong nationalists pursuing other political agendas. Then the audience was given a close reading of the 1909 Adana massacres as evidence of this non-engagement by the Armenians, who had not wanted to compromise. According to one of the experts called on in this episode – who was also at the Istanbul Bar Association event discussed above – the Balkan refugees who had arrived after the end of the Balkan Wars had contributed to the 'emerging polarisation of Anatolia' on this issue. This was certainly an interesting observation, but it did not explain why such tensions had been created; instead, it implicitly suggested that local Armenians had been hostile to the incoming refugees, who were largely Muslim Turks. The episode then considered the local Armenian Ottomans who had decided to join the Russians to fight against the Ottoman Empire. According to the above-mentioned expert, these had numbered 'around 84,000, and there were another 80,000 Armenians who were part of the Russian army. . . . You can see altogether these numbers are very large and present a real threat to the

Ottoman government' (Akyol 2015). At this moment in the episode, all of these factors came together to outline the reasons leading up to the arrests in Istanbul on 24 April 1915. The audience was told that '235 public figures were arrested in Istanbul and sent to Çankırı. These were not to come back but to lose their lives' (Akyol 2015).

Akyol ended this episode by stating that 'the decision to deport can be understood due to both wartime conditions and security concerns, but there are tragic aspects from a humanitarian perspective'. Throughout its seventh, eighth and ninth episodes, the documentary series established the content of an argument that showed how the 1915 deportation decision had been taken and why it had been rational under wartime conditions, given the subversive Armenian activities across time and across Anatolia. In this narrative arc, not only were the 1915 deportations justified, but the documentary series also claimed to have provided a response to the 'so-called genocide claims'. The audience was given an in-depth historical analysis of particular events in order to deepen their understanding of events that were already known to the public through the public memory repertoire, grounded broadly in what they had learned at school.

The tenth and final episode introduced the critical move of the series. It argued that the incontrovertible historical knowledge presented during the series should reassure us that Muslim Turks had in fact been the victims, both in 1915 and before. But the audience was told we still needed to acknowledge Armenian suffering in 1915 as a humanitarian concern. According to an expert interviewed in this episode, 'this is not an ideal position, but at least the existence of Armenians and their suffering is acknowledged. So, they are not just ignored'. This acknowledgement subsumed Armenian voices, memories and knowledge about the genocide under the national and nationalist Turkish public memory that led the discussion. I will now look at episode 10 to highlight how this subsumption worked.

Although the series' final episode was highlighted as focusing on Armenian suffering in order to understand Armenians' experiences during the deportations, the episode did little to engage in any discussion. It began with Akyol stating:

We will focus on the Armenian deportation [*tehcir*], that is to say, Armenian deportations and resettlement [*iskan*]. No doubt Armenians experienced a great disaster. Did the Ottomans do it because of racism or Turkishness, or did they do it under wartime conditions as a military measure, as a security operation? This is the fundamental question. (2015)

The first, 23-minute segment of the episode, entitled 'Towards Deportation', recapped events by focusing on the activities of Armenian armed groups: how they had armed themselves across Anatolia, and how Armenians had supported the Russian army. It particularly emphasized that the Russians had managed to occupy Van and Bitlis thanks to the support of Armenian armed groups. It also argued that it was only after these events, in which '30,000 Muslims were killed', that the Ottoman government had realized the danger posed to other areas. By relying on the views of a few international military strategy experts, the segment aimed to highlight that this situation had created a major security and military risk to the Ottoman government in 1914, which had just entered the war and lacked sufficient resources to deal with an 'internal rebellion'. According to one Turkish historian, further risks had also been created by desertions from the Ottoman army:

> Ottoman soldiers fighting against the enemy on many fronts, realising that behind those fronts fathers, mothers, sisters left behind were being raped and violently slaughtered by the Armenian armed groups and the rebels, these soldiers deserted from the army. . . . These [desertions] were all caused by Armenian raids on Muslim villages and the massacres they committed, rapes and razing during those raids. (Akyol 2015)

Thus, the historian argued that the deportation policy had been a reasonable and justified response. Akyol emphasized that given the threat posed by the Armenian rebellion, there had been a fear of its spread, and these armed groups had presented a major potential problem for military logistics and communication lines in Anatolia. He then reasoned that such concerns meant the decision to deport Armenians had been taken not on racist grounds but as a defensive measure. The deportations had started in the eastern provinces and been rigidly applied. Akyol then asked: 'But they were also carried out in the western regions. Why?' This rhetorical question was answered by the subsequent segment, which looked at the arrests of public figures in Istanbul by presenting them as political activists who had supported the Armenian rebellion. The segment suggested that many Armenians had been left in the western regions. The overall narrative conveyed that Armenians had betrayed the Ottoman government and the Muslim Turks in Anatolia, pointing out that the Ottoman government's response had nonetheless been one of restraint. It stated that the limited nature of the deportations from the west of the country indicated this restraint and care. It also argued that this was the reason why the 'so-called genocide claims' did not make sense.

It seems that the aim of this segment was to ensure that even those who had not seen the previous episodes would clearly understand the baseline from which Akyol's question could be answered. Indeed, Akyol helped the audience by answering his own question: 'It is the truth that the decision to deport was taken due to military concerns.' He again repeated all the military reasons behind that decision, adding that these military factors were evidence that the genocide characterization was wrong. But he added: 'On the other hand, in the deportations there were humanitarian disasters' (Akyol 2015).

After establishing this position, the next segment moved on to introduce the idea that all the disasters that Armenians mentioned in their narratives had resulted from the behaviour of various groups. Akyol pointed out that Armenians had experienced disasters during the deportations: 'Talat Pasha recognised that massacres and robberies were committed by irresponsible actors. Local bandits, merciless, pillaging civil servants and political fanatics committed massacres and robberies' (2015). Akyol accepted that together with the 'guilty Armenians, other innocent Armenians also suffered [*kurunun yanında yaş da yandı*]' (Akyol 2015). The segment elaborated on these points by referring to Talat Pasha's autobiography, in which he condemned those who had acted unlawfully during the deportations out of self-interest and political zealotry. In addition, Akyol introduced a discussion of the scramble for land by Kurds and other groups during the period as one of the causes of the disastrous situation for Armenians. Then an expert discussed how the Ottoman government had not had the authority or the resources to control the situation in Anatolia or secure the Armenian deportees once they had been en route. The next explanation given in the episode for the scale of the Armenian deaths was contagious diseases. Akyol described the prevalence of such diseases, from which even the Ottoman army itself had suffered. In relation to the contested numbers of Armenian deaths, one expert gave his own calculations. After suggesting that up to 700,000 Armenians had been sent to Syria, he said: 'There were between 350,000 to 500,000 Armenians who had gone to the Caucasus on their own initiative [*kendiliklerinden*].' He then argued that calculations after the event had shown that 'between 400,000 and 700,000 Armenians were lost [*kaybolmustur*]'. Here again, these numbers were presented as if they were explanations of the lives lost, but without any real explanation as to why such a large group of people would make the decision to move to the Caucasus, or how so many people from one community could be lost in Anatolia. At this stage the presentation moved on to the investigation and trial of the people who had abused Armenians, which had been limited due to the wartime conditions. The final part of the episode also considered the Turks who had protected their Armenian neighbours or officials during the deportations, pointing out that 'in some western provinces [in İzmir and in Kütahya], some governors did not implement the deportations orders, and the CUP government did not react to this'. According to Akyol, these instances were important in showing that despite the claims of Armenian scholars, there had been nothing genocidal about Muslim-Turkish attitudes in Anatolia.

More than half of this final episode was dedicated to showing, repeating and instilling the idea that the Ottoman government had taken the deportation decision under duress. The decision had been rigidly implemented in many areas, but on the whole it had been other actors that had been responsible for the violence experienced by the Armenian deportees. The last segment of the episode discussed violence against the Muslim-Turkish population by repeating all the Armenian atrocities that had been covered in previous episodes. The audience was told that to deny either these massacres or the massacres suffered by Armenians would be against morality and history. Akyol then went back to describe the bloody Armenian nationalist terrorist attacks in eastern Anatolia from the 1870s onwards. The episode ended with an important statement by Akyol:

> Today, Turks and Armenians should again turn their faces towards peace. We cannot deny the suffering of Armenians in the deportations. Children, women, men were ripped away from their homes to be deported hundreds, thousands of kilometres away to Syria, and thousands of children died on the road. We must feel and share Armenian pain. And Armenians should think that this [the deportations] did not happen without a reason: it was a reaction to the Muslims who had been deported from the Caucasus with similar pain, the creation of rebellions in Van and Bitlis during the bloody battles of Çanakkale, massacres by Armenian voluntary regiments. After the Adana massacres, Armenian nationalists and CUP leaders tried to find a common solution, saying that we have to live together. A good solution could have been found. But the war interrupted this. Today, putting psychological warfare to one side, we must understand each other, and we must reach out [el uzatmalıyız]. We all experienced great pain during World War I. The insistence on genocide does not bring a solution. It locks out the solution. The name of the disasters that were lived is 'joint pain'. A hundred years have passed. There is no reason to carry on with the historical fight and scratch [kaşımaya] the pain. With mutual understanding, we are obliged to develop a moderate language that can open the way to reconciliation [mutabakat]. Historical pain should remain in history. The foundation of the future should be peace. (2015)

There are remarkable aspects to this documentary series and its presentation of how 'we' should think about the contentious question of 'the so-called genocide' as it is framed in Turkey. The central message of the presentation highlighted Armenian suffering and then repeatedly argued that the deportations had been inevitable given how Armenians had behaved before and during the First World War. The series repeated 'our' story and provided further details to deepen 'our' knowledge of those events in order to strengthen the veracity claims of what the public already knew from the public memory repertoire. It aimed to silence any knowledge Armenians might wish to present, and it also rendered that knowledge difficult to absorb. It was through this mechanism that the documentary aimed to educate the public, in addition to urging them to be confident about what they knew through the public memory repertoire.

The narratives that constitute the public memory repertoire underwrote the content communicated by this documentary series. The series was built on the repertoire's 'schemata', which act as 'instruments of learning and forgetting', providing a language and the rules of what can be thought within that language (Luhmann 2000: 109). These rules enabled both the comprehensibility of the series' content and the different ways of thinking within the public memory. In the documentary series, Akyol's last statement – a call to share the suffering and pain – appeared to be a new variation within the public memory. But it did not change the ontology, boundaries or comprehensibility conditions of the genocide denial. The series remained within the rules provided by that ontology, categorically designating Turks as victims and Armenians as villains. In this respect, the memory repertoire is not simply about recurring images (such as some of the photos used in the documentary); it also 'enable[s] recursions, retrospective reference to the familiar, and repetition' of the language that allows remembering (Luhmann 2000: 109).

Through this documentary series, the audience was given a causal story that explained and justified what Armenians had experienced in 1915 and afterwards. The series made three categorical assertions to frame its narrative: (1) the question of violence entailed a discussion of 1915–16, and the wartime context underwrote the decisions taken by the Ottoman government to deal with the Armenian insurgency; (2) apart from Armenians, many other subjects of the empire had died too, including Muslim subjects, and this created an equivalence between the war dead and the dead civilians who had been targeted as a policy of their own government; (3) there was no genocide, and the history shown in the documentary supported this conclusion. In this way, the documentary provided 'simplified causal attributions that generate judgements, emotions, calls, protests'

(Luhmann 2000: 77). This view might suggest that individuals watching this series (or other similar documentaries) were being invited to engage with this knowledge and to develop their own denialist positions. The ability to do so rests on the possibility of comparing what you are watching against what you might already know. However, in the present case there were very few if any differences between what people had learned during their education, what they had heard in public discussions and what was presented in the documentary series. What was communicated broadly fitted with the public memory repertoire. As a result, individuals could not contest the premises of the documentary, as they had no alternative knowledge. In light of all this, the public could only evaluate what they were watching on the basis of how far it confirmed their broad understanding based on a logic of 'us and them'. As a method, the presentation aimed to reprise and maintain societal anger against Armenian narratives of the genocide.

The repeated broadcasting of programmes such as the series discussed above aimed not only to refresh the public's memory but also to engage new generations in its knowledge. This engagement, exemplified by the documentary series (and also observed in the use of *Sarı Gelin* in schools), reiterated what needed to be remembered and its 'co-occurring discrimination' (Luhmann 2000: 101), that is, what needed to remain erased. Here, detailed descriptions of events such as specific rebellions (e.g. in Bitlis and Van) or massacres in which Muslim Turks were killed acted as interventions to establish what should be remembered as part of the public memory repertoire. They intervened to prevent something else from being remembered or to prevent erased voices from emerging due to the commemorations in 2015. By repeating its message – by repeating the categories of 'us and them' and attaching them to the status of 'victims versus villains' – these documentaries 'reimpregnated' the public memory (Luhmann 2000: 101–9) to protect it against the challenge presented by the genocide commemorations.

In his role as producer and presenter, Akyol facilitated this process. He was 'making distinctions to describe something' (Luhmann 2000: 95). What he was describing included a set of justifications for the deportations, which were categorically presented as the acceptable way to think through the public memory repertoire rather than to question it. While Armenians were mentioned many times, and the audience was even asked to share their pain, Armenian voices describing their own experiences were entirely absent. Akyol's descriptions framed 'how the world was', underwriting how 1915 should be understood today. No doubt there was an underlying moral position in Akyol's descriptions. This was clearly marked by his tone of regretful loss combined with rightful demand that the audience should agree with him in solidarity. He was emphasizing the inevitable 'truth' value of his descriptions and implicitly asserting that another claim was untruthful. In this way, he stressed the Turkish innocence and the difficulty of taking unpleasant decisions under duress.

While Armenians were negatively included in these descriptions and given no voice, the documentary series relied on Talat Pasha's autobiography to establish the truth value of the facts it presented. The programme used this autobiography – which Talat wrote in Berlin after his escape from Turkey at the end of the First World War – as evidence that the Ottoman government had not intended to massacre Armenians and that Talat had in fact been unhappy about the Armenians' suffering during their deportation. The repeated use of this material gave the audience the impression that thousands upon thousands of Armenians had died during this period because of uncontrolled and unpredictable conditions. The presentation seemed to imply that it was just *really* bad luck. In addition, throughout the documentary series it was made clear that no formal responsibility should be attributed to decision makers such as Talat and the many others who had initiated and implemented the process. Yet all throughout the series, it was also implied that the Armenians themselves bore significant responsibility for their own massacre.

The knowledge this documentary series produced to establish the reasons why the Armenian deaths and suffering during the deportations did not amount to genocide raises significant questions. The series was a comprehensively denialist construction that produced possible humanitarian moral positions for the public to occupy without accepting the facticity of the genocide. Drawing on expert opinion, it argued that the survival of some Armenians, particularly in Istanbul and some other western cities, in addition to the existence of a few remaining Armenian civil servants and members of parliament after the end of the war, demonstrated the absence of genocidal intent. The series seemed here to be using backwards causation: the survival of some was evidence against genocidal intent. Using the survival of a few to silence the question why the majority had disappeared from their native homelands is a highly questionable method of argumentation.

At the end of the series, the audience were asked to share the pain. But the content of the series did not allow the audience to think from a perspective that would allow them to understand the experiences of Armenians independently of the public memory, or to ask questions about what had happened to those who had survived, what had happened to the Armenian property left behind, what measures had been taken once the new republic had been established or how Armenians both inside and outside Turkey had lived since 1922 with a memory that had not accepted for a long time and is still not accepted in Turkey today. These questions are not simply about the responsibility of the Ottoman government of the time. They are also about the responsibility of subsequent political authorities, including those who produce the kind of knowledge exemplified by this documentary series to reiterate the Turkish public memory repertoire and limit the Turkish public's thinking.

Conclusion

To conclude this chapter, I will reflect both on the implications of the academic research presented at various conferences, workshops and similar venues and on Akyol's final statement at the end of his documentary series. What does the trajectory of the academic research I have traced here mean?

The symposium I described above raised especially central questions for me about the direction of travel of historical research in Turkey. The presentations were by academics from across the country and researchers at different phases of their careers. It seemed that a new generation of researchers in this area was focused on specific cases or episodes of Armenian violence that were then used as evidence to support the view of the previous generation of historians that Armenians were the enemy within. Overall, the research presented revealed a sedimentation of denialist historical narratives. It was clear to me that a system of thinking had emerged in which new historical research was taking narratives that were internal to the system to guide its research questions and the historical resources it preferred to use. This academic endeavour seemed to be about the total destruction of what Marc Nichanian (2002: 13) calls 'the archive' of the lives and sociability of those who had been systematically violated and obliterated. Thinking about republican history seemed to require the further erasure of this archive of the lives of different groups and cultures as part of a broader sociability under the Ottoman Empire. This erasure also erased the dynamics of the majority's severe violence against some of these groups. As a result, the violence inflicted was constructed and could only be understood as violence against a tolerant and benevolent majority (as also evident in the documentaries discussed above). Overall, the obliteration of the archive since 1915 blocked public memory from remembering differently. It erased the archive of a different way of *being* and *being with others* for all parties involved. What was being erased here, as Nichanian (2002: 13–14) says, was 'about nonexistent archives, about a nothingness of the archive', indicating the emergence over time of another archive supported by academic research in Turkey that established what could be remembered. This process rewrote the archive based on the exclusivity of the majority imagined by the foundation of the Republic of Turkey. The denialist research highlighted above, with its implications for the education system, is a central mechanism that creates that nothingness. What remains for the Turkish public to rely on, over 100 years after the event, is the archive constructed contra Armenians, the genocide and knowledge about the genocide. This archive is the knowledge base that grows further through the kind of research discussed above, as the different narratives that comprise what I have labelled the repertoire of public memory.

In its didactic form, Akyol's acknowledgement of the Armenian dead and their pain at the end of his *1914/1915* documentary series aimed to guide public thinking. It represented the paradigmatic position conveyed in the public memory repertoire in its apparently humanitarian form. This position is now commonly observed in many forums, including in formal statements by Turkish government representatives. Many nationalists in Turkey object to such statements as a dilution of Turkish innocence in the face of Armenian accusations. But such statements do not in fact change the overall position: they still rest on the point that many people in general died during the First World War. They highlight that 'we' all share the memory of being part of the war and the pain of those who were lost. This approach allows both politicians and Turks to present a humanitarian outlook while sidestepping the question of why certain civilian groups were targeted and died in such huge numbers that their presence is barely detectable in Turkey today. Akyol's final statement not only instils a position based on pure interpretive denialism as described by Cohen (2001) but also expects the public to comply by following and using the same argument. Furthermore, as it makes historical truth claims, it prevents other memories, and through them different archives, from emerging or being relevant. In this way, it also expects and solicits Armenians' compliance with this view, regardless of their own memories and experiences. It presents this denialism and its acceptance by all, including Armenian Turks, as the grounds for solidarity in Turkey as a community. This, it says, is the route Armenians must follow if they wish to have peaceful relations with Turkey. Ultimately, while the position propagated in Akyol's documentary series acknowledges Armenian suffering and pain, it entirely ignores other voices, memories and questions. The explicit invitation to ignore, as Zerubavel highlights, is 'a product of social norms of attention designed to separate what we conventionally consider "noteworthy" from what we come to disregard as mere background "noise"' (2007: 25). The documentary creates a pressure demanding ignorance of the following questions: What was the reason for inflicting what appears to have been communal punishment to such an extent that entire populations disappeared from Anatolia? If this was not an ethnically orientated action, an ethnic cleansing, then what was it? How can different groups build solidarity and peace if they cannot even ask these questions and seek the answers?

7

Conclusion

In this concluding chapter, I will summarize the overall discussion I have developed throughout the book. Then I will focus on some questions I think readers might want to ask, before moving on to suggest some policies to tackle denialism.

Summary of the argument

This book has focused on the ways in which the Turkish public's current understanding of the Armenian genocide is structured. I have used the concept of grammar to refer to this structure. I have argued that there is a set of norms and rules for speaking about Armenians and the Armenian genocide that creates the comprehensibility of speech on these topics within Turkish society. In this way, my work contributes to the understanding of the mechanisms that produce and reproduce pervasive, normalized denialism among the Muslim-Sunni Turkish majority in Turkey today. I have argued that the language used on this issue and the knowledge that is recalled by that language establish the norms and rules of comprehensibility with regard to belonging to Turkey or Turkish history. Furthermore, by setting the boundaries or threshold for belonging, this linguistic process controls the sociopolitical imaginary of being Turkish. The knowledge that 'we' as part of the Turkish public claim to have in public discussions originates from the foundational stages of the creation of a new imagined community, the Republic of Turkey. What is communicated as knowledge about the events of 1915 informs the public's ability to evaluate discussions of the violence experienced by Armenians and its genocidal nature.

I have examined this dynamic relationship between language, knowledge and language use through the analytical lens provided by the concept of public memory. This is a particularly relevant concept, as the time gap between the events of 1915 and the present is vast. The public in Turkey relies on knowledge claims that are based on a national historiography. As my analysis of historical research material has revealed, there is a set of narratives that is repeated as the knowledge base of the Turkish understanding of the past and the public's relationship to it. The argument of this book is that these narratives constitute a repertoire that is deployed when members of the public are confronted by questions (or unexpected knowledge) about the Armenian genocide – or, as it is framed by those narratives, the 'Armenian issue' (*Ermeni Meselesi*). I have broken down this repertoire into a typology, identifying specific narratives that are commonly observed in public discussions and used by people taking part in those discussions. These narratives are repeated time and again. While some of them have a long lineage that extends all the way back to the 1918 Constantinople trials, some have been repurposed so that they can be used in response both to the gradually increasing knowledge base and the international recognition of the Armenian genocide. I have observed that these narratives are used as public memory, a cognitive resource that enables people to participate in discussions when they are asked questions about the Armenian genocide. The expectation is that these narratives will help the public to counter such questions.

Over time, these narratives have become sedimented in such a way that they have become the basis of knowledge about the Armenian genocide in the Turkish public's collective memory. This memory is collective because it underpins the understanding of being Turkish. Each time the language of this public memory is deployed, it enables people to comprehend one another as belonging to that Turkish identity. This language (for instance, the term 'the Armenian issue') makes it possible to remember who 'we' are and how 'we' fit into 'our' history against the Other. This remembering involves the erasure of other possible memories and histories.

It is important to study present-day manifestations of this public memory repertoire in order to show the comprehensive domination of public discussions by the repertoire's narratives. By limiting the collective memory, these narratives also limit the available possibilities for individual members of the public to locate and think about themselves in relation to the past. It is in this cognitive state, in each deployment of a history (in this case, the narratives), that a community and individuals remember a past. This integration highlights the historicization of the past as a constitutive element of the self-understanding of a community and individuals in the present. As I have highlighted, some of the narratives in the public memory are being reformulated to respond to the changing environment. However, their overall message has endured across generations. I have brought these narratives together as a repertoire that is used in public discussions to facilitate public recall and at the same time limit what can be known about the Armenian genocide. This recall takes place in the public memoryscape constituted by the repertoire. Thus, what is remembered remains limited. I argue that over time, for the majority of the public, any other knowledge – perhaps the knowledge that is available to Armenians, Kurds or Alevis – gets erased.

Paul Ricoeur (2004: 440) describes this process as a 'forgetting by effacement of traces', and he talks about memories' 'removal from the vigilance of consciousness'. In his view, it is through language that such effacements can suddenly be reversed as unexpected memories reveal themselves. As he says, 'language contains in itself what was learned, felt and heard' (Ricoeur 2004: 400). But this assumes that the language still carries some of that which has been erased. I suggest that in the Turkish case, new language policies have changed the context of this process by teaching new feelings and new histories in order to develop new forms of belonging. Therefore, what the language can reveal is limited to the national history and the narratives of the memory repertoire. Little remains as traces in this new language to remind new generations of any of the things that have been erased. Thinking about the language that is prescribed and used matters greatly for a society and its own approach to itself – what one might call its self-management policies. The challenge of prescribed language is captured by Victor Klemperer (2013). In the introduction to *The Language of the Third Reich*, he writes:

> But language does not simply write and think for me, it also increasingly dictates my feelings and governs my entire spiritual being the more unquestioningly and unconsciously I abandon myself to it. And what happens if the cultivated language is made up of poisonous elements or has been made the bearer of poison? (Klemperer 2013: 14)

Can the Armenian genocide be spoken in Turkish? Can the language allow the remembering of experiences and memories of the Other, beyond what is already given nationally? This question goes to the heart of the relationship between memory, erasure and the possibility of remembering. What is remembered relates to the possibility of recalling what was once known but has been forgotten. But what gets erased over time – in this case, Armenians' lives and experiences of violence – does not appear as knowledge in the first place; being unknown, it cannot be forgotten, and thus it cannot be recalled. For new generations, the knowledge has not simply been forgotten; it has never been given as a cognitive resource for them to think with in their everyday lives. As part of this process, which is a 'type of unique disappearance' (Ophir 2005: 83), certain subject positions become unavailable to be claimed in public, and their traces gradually disappear, as do the traces of the process itself. The consistent use of this repertoire as the public memory demonstrates a persistent ideological approach to erase different sources of knowledge based on different subjectivities, and what might be remembered through them. Melanie Altanian eloquently frames this process as an epistemic injustice (2021; also see Oranlı 2021).

The public memory repertoire plays a central role in this erasure by maintaining the primacy of a set of narratives as the condition of public comprehensibility for new generations. To remain functional, the repertoire needs to be reproduced intergenerationally in public relations to think about Armenians and the Armenian genocide in Turkey. I have considered this reproduction processes throughout the chapters of this book. I started with a close look at how it was deployed around the commemorations of the centennial of the genocide in 2015. I then considered how the education system introduces and reproduces the narratives by creating the public memory repertoire, as well as the role of the media in maintaining the centrality of that repertoire in public life. I also identified another aspect of this process in the way in which the use of the repertoire's narratives establishes the boundaries of the public comprehensibility, of being a Turkish citizen. I pointed out that this imaginary and the rules and norms of belonging were developed as specific public policies on language and history during the early years of the Republic of Turkey from the mid-1920s onwards. The policies on language and the changes they initiated aimed to create a Turkish nation out of the remains of the multilingual and multicultural Ottoman Empire. A central mechanism to achieve this aim was the Turkification of people, regardless of their other identities, in order to enable them to become members of the new polity. In other words, it was a policy to create a set of markers of Turkishness to enable all citizens to claim to be part of the new republic. A unitary language and history were unquestionable requirements of citizens' belonging to the prescribed Turkishness. The repeated deployment of those views since those years has underwritten the narratives of the public memory repertoire. Over the decades they have become embedded and normalized through education policies that aim to homogenize Turkish society by creating acceptable citizens. A central condition of acceptability, and comprehensibility, is that one belongs to a specific historical narrative about being Turkish and performs that belonging publicly. Thus, the narratives of the public memory repertoire provide knowledge about the history to which 'we' all belong and which claims all Turkish citizens, and this must then be performed in public discussions.

In summary, the process began by imagining a homogenous society around a single language and a single history of the new republic to set the boundaries of belonging. This approach by its nature excluded other identities. Therefore, it began by denying the relevance to Turkishness of Others' identities; indeed, Turkishness was arguably constructed *against* Others' identities. This also meant that Others' knowledge of their own experiences became irrelevant to the new imaginary of the national community. Knowledge about the genocidal violence experienced by Armenians in 1915 – and about the similar experiences of other groups, such as Pontic Greeks during the same period, or Alevi Turks, Alevi Kurds and converted Armenians in Dersim during 1937-8 – was foundationally excluded from the self-understanding of Turkish society. In that self-understanding, these violent episodes are either reinterpreted and presented as political necessities for security reasons or simply denied as significant events at all.

It is thus clear that genocide denialism goes back to foundational discussions that aimed to distance the new Turkish republic from the Ottoman past and forge a new community. This aim is manifest not only in the new language policies but also in the drive to produce a national historiography to instil a sense of righteousness. There was also an aim to provide new generations of the public with a new interpretation of the violence and atrocities that were known to the republic's founding generation. Perhaps, as Alex Gillespie (2020: 382) argues, the new language and history policies were 'defensive tactics' – an attempt to prevent what was seen as the past from disrupting the founding of the republic. It opened up a space for information to be 'repressed, disavowed, pushed aside or reinterpreted' (Cohen 2001: 1) by the creation of a national knowledge. This denialist knowledge production and the knowledge it produced became part of the national identity formation as the boundary conditions of belonging. As a result, the national identity that new generations encountered over time became defensive and denialist. The success or failure of such tactics, according to Gillespie (2020: 385), 'rests upon the defensive tactics used and specifically how their use is viewed by the audience'. I argue that in the Turkish case, these defensive tactics have been integrated into the mechanisms that produce the cognitive resources available for members of the public to be able to think as members of this new polity. The tactics informed the new identity formation as foundational components.

Over time, the intergenerational diffusion of this approach based on a national knowledge of self and Other became the basis of what can be known in public today. The denialism that forged the national identity in contradistinction to the other identities that existed in the Ottoman Empire remains the glue for national solidarity in Turkey. For younger generations who lack experience of the past, their engagement with these issues is mediated by the normalized national knowledge they find as given in their everyday experience, whether through their social interactions or through their formal education. Today, it is this knowledge – constructed, directed and reproduced time and again – that controls what one needs to know if one is to be part of the national community. In Gillespie's terms, the public performance of naturalized denialism by the majority of the audience indicates the success of the defensive tactics.

The main point demonstrated in this book is that most of the audience in Turkey today do not have the cognitive space to engage critically with these denialist defensive tactics or even to observe that what they know is underwritten by denialism. The knowledge they claim to have is normalized as truth claims that are reinforced in a circular manner by what they learn in everyday life and the education system and what they hear from opinion makers. Audience approval is mediated by a diffused and normalized denialism that hides its own antecedents. By analysing various dimensions of this reinforcement process, this book has highlighted how the grammar of denialism has been normalized and reinforced by the reproduction of the narratives that constitute the public memory, thereby limiting the cognitive resources available to the public.

Questions

In this part of the chapter, I provide brief answers to a set of questions that I think my analysis might have generated for the reader.

Does your analysis perhaps overstate the pervasiveness of denialism?

Looking at the available material, I think genocide denialism is very pervasive. It is normalized in everyday interactions in Turkey. Its language and narratives are used in public to emphasize 'our' innocence and the accuracy of 'our' knowledge on this question. The possibility of this public stance is a function of the denialist historiography that has become widely available through different mechanisms, including the education system. I will give two examples to highlight this normalized denialism. The first example is a formal exchange between the

UN and the government of Turkey that was covered at the time in the daily news media; it highlights the centrality of the public memory repertoire for the institutional position. The second is from a social media exchange, and it highlights how the idea of 'Armenian' is used to indicate a general discomfort that is central to the public memory.

On 25 March 2019, the Turkish government was sent a formal letter by three special rapporteurs of the UN Human Rights Working Group on Enforced or Involuntary Disappearances; the special rapporteur on the promotion of truth, justice, reparation and guarantees of non-recurrence and the special rapporteur on the promotion and protection of the right to freedom of opinion and expression. The letter stated that the writers had received information 'alleging violations attributable to Turkey in relation to the tragic events that affected the Armenian minority from 1915 to 1923, and their consequences for the population concerned' (UNHR 2019a). It solicited the Turkish government's comments on the allegations, requesting clarification on a number of points:

1. Please provide any information and/or comment(s) you may have on the allegations.
2. What policies have been put in place by your Excellency's Government to respond to these allegations?
3. What measures has Turkey taken to establish the facts, including the fate or whereabouts of Armenians who were subjected to forced internal displacement, detention, extrajudicial killings and enforced disappearances during the period of 1915–23?
4. What measures have been taken to ensure the right of victims and of society as a whole to know the truth about these events and to ensure the right of victims to justice and reparations for the damage suffered? (UNHR 2019a)

The formal response to this letter came on 19 May 2019 from the permanent representative of the Republic of Turkey to the UN in Geneva. The strongly worded response reminded the rapporteurs that the UN operated under specific principles of objectivity and impartiality. It stated that the UN letter had gone beyond those principles and that the questions it had asked had thus exceeded the UN's mandate:

> Let me just express that by taking up some wartime historical events that date back to 104 years ago, long before the UN was established, and trying to link these events through some dubious connections to the present day in an

attempt to make them somehow relevant, the communication is unfortunately ill-intended and politically motivated. . . . When one reads between the lines, it is very easy to identify who is behind these 'allegations' and that this is a biased exercise. The communication, in the way it is formulated, only serves the political motives of a well-known party. . . . The communication builds upon and makes presumptions about some historical events, which are and can only be under the care of historians. (UNHR 2019b)

The response then pointed out that these debates were not a matter for the UN. It went on:

> The period in question needs to be understood in its entirety, and the memory of so many lives lost has to be properly respected. Such an exercise requires a reliable factual basis and approach, and empathy. All of which I regret to say are lacking in this communication. (UNHR 2019b)

It further pointed out that in 2005 the Turkish government had issued an invitation to create a multinational history commission, in which the Armenians had been reluctant to participate. The UN was also reminded that 'in Turkey, the issue of the events 1915 is not a taboo. Although the events of 1915 are freely debated in Turkey, the opposite is implicitly not allowed in some countries where there is no room for debate' (UNHR 2019b). From there the response letter moved on to state that the government of Turkey would not answer the questions posed as they were against the UN's own principles of impartiality. This governmental response followed a language linked to the narratives of public memory. Those narratives provided a set of justifications for the response: the time gap between the events and the UN mandate; the importance of recognizing all victims; and importantly, the emphasis on not recognizing the history of the Other, which was dismissed as presumptuous and as mere allegations. A similar language is also observable in another formal letter sent by the then Turkish ambassador in Paris to a French government committee looking at the way in which to include knowledge about genocides and crimes against humanity into the education materials (Musa 2018). Not only does this reveal how the logic of the narratives is diffused throughout the system, but it also demonstrates how this logic can be repurposed to respond to new situations without altering the foundational denialism: having rejected the relevance of the concept of genocide on the grounds of the chronology of the events and the UN convention, the Turkish government now also sees the UN itself from the same logical position.

As I write this conclusion, in early December 2022, a Twitter exchange is attracting attention in Turkey. Kemal Kılıçdaroğlu, the leader of the Republican

People's Party (Cumhuriyet Halk Partisi, CHP), has been consulting with many experts on a range of policy proposals in the run-up to the elections scheduled for spring 2023. One of these experts is a well-known economist from the Massachusetts Institute of Technology; his name is Daron Acemoğlu, and he happens to be an Armenian Turk. In a press statement, Kılıçdaroğlu mentioned that Acemoğlu had joined their meeting via internet link from Boston. Subsequently, on 3 December, the well-known conservative journalist Necmi Batırel tweeted: 'armenian [*ermeni*] Daron Acemoğlu, who was praised by FETÖ [an Islamic group that was banned in Turkey in 2016], seems to have prepared Kılıçdaroğlu's vision document, their blood must have been drawn to each other [*Kılıçdaroğlu'nun vizyon belgesini FETÖ'nün övdüğü ermeni Daron Acemoğlu hazırlamış, kan çekmiştir*]' (Batırel 2022). After receiving numerous complaints, Batırel later tweeted an apology. Batırel's use of the lower-case initial in the word *ermeni* ('armenian') is significant here. It was not simply telling the reader that the person in question was Armenian. Written in the lower case, it seemed to emphasize the unease and distrust that this category communicates in some of the public memory narratives. One might wonder whether it was simply a typing error, but if one looks at the whole tweet, it is clear that it was intentional – when the tweet refers to other actors, all the usual case conventions are observed. Thus, the use of *ermeni* reveals that the author was trying to signal to the public a sense of distrust and suspicion attached to Armenian identity. By using this language, he was perhaps hoping to connect members of the public with what they could recall from within what they already knew about 'these kinds of people' in order to evaluate the wisdom of the CHP's relationship with this academic. Furthermore, by attaching this to the idea of 'shared blood', the tweet seemed to raise interrelated questions about Kılıçdaroğlu's belonging and his fitness for political office.

Many people confronted Batırel, pointing out the racist nature of his tweet and its total inappropriateness. An immediate tweet by the academic Özgür Demirtaş set the tone for many of these strongly critical statements. His tweet pointed out that Acemoğlu was a Turkish citizen, and it highlighted his Turkishness. While one can observe the anti-racist sentiments expressed in these exchanges, it is also interesting that some of those anti-racist statements themselves emphasized Turkishness and Turkish citizenship as markers of belonging. It appears that even for more critical Turkish commentators, foundational assumptions about being Turkish are taken as unproblematic. Thus, these defences of Acemoğlu also operated within the broader context of the public memory repertoire where belonging is claimed automatically for all citizens on the basis that they naturally agree with foundational assumptions about being Turkish. This highlights the conditions of belonging for minoritized groups as 'Turkish X' – in this case, 'Turkish Armenian'. The second identity qualifier is subsumed under being Turkish, which is the primary belonging. It is hard not to wonder whether Armenians (or others) would be so strongly welcomed or defended if they were to voice claims about their own experiences and memories of belonging as Armenian-Turkish members of society without subsuming their Armenian identity under some public Turkishness. Such claims would question the national historiography.

You have talked about the availability in Turkey of many critical books and symposia on the Armenian genocide. Does this not contradict your argument about the pervasiveness of the public memory repertoire?

Indeed, many books have been published on the Armenian genocide, and they are available in at least some of the bookshops in Turkey's big cities. In addition to the many works translated into Turkish, there are also numerous such books written by Turkish academics, researchers and public intellectuals. For instance, Hasan Cemal's (2012) groundbreaking book was simply entitled *1915: The Armenian Genocide* (*1915: Ermeni Soykırımı*). The publication and availability of these books are very important. But there are several reasons why the availability of such literature might not produce significant change. As I have tried to demonstrate in this book, for most of the public audience, the question is about finding good reasons to read these books from within what they already know, which is structured in the first place to make them suspicious of any use of the term 'Armenian genocide'. They then need to have the cognitive space to read the books from a critical viewpoint in order to think against the grain of the already-given knowledge.

The difficulty here arises from the way the structure I discussed in previous chapters creates a reinforcement mechanism for denial. What one reads and hears is validated in other forums to settle any questions one might have. The knowledge these books create about the Armenian experience and the genocide is not located within that validation system. Instead, it is located within the denialist mechanism, where it is invalidated. So, the knowledge the books provide is not enforced in any public process, and especially not at any level of the education system. Without any reinforcement, their impact within the system is limited. Furthermore, in practice the availability of these books is variable: many of them soon become unavailable, as they often have small print runs, and most of them do not reappear in further editions.

Can we really say it was a genocide?

This question in turn raises two subsidiary questions. First, do we have clear evidence that an entire group was targeted and killed in 1915 – for instance, a physical document ordering the violence and murders? Second, were the numbers killed in 1915 large enough to qualify as a genocide? Another factor here is that the Armenian suffering during the First World War I is now formally recognized as an outcome of wartime conditions. I consider these questions to be attempts to validate denialist positions against the facticity of the genocide. They sideline and divert attention from the disappearance of actual lives in particular sociopolitical contexts. Timothy Snyder (2011: 400) suggests that questions that heavily focus on numbers to ascertain the nature of events are attempts at 'grasping at their [victims'] deaths' as objectified multitudes rather than lives and communities lost. I would add that in this case they are also attempts to justify denialist games with documents and numbers, ignoring the fact that 'the victims were people' with everyday lives (Snyder 2011: 400). Therefore, taking the initial question seriously, I will answer it via a different route.

Earlier in this book I explained why I consider the events of 1915 to constitute a genocide by using Lemkin's definition. I think it is important to return to this definition and reflect on its implications for my analysis as I conclude the book. Lemkin argues:

> Genocide has two phases: one, destruction of the national pattern of the oppressed group; the other, the imposition of the national pattern of the oppressor. This imposition, in turn, may be made upon the oppressed population which is allowed to remain or upon the territory alone, after the removal of the population and the colonization of the oppressor's own nationals. (Lemkin 1944: 79)

He further argues that the process of killing the 'foundations of life' of a given community follows targeted policies to destroy 'the political and social institutions, of culture, language, national feelings, religion, and economic existence of national groups and the destruction of personal security, liberty, health, dignity' (Lemkin 1944: 79). This has a number of implications for the question of whether the events of 1915 amounted to a genocide. It certainly was a genocide given the violence experienced by a targeted community across a whole social geography. However, the genocidal process marked by the events of 1915 was much longer: it began before 1915 and continued after that date. Lemkin's broader conceptualization takes the sociocultural and economic infrastructure of the group into consideration. A community's ability to think through their memories publicly as part of society is important here because remembering the past gives coherence to their lives. The loss of human life is a great tragedy, as many wars have demonstrated. Under all kinds of wartime conditions, significant crimes against humanity have been committed. The loss of both a community's sociocultural life and its infrastructure potentially turns such crimes into a broader sustained problem for that community's future survival in a given context. In other words, while recognizing individual deaths within the broader context of war highlights an important loss, it does not enable an understanding of the conditions under which a specific group is targeted and killed. In the present case, it is clear that during the First World War I many Armenians were killed or assimilated by conversion – particularly women and children in the latter case – simply because they were Armenians. To treat these as casualties of war, and even in some cases as crimes against humanity committed unsystematically, hides the targeting of the community, the nature of that targeting and its destruction of not only lives but also the infrastructure required for the community's future survival (Sands 2017: 376–87).

If one looks at the historical conditions of the violence against Armenians, it is clear that their gradual marginalization led to their becoming the 'enemy within' as the target of the political authority of the Ottoman Empire. During both the Hamidian massacres of the mid-1890s and the Adana massacres of 1909, Armenians were the main targets of the violence. If we consider the violence of 1915–18 and the Turkish War of Independence from 1919 onwards in terms of Lemkin's periodization, this was a long period of the violent destruction of the national pattern of an oppressed group. The second phase of the genocide, in which the oppressor imposes its own national pattern on the oppressed, corresponds in this case to the period from the formation of the new Turkish republic to the present day. During this phase, the Armenian survivors of the violence in Turkey found themselves having to accept a new pattern of life in order to survive in the new political configuration. This period has been marked by a series of policies on language and history that not only aim to destroy Armenians' self-knowledge and memory of the genocide, but also establish the baseline for the new Turkey in such a way that in order to maintain their own dignity and economic existence (among many other things), Armenians have to conform to the new national identity and its narration of national history, which underwrite their belonging to Turkish society. The analysis provided in this book has shown that the public memory continues to maintain these positions, marginalizing the Armenian community and at times targeting them, as the Twitter debacle discussed above demonstrates. In light of all this, there are serious questions about the designation of Turkey today as a post-genocide society. I think the balance of evidence points instead to the ongoing continuation of a long genocidal period.

So, the answer is yes. The events experienced by the Armenian population during the Ottoman Empire constituted the first phase of a genocide in that they included targeted acts of violence as well as attempts to eradicate signs of Armenian lives across Anatolia by appropriating the community's cultural, economic, religious and personal properties. But the genocide then entered its second phase, which is still ongoing today: the public memory with which we live in Turkey has erased and is still erasing the possibility of thinking about the Armenians who were killed. Armenians have no voice with which to publicly engage in their own knowledge production about the violence they experienced, or the memories of it with which they have lived ever since, as part of a rethinking of national history. Instead, as I have highlighted in this book, in many of the narratives of public memory and in the manifestation of those narratives in public or policy discussions, Armenians are invited to agree with their own erasure and to understand themselves from the perspective of national history.

What could be done?

There is one further question: Can anything be done? Are we locked into denialism forever? Some readers of this book might have drawn the conclusion that I think that we are. But no, that is not my view.

Genocide denialism has a long history in Turkey. Some scholars and researchers take the view that the issue of the Armenian genocide tends to disappear for long periods, only re-emerging in response to events such as the fiftieth anniversary of the genocide in 1965 and the Armenian Secret Army for the Liberation of Armenia's assassination of Turkish diplomats in the 1970s and 1980s. But for me, this notion that the genocide issue only resurfaces in Turkey in reaction to international debates is inaccurate. The Turkish state has remained focused and vigilant with regard to the issue since its inception. Education policies do significant work to intergenerationally instil the narratives of the public memory as the source of our self-understanding, and the media then repeats those narratives time and again to remind us of them. In this process, there is a double movement of erasure: following Cohen (2001: 243), the 'eradication' of other memories of the past, of the genocide, needs to be actively pursued and maintained over generations; at the same time, 'our' history needs to be constantly centred to underwrite public debates. This double process has been part of public policy thinking since the foundation of the republic, and it has also become part of the work that is done by many small community groups – for instance, organizing local independence commemoration days. One of the central findings of my research follows on from this understanding.

While denialism is normalized as part of everyday culture and at times feels suffocatingly inescapable, the system evidently needs to control, reproduce and monitor the constant normalization of denialism as a regular policy concern. However, this constant policy work to deny and dismiss the relevance of any knowledge that does not align with 'our' public memory indicates the weakness of that position. Furthermore, as I have discussed in this book, the need to intervene – to use the narratives to bolster denialist public memory, to remind the public of their duty to remember those narratives and to facilitate the public's adherence to them – suggests the fragility of the public's perception should they be exposed to the knowledge available from other sources. Given this weakness and fragility, it is important to think about what can be done to change the situation.

There are several possible avenues to follow. One path that has become common in recent years is for governments to issue formal apologies for past atrocities. Such apologies are no doubt important to formally acknowledge not only what happened in the past but also what is still happening now. Whether an apology alone is enough to initiate a new era is an open question (Barkan 2000; Nobles 2008; Cunningham 2014). I suggest two central reasons for the possible ineffectiveness of apologies. First, the formal apology process is based on pragmatic political expediency rather than a desire to change social relations. Once the actor has apologized, it is assumed that the work has been done and the parties can follow their own trajectories. The main obstacle here is the instrumentalization of the apology process for the state's policy interests, since an apology would constitute evidence for social change in the rejection of denialism. Whether the reality of institutional denialism would permit such a change is an open question. Second, apology is considered to be a process of inclusion for those who have been excluded from mainstream society by various kinds of discrimination. The aim of an apology might therefore be to bring the excluded into the national fold, without mainstream society necessarily changing the underlying assumptions that regulate social relations. The newly included people and their experiences might be added to pre-existing historical or social narratives, but the process would not be intended to lead to a major shift in how the mainstream thinks about itself. The parliamentary incident with which I opened the book exemplifies this: we can accommodate an Armenian-Turkish member of parliament, but we cannot allow him to rethink national history on the basis of his own experience.

Contrary to these possible situations, for an apology to be effective, it needs to be meaningful. That is, it needs to be clear who is apologizing to whom and for what, and the apology itself – in this case, both for the genocide and for the institutionalized denialism – needs to be underwritten by policies that highlight the trajectory of change that the apology is supposed to initiate. Given the involvement of Turkey's political authorities both in the events of 1915 and in the subsequent institutionalization of denialism, this process needs to be systematically initiated and led by the state, as some aspects of the change required need to be implemented by the political authority itself. This will no doubt be a difficult process. What follows is a list of potential policies that I think would make sense to engage with the necessary changes in public thinking and public life.

Citizenship

To support the apology process, mechanisms must be developed to change public perceptions by integrating the histories of the Other into the sociocultural imaginary. One part of this is to establish formal recognition by granting citizenship to all descendants of Armenian subjects of the Ottoman Empire who were either killed or forced to leave their homelands. This will turn the passive process of issuing an apology into active recognition and the responsibility to deliver on that recognition. Some of my Armenian colleagues have questioned this suggestion, not by objecting to its spirit but by asking whether Armenians outside Turkey would want to rejoin a polity that has become significantly undemocratic in its treatment of different communities, including Alevis and Kurds. This is an interesting point, but I still think citizenship would be a significant step, both for Turkey and for the descendants of those who were deported and massacred. Citizenship would not only be an important sign of recognition, but it would also help to unpick the nature of didactic Turkishness as a way of moving away from institutional denialism. Spain and Portugal provide good examples of the practicalities of this process in relation to the Jewish descendants of those who were expelled from 1492 onwards.

Education

Significant change in the education system is required at all levels, including in the academic historical research that informs both teachers' and students' education. Given the mechanism through which history and the Other are apprehended, there is a need not only to look at the events of 1915 as a singular historical event, but also to consider Armenians' experiences in 1915 as a process of genocidal violence that extends across history into the present. It is critical to deconstruct the narratives of the public memory in order to open a new space that does not begin from an exclusively nationalist position, grammar of comprehensibility. A rethinking of the school curriculum is required to break away from the framework that aims to create acceptable citizens according to an exclusively nationalist model of citizenship.

Recognition: A process of knowledge creation

There is a need for policy to build knowledge through everyday encounters with the past. I suggest two ways to achieve this. One concerns memorials. This would be a policy to install plaques on buildings from which Armenians were deported, to mark the fact that these Armenians lived; were part of wider society and were then attacked, deported and killed. It is also important to create a chain of memorials along the deportation routes in towns and cities across Turkey, to highlight what the process was like, what happened during the deportations and what happened when people arrived at the end of these routes. No doubt the same method could also be used to mark events and produce knowledge about people from the Greek/*Rum*, Jewish, Kurdish and Alevi communities. Again, there are many cities and countries that already have such programmes, including Germany and France, and they can provide insights into the practicalities of rolling out such a programme in Turkey.

Second, public spaces can be renamed to encourage the public to reflect on the individuals and lives lost. The first person I have in mind is Gomidas (Komitas) Vartabet, a well-known priest who was highly respected for his work on Anatolian musicology and his compositions based on his research. He was arrested on 24 April 1915 in Istanbul and sent with others to Çankırı in central Anatolia. After interventions by Turkish public figures – including no less a person than Talat Pasha, the Ottoman grand vizier and one of the central architects of the genocide – Gomidas was returned to Istanbul, and in the spring of 1916 he was hospitalized on a psychiatric ward due to his traumatic experiences during the deportations. In 1919 he moved to Paris, where he died in a psychiatric hospital in 1935. One of the university music conservatories in Istanbul could be named after him. This would be both a fitting tribute to his work and a fitting recognition of his suffering. It would also help the public to recognize his contributions and to understand his life as one of the lenses through which they can look at the past.

Another personality whose name could be given to a public hospital or university medical school is Dr Zaruhi S. Kavalcıyan. The Istanbul Medical Chamber (İstanbul Tabip Odası) already recognizes her as Turkey's first female doctor (Ether 2021). She was born in 1877 in Adapazari. In 1903 she completed her medical degree at Boston University School of Medicine, returning to Adapazari to practise medicine until 1921, when she went to Istanbul to practise. Other similar personalities mentioned by Şeref Ether (2021) are Dr Ofelya Nergararyan-Kasabyan of Izmir and Dr Amália Frisch of Edirne. Again, their names could be given to medical institutions to highlight the individuals' importance for the development of clinical medicine in Turkey. It would also be very appropriate to name a school of architecture or a central city square in Istanbul after the Balian (Balyan) family. From the end of the seventeenth century to the nineteenth century, many members of that family served as court architects (Wharton 2015). They designed and built palaces, mosques, mansions, fountains and other buildings across Istanbul, creating some of the most familiar views of the city that people can see today.

The list above is certainly not exhaustive. There are many other candidates from different walks of life. Memorializing them and their lives would help Turkish society to remember and hopefully behave differently.

Restitution (to produce knowledge)

This is the most contentious suggestion of all. Arguably, restitution is a central concern that fuels institutional denialism in Turkey. One of the central arguments is that the Republic of Turkey formally severed its links with the Ottoman Empire and thus cannot be held responsible for restitution claims. This is a difficult question. It requires us to unpack the actions of the new republic after 1923, when Armenian Ottomans were permitted to return to claim their property. Taner Akçam and Ümit Kurt (2017; see also Öz 2020: 34–53) among others have shown that the genocidal process included the dispossession of Armenians over an extended period through the issuing of various laws by the late Ottoman government as well as by the Republic of Turkey (Polatel 2012; Çelik and Dinç 2015: 258–73; Ter Minassian 2015). Another argument concerns the time factor. For over three generations, different people have been living in properties that might potentially be reclaimed by Armenians: What about those people's right to live in the places they consider to be their homes? When they acquired their property, particularly if they did so recently, they would not have known the property's history, and they entered an exchange relationship in good faith.

This last argument in particular is persuasive. A policy that is based on evicting people from their homes and lands in response to restitution demands would not be reasonable. It would lead to a new wave of significant animosity. However, it is also true that many descendants of the deported and killed Armenians might still possess their property deeds, on the basis of which claims might be made. This certainly requires acknowledgement and response. Furthermore, even if they do not have the property deeds, some people can still trace their lineage to specific locations. And it is not only various forms of property that are at issue: other economically important assets, including insurance payments, were transferred to Muslim-Sunni Turks, facilitated by the state and by specially created laws that allowed unclaimed property to be redistributed (Der Bedrossian 2011). It seems that religious and cultural properties were also part of this redistributive system.

The dispossession of Armenian communities across Turkey is not in doubt. It would also be possible to assess the scale of the overall dispossession. Perhaps the central question is who should respond to such claims. It is clear that the Republic of Turkey is the authority to think and act on this. There are different models to follow, including for the assessment of documents and the compensation of some claims on the basis of them. Another possible model is collective compensation based on the assessed overall value of the dispossession. That value could then be invested in the creation of an independent national institution for the multidimensional study of Armenian culture, lives and genocide experiences together with other community experiences of violence in Turkey. This would be accompanied by investment in the renovation of the cultural and religious properties of the Armenian community across Turkey, creating a network of institutions, memorials and research in local areas. These two models could even work together, compensating those who have documents and creating significant institutions with the remaining unclaimed resources.

Final remarks

My policy suggestions above are not random. They are the building blocks required to tackle institutional denialism by targeting its reproduction mechanism. They aim to create a space to challenge denialism publicly in order to initiate a change. The other important point I wish to make as I conclude the book is the role of members of the public. While the political authority – that is, the state in its various manifestations – needs to lead in a number of ways, members of the public also have a central role. They need to have the courage to question what they know as given and to question their own identities built on that knowledge.

When part of a society is forgotten, the rest of the society not only forgets but also becomes involved in the reproduction of that forgetting, which eventually becomes an erasure. It is one thing not to have a memory. But not even to search for that memory when there are so many resources to consider is wilful ignorance. It begins to implicate people today in the perpetuation of a false memory, essentially linking them to the genocidal process. They become implicated in what happened not only in 1915 but also during the subsequent period up to the present day. At this juncture, the events of 1915 and their implications for the present are matters of concern for Turkish society in general in the form of the essentialized 'Turkishness' to which most people in Turkey subscribe. Claims are being made on people's behalf. Public claims regarding what Turks might or would have done place a burden of responsibility on present generations to refuse to be homogenized in this manner.

I am getting at the difficulty of everyday experience. Do people deny the genocide as individuals? Or are generations of citizens made to deny it? My view is the latter. People are made to deny the genocide by being conditioned to think in particular ways. Their forgetting is a sign that institutionally denialist politics is being produced and reproduced intergenerationally. Following Ricoeur (2001: 452), one can argue that the state recounts one drama and makes the other forgotten – or in Cohen's (2001) terms, eradicated. The state thus carries a major burden of responsibility regarding this issue. Turkish people today also face the question of whether they are not only descendants of the perpetrating community but are also perpetrators themselves, insofar as they position themselves within and defend the denialist public memory. Given the availability of other memories and knowledge, will they take on Ricoeur's (2001: 449) reformulated challenge individually and dare to give an account themselves?

References

AA (2015) *TSK Arsivlerinden 1915 olaylarının bilinmeyen yüzü*. 23 April. https://www.aa.com.tr/tr/turkiye/tsk-arsivlerinden-1915-olaylarinin-bilinmeyen-yuzu/54605 (accessed January 2023).

Adanır, Fikret and Oktay Özel (2015) *1915, Siyaset, Tehcir, Soykirim* (1915 Politics, Deportations, Genocide). İstanbul: Tarih Vakfı Yurt Yayınları.

Adiguzel, Huseyin (2015) *Yer Değistirmenin 100. Yılında Ermeniler ve Ermeni Meselesi*. İstanbul: Bilgeoğuz.

Agos (2004) *Sabiha Hatun'un Sırrı*. 6 Şubat. Istanbul.

Agos (2009) *1919'a bile gelemedik*. 24 Nisan. İstanbul: Agos.

Akarca, Mehmet (2015) 'Hakkı Kötek olanlar'. *Takvim*, 25 April. https://www.takvim.com.tr/yazarlar/mehmet_akarca/2015/04/25/hakki-kotek-olanlar (accessed January 2023).

Akçam, Taner (2010) *1915 Yazıları*. Istanbul: İletişim.

Akçam, Taner (2013) *From Empire to Republic: Turkish Nationalism and the Armenian Genocide*. London: Zed Books.

Akçam, Taner (2014) *Ermenilerin Zorla Müslümanlaştırılması, Sesizlik, İnkar ve Assimilasyon*. Istanbul: İletişim.

Akçam, Taner (2018) *Killing Orders: Talat Pasha's Telegrams and the Armenian Genocide*. London: Palgrave Macmillan.

Akçam, Taner and V. N. Dadrian (2008) *Tehcir ve Taktil Divan-I Harb-i Örfî Zabıtları: İttihad ve Terraki'nin Yargılanması 1919–1922*. Istanbul: Bilgi Üniversitesi Yayınları.

Akçam, Taner and Ümit Kurt (2017) *The Spirit of the Laws: The Plunder of Wealth in the Armenian Genocide*. Oxford: Berghahn.

Akçay, Deniz (2016) 'AİHM' in Perinçek Kararı: "Soykırım İnkarı"/İfade Özgürlüğü İkileminin Aşilabilirliği'. *Ermeni Araştırmaları* 53: 261–300. https://avim.org.tr/tr/Dergi/Ermeni-Arastirmalari/53/pdf (accessed February 2023).

Aktar, Ayhan (2015) '"Ermeniler İsyan" etti palavrası'. *Taraf*, 24 April, 7 https://www.academia.edu/12102347/Ermeniler_%C4%B0syan_Etti_Palavras%C4%B1_Tall_tale_of_Armenian_Revolt_in_1915_Taraf_24_Nisan_2015 (accessed January 2023).

Akyol, Taha (2015) Documentary 1914/1915 by Taha Akyol. https://www.youtube.com/watch?v=Y53O6LTxroA (accessed 18 November 2022).

Altanian, Melanie (2021) 'Genocide Denial as Testimonial Oppression'. *Social Epistemology* 35(2): 133–46.

Altaylı, Fatih (2010) 'Teke Tek 9 Mart 2010'. *HaberTürk*. https://www.youtube.com/watch?v=0xkrrYsU9Og (accessed February 2023).

Altınok, Metin (2015) '100'üncü yılında ekşiekşi ittihatçılık' Sabah 26 Nisan. https://www.sabah.com.tr/yazarlar/melihaltinok/2015/04/25/100uncu-yilinda-eksi-eksi-ittihatcilik (accessed September 2023).

Anderson, Benedict (2006) *Imagined Communities: Reflections on the Origin and Spread of Nationalism*. London: Verso.

Anscombe, G. E. M. (2000) *Intention*. Cambridge, MA: Harvard University Press.

Arslan, Ali, Halil Bal, and Hasan Demirhan (2012) *Tarihi ve Stratejik Boyutlarıyla Ermeni Meselesi*. İstanbul: İdil Yayincilik.

Aslan, Ali H. (2015) 'Obama 24 Nisan'da "soykırım" demeyecek'. *Zaman*, 23 Nisan, 15.

Assmann J. (2013) *Conversation with Jan Assmann: Memory Goes Hand-in-hand with Forgetting* [Interview lead by Caroline Gaudriault]. http://www.zigzag-blog.com/spip.php?page=article&id_article=3 (accessed May 2019).

Ata, Feridun (2017) *1915'e Hapsedilen Tarih: Ermeni Meselesi*. İstanbul: Palet.

Atay, Falih Rıfkı (1936) 'Dil Bayramı [Language Festival]'. *Ulus*, 26 September No 5448. https://www.gastearsivi.com/gazete/ulus/1936-09-26/1 (accessed 23 November 2022).

Aydın, M., M. Güvenç, O. Z. Zaim, B. B. Hawks, M. Çelikpala, E. Karaoğuz, C. Dizdaroğlu, M. G. Kösen, and B. A. Akıncı (2019) *Türkiye Sosyal-Siyasal Eğilimler Araştırması 2018–30 Ocak 2019*. https://www.khas.edu.tr/sites/khas.edu.tr/files/inline-files/TSSEA-2018-TR.pdf.

Aydınlık (2015a) 'Diaspora Şaşkın'. *Aydınlık*, 24 Nisan. https://egazete.aydinlik.com.tr/sites/default/files/dergi-arsivi/2015/04/24_04_2015.pdf (accessed January 2023).

Aydınlık (2015b) 'Büyük Felaket Sensin'. *Aydınlık*, 25 April. https://egazete.aydinlik.com.tr/sites/default/files/dergi-arsivi/2015/04/25_04_2015.pdf (accessed Januarry 2023).

Aytar, Mustafa (2016) 'Nereden Yeştişdirdiğin değil, Nasıl Yetiştirdiğin önemli'. http://emekliasubaylar.org/yazarlar/item/1549 (accessed February 2023).

Ayverdi, Samiha (2005) *Türkiye'nin Ermeni Meselesi*. Istanbul: Kubbealtı.

Babacan, Ali (2009a) '25 Nisan 2009, ABD Başkanı Obama'nın "Ermeni Anma Gününde" Vesilesiyle Yaptığı Yazılı Açıklama Hakkında'. https://www.mfa.gov.tr/no_58_-25-nisan-2009_-abd-baskani-obama_nin-_ermeni-anma-gunu_-vesilesiyle-yaptigi-yazili-aciklama-hk_.tr.mfa (accessed February 2023).

Babacan, Ali (2009b) 'O yorumu kabul etmeyiz'. *Hürriyet*, 26 April, 27.

Baecker, Dirk (2001) 'Why Systems? Theory'. *Culture & Society* 18(1): 59–74.

Bahçeli, Devlet (2009) 'Genel Başkanımız Sayın Devlet Bahçeli'nin TBMM Grup Toplantısında Yapmış Olduğu Konuşma, 7 Nisan 2009'. https://www.mhp.org.tr/htmldocs/genel_baskan/konusma/652/index.html (accessed March 2023).

Balakyan, Krikor (2014) *Ermenilerin Golgothası*. İstanbul: Belge yayınları.

Balancar, F. (ed.) (2012) *The Sounds of Silence: Turkey's Armenians Speak*. İstanbul: Hrant Dink Foundation Publications.

Balancar, F. (ed.) (2013) *The Sounds of Silence II: Diyarbakır's Armenians Speak*. İstanbul: Hrant Dink Foundation Publications.

Balancar, F. (ed.) (2015) *The Sounds of Silence III: Ankara's Armenians Speak*. İstanbul: Hrant Dink Foundation Publications.

Balancar, F. (ed.) (2016) *The Sounds of Silence IV: Izmit's Armenians Speak*. İstanbul: Hrant Dink Foundation Publications.

Bali, Rifat (2005) *Cumhuriyet Yıllarında Türkiye Yahudileri Bir Türklestirme Serüveni (1923–1945)*. İstanbul: İletişim.

Bardakçı, Murat (2008) *Talât Paşa'nin Evrak-ı Metrûkesi: Sadrazam Talât Paşa'nin özel arşivindende bulunan Ermeni tehciri konusundaki belgeler ve hususi yazışmalar*. İstanbul: Everest.

Bariş, Linda (2021) *Türkiyede Ermeni Okulları ve Ermeni Kimliği*. İstanbul: İletişim.

Barkan, Elazar (2000) *The Guilt of Nations: Restitution and Negotiating Historical Injustice*. New York: W.W. Norton & Comp.

Başar, Zeki (1978) 'ABD'leri Kongresine Sesleniş -1975'. In Z. Başar (ed.), *Ermeniler Hakkında Makaleler ve Derlemeler – Atatürk Üniversitesi Kuruluşunun XX. Yıl Armağanı*. Ankara: Atatürk Üniversitesi Yayınları, 23–8.

Batırel, Necmi (2022) *Tweet*. https://twitter.com/necmbatirel/status/1599675538817228800?ref_src=twsrc%5Etfw (accessed 10 December 2022).

Battal, Peyami (2015) *100. Yılında Ermeni Meselesi ve Gerçekler Sempozyumu 28 Mayıs Yüzüncü Yıl Üniversitesi, Van*. https://www.yyu.edu.tr/images/files/2015%281%29.pdf (accessed March 2023).

Bayer, Yalçın (2015) 'HER yıl 24 Nisan öncesinde ve sonrasında, Ermenilerin dünya çapında yaptıkları azginlıklar doğrusu gına getirdi'. *Hürriyet*, 22 April. https://www.hurriyet.com.tr/yazarlar/yalcin-bayer/ermeniler-gina-getirdi-28801662 (accessed December 2022).

Bayraktar, Seyhan (2015) 'The Grammar of Denial: State, Society, and Turkish–Armenian Relations'. *International Journal of Middle East Studies* 47(4): 801–6.

Benjamin, Walter (1968) 'Theses on the Philosophy of History'. In H. Arendt (ed.), *Illuminations*, trans. Harry Zohn. New York: Schocken Books, 253–64.

Bernard-Donals, Michael (2009) *Forgetful Memory: Representation and Remembrance in the Wake of the Holocaust*. New York: State University of New York Press.

Beyleryan, Nazli Temir (2019) 'Arméniens en Turquie: Entre déni ordinaire et pluralité des mémoires'. *Études arméniennes contemporaines* 12: 67–90.

Bianet (2009a) 'MEB'in Özrü Kabahetinden Büyük: Sarı Gelin Tarih Öğretmenleri İçindi'. 19 February. https://m.bianet.org/bianet/azinliklar/112667-meb-in-ozru-kabahatinden-buyuk-sari-gelin-tarih-ogretmenleri-icindi (accessed February 2023).

Bianet (2009b) 'Başbakana 501 imzalı Mektup: Okullarda "Sarı Gelini" Engeleyin'. 18 February. https://bianet.org/bianet/siyaset/112658-basbakana-510-imzali-mektup-okullarda-sari-gelin-i-engelleyin (accessed February 2023).

Bianet (2014) 'Erdoğan: Afedersin Ermeni Diyen oldu'. https://m.bianet.org/bianet/toplum/157616-erdogan-afedersin-ermeni-diyen-oldu.

Biden, J. (2021) *Statement by President Joe Biden on Armenian Remembrance Day*. https://www.whitehouse.gov/briefing-room/statements-releases/2021/04/24/statement-by-president-joe-biden-on-armenian-remembrance-day/ (accessed May 2022).

Bilgi, Nejdet (2006) *Yozgat Ermeni Tehciri Davası*. İstanbul: Kitabevi.

Biner Zerrin, Özlem (2010) 'Acts of Defacement, Memories of Loss: Ghostly Effects of the "Armenian Crisis" in Mardin, Southeastern Turkey'. *History and Memory* 22(2): 68–94.

Bjørnlund, Matthias (2008) 'The 1914 Cleansing of Aegean Greeks as a Case of Violent Turkification'. *Journal of Genocide Research* 10(1): 41–58.

Boggs, Carl (1976) *Gramsci's Marxism*. London: Pluto Press.

Bozkir, Volkan (2015) 'Üçüncü Şahıslar Aramızdan Çekilsin'. *Habertürk*, 22 April, 22.

Brendon, Cannon J. (2016) *Legislating Reality and Politicizing History: Contextualizing Armenian Claims of Genocide*. Offenbach am Main: Manzara Verlag.

Çarkoğlu,Ali ve Kalaycıoğlu, Ersin (2014) *Türkiye'de ve Dünyada Vatandaşlık*. Istanbul Policy Center At SABANCI University. https://bilimakademisi.org/wp-content/uploads/2015/12/T%C3%BCrkiyede-ve-Dunyada-Vatandaslik-2014-1.pdf (accessed June 2023).

Çelik, Adnan and Namık Kemal Dinç (2015) *1915 Diyarbakır: Yüz Yıllık Ah Toplumsal Hafızanın İzinde*. Istanbul: IBV Ismail Beşikci Vakfı Yayınları.

Cemal, Hasan (2012) *1915: Ermeni Soykırımı*. İstanbul: Everest Yayınları.

Çetin, Fethiye (2004) *Anneannem*. İstanbul: Metis.

Çetin, Fethiye and Ayşe Gül Altınay (2009) *Torunlar*. Istanbul: Metis.

Çiçek, Kemal (2020) *Ermenilerin Zorunlu Göçü 1915-1917*. İstanbul: Cedit.

Cıvaoğlu, Güneri (2015) 'Belgeyse, işte "belge"'. *Milliyet*, 25 April. https://www.milliyet.com.tr/yazarlar/guneri-civaoglu/belgeyse-iste-belge-2049350 (accessed January 2022).

CNN.Türk (2008) *Ermenilerden Özür Kampanyası Başlıyor* (The campaign to apologies from Armenians Begins). https://www.cnnturk.com/turkiye/ermenilerden-ozur-kampanyasi-basliyor (accessed October 2022).

Cohen, Stanley (2001) *States of Denial: Knowing About Atrocities and Suffering*. London: Polity Press.

Çölaşan, E. (2004a) 'Sabiha Gökçen'. *Hürriyet*, 22 Şubat. https://www.hurriyet.com.tr/sabiha-gokcen-204333 (accessed February 2023).

Çölaşan, E. (2004b) 'Ermeni imiş?'. *Hürriyet*, 24 February. https://www.hurriyet.com.tr/yazarlar/emin-colasan/?p=132 (accessed February 2023).

Çölaşan, Emin (2015a) 'Sen Kime taziye veriyorsun ey Ahmet?'. *Sözcü*, 22 April. https://www.sozcu.com.tr/2015/yazarlar/emin-colasan/sen-kime-taziye-veriyorsun-ey-ahmet-810431/ (accessed January 2023).

Çölaşan, Emin (2015b) 'Hepimiz Ermeniyiz!'. *Sözcü*, 25 April. https://www.sozcu.com.tr/2015/yazarlar/emin-colasan/hepimiz-ermeniyiz-813834/ (accessed January 2023).

Cooper, Robert L (2000) *Language Planning and Social Change*. Cambridge: Cambridge University Press.

Çubukçu, Aydın, Nevzat Onaran, C. Hakki Zariç, and Onur Öztürk (2015) *Onur ve Utanç-1915-2015 Ermeni Soykırımı'nın 100.yılı* (Honour and Shame 1915-2015 Centennial of the Armenian Genocide). İstanbul: Evrensel Basım Yayın.

Cuma, Atacan (2009) 'Diaspora, PKK'lılar gibi, para vermeyen Ermenilerin evini basıyor'. *Zaman*, 22 April, 19.

Cumhuriyet (2015a) 'Front Page'. *Cumhuriyet*, 24 April. https://www.gazeteoku.com/gazeteler/2015-04-24/cumhuriyet-gazetesi-manseti (accessed January 2023).

Cumhuriyet (2015b) 'Tehcirde Ermenilerin Güvenligini sağlayın'. *Cumhuriyet*, 24 Nisan, 12.

Cunningham, Michael (2014) *States of Apology*. Manchester: Manchester University Press.

Dadrian, Vahank N. and Taner Akcam (2011) *Judgement at Istanbul. The Armenian Genocide Trials*. New York: Berghahn Books.

Daily Sabah (2018) *Turkey's Minority Leaders Sign a Joint Declaration Denying 'Pressure' on Communities*. https://www.dailysabah.com/minorities/2018/07/31/turkeys-minority-leaders-sign-joint-declaration-denying-pressure-on-communities (accessed October 2022).

Davutoglu, Ahmet (2015) *Davutoglu Hopes 2015 Renews Turkey, Armenian Friendship*. https://www.aa.com.tr/en/politics/davutoglu-hopes-2015-renews-turkey-armenia-friendship/82328# (accessed January 2017).

Deli, Yunus Emre (2015) *Ermeni Meselesi: Kafası Karışanlar için 100. Yılında*. İstanbul: Divan.

Demircioğlu, İ Hakkı (2013) 'Tarih Ders Kitabı Yazımında Yeni Yaklaşımlar'. *Karadeniz Araştırmaları* 38: 119–33.

Demirel, İdil (2007) 'ABD'de Maalesef Lobi Faliyetleri yetersiz'. *Sabah*, 13 March. http://arsiv.sabah.com.tr/2007/03/13/gnd107.html (accessed July 2023).

Der Matossian, Bedross (2011) 'The Taboo within the Taboo: The Fate of "Armenian Capital" at the End of the Ottoman Empire'. *European Journal of Turkish Studies*. http://ejts.revues.org/4411 (accessed February 2023).

Der Matossian, Bedross (2022) *The Horrors of Adana: Revolution and Violence in the Early Twentieth Century*. Stanford: Stanford University Press.

Descombes, Vincent (2014) *The Institutions of Meaning: A Defence of Anthropological Holism*. Cambridge, MA: Harvard University Press.

Diken (2015) 'Gökçek, kendisine "Ermeni" diyen Hayko Bağdat'a hakaret davası açtı'. https://www.diken.com.tr/gokcek-kendisine-ermeni-denmesinden-tiksinti-duyup-gazeteci-hayko-bagdata-hakaret-davasi-acti/ (accessed February 2019).

Dincer, Selim (2013) 'The Armenian Massacre in Istanbul (1896)'. *Tijdschrift voor Sociale en Economische Geschiedenis* 10(4): 20–45.

Dixon, Jennifer M. (2015) 'Norms, Narratives, and Scholarship on the Armenian Genocide'. *International Journal of Middle East Studies* 47: 796–800.

Ekşi, Oktay (2004) 'Sabiha Gökçen tartışması'. *Hürriyet*, 24 Şubat. https://www.hurriyet.com.tr/sabiha-gokcen-tartismasi-204774 (accessed February 2023).

Ekşi, Oktay (2009) 'Laf Cambazı'. *Hürriyet*, 26 April. https://www.hurriyet.com.tr/laf-cambazi-11514819 (accessed January 2023).

Ekşi, Oktay (2010) 'Hukuk ve Soykırım'. *Hürriyet*, 24 April. https://www.hurriyet.com.tr/hukuk-ve-soykirim-14516061 (accessed January 2023).

Eldem, Ethem (2018) *Mitler, Gerçekler ve Yöntem. Osmanlı Tarihinde Aklıma Takılanlar.* Istanbul: Tarih Vakfı Yurt Yayınları.
Erdoğan, Recep Tayyip (2014) *The Unofficial Translation of the Message of H.E. President Recep Tayyip Erdoğan, the then Prime Minister of the Republic of Turkey, on the Events of 1915.* 23 April. https://www.mfa.gov.tr/turkish-prime-minister-mr_-recep-tayyip-erdo%C4%9Fan-published-a-message-on-the-events-of-1915_-23-april-2014.en.mfa (accessed June 2022).
Erdoğan, Recep Tayyip (2015a). 'Message Sent by H.E. Mr. Recep Tayyip Erdoğan, President of the Republic of Turkey, to the Religious Ceremony Held in the Armenian Patriarchate of Istanbul on 24 April 2015'. https://www.mfa.gov.tr/message-sent-by-h_e_-mr_-recep-tayyip-Erdogan_-president-of-the-republic-of-turkey_-to-the-religious-ceremony-held-in-the-arme.en.mfa (accessed June 2022).
Erdoğan, Recep Tayyip (2015b) *Çanakkale 100. Yıl Barış Zirvesinde Yaptıkları Konuşma.* https://www.tccb.gov.tr/konusmalar/353/32664/canakkale-100-yil-baris-zirvesinde-yaptiklari-konusma (accessed January 2022).
Erdoğan, Recep Tayyip (2022) 'April 24 Message from Erdoğan to Turkish Armenians'. https://massispost.com/2022/04/april-24-message-from-Erdogan-to-turkish-armenians/ (accessed November 2022).
Eroler, Elif Gençkal (2019) *Dindar Nesil Yetiştirmek: Türkiye'nin Eğitim Politikalarında Ulus ve Vatandaş İnşası (2002–2016).* İstanbul: İletişim.
Ersanlı, Büşra (2011) *İktidar ve Tarih, Türkiye'de 'Resmî Tarih' Tezinin Oluşumu (1929–1937),* 4th ed. İstanbul, İletişim Yayınları, 104–5.
Ersoy, Pinar (2015) 'Amerikalı Türkler 25 Nisan Nöbetinde'. *Milliyet,* 24 April, 8.
Esin, Taylan and Zeliha Etöz (2015) *1916 Ankara Yangını [1916 Ankara Fire].* Istanbul: İletişim.
Ether, Şeref (2021) *Dr. Zaruhi S. Kavalcıyan, Turkiyenin İlk Türk Kadın Hekimi.* https://www.istabip.org.tr/6743-dr-zaruhi-s-kavalciyan-turkiye-nin-ilk-kadin-hekimi-seref-etker.html (accessed 16 December 2022).
Fikriyat (2019) 'Şark Fatihi: Kazım Karabekir'. https://www.fikriyat.com/tarih/2019/01/25/sark-fatihi-kazim-karabekir (accessed February 2023).
Gallagher Charles, F. (1971) 'Language Reform and Social Modernization in Turkey'. In Joan Rubin and Jernudd H. Björn (eds), *Can Language be Planned? Sociolinguistic Theory for Developing Countries.* New York: University of Hawaii Press, 152–69.
General Staff (2004) *Genelkurmay Başkanlığı'nın Sabiha Gökçen haberi açıklaması.* 22 Subat, Bianet. https://m.bianet.org/bianet/siyaset/30301-genelkurmay-gokcen-turk-kadini-sembolu (accessed June 2023).
Gensburger, Sarah (2016) 'Halbwach's Studies in Collective Memory: A Founding Text for Contemporary "Memory Studies?"'. *Journal of Classical Sociology* 16(4): 396–413.
Giddens, Anthony (1997) *Sociology,* 3rd ed. Cambridge: Polity Press.
Gillespie, Alex (2020) 'Disruption, Self-Presentation, and Defensive Tactics at the Threshold of Learning'. *Review of General Psychology* 24(4): 382–96.
Göçek, Fatma Müge (2014) *Denial of Violence: Ottoman Past, Turkish Present and Collective Violence Against Armenians 1789–2009.* Oxford: Oxford University Press.

Goffman, Erving (1990) *Stigma: Notes on the Management of Spoiled Identity*. London: Penguin.

Görke, Alexander and Armine Scholl (2006) 'Niklas Luhmann's Theory of Social Systems and Journalism Research'. *Journalism Studies* 7(4): 644–55.

Gül, Abdullah (2009) 'Yüz binlerce Türk'ü de ansaydın'. *Hürriyet*, 26 April, 27.

Güller, Mehmet Ali (2015) 'AKP'nin Obama'yla soykırım Pazarlığı'. *Aydınlık*, 23 April, 9. https://egazete.aydinlik.com.tr/sites/default/files/dergi-arsivi/2015/04/23_04_2015 .pdf (accessed December 2022).

Gürsel, Burcu (2015) 'The Mythical Interface of Turkish Intellectuals' Orientation toward the Armenian Genocide'. *International Journal of Middle East Studies* 47: 791–4.

Gürün, Kâmuran (1988) *Ermeni Dosyası*. İstanbul: Remzi Kitap.

Gust, Wolfgang (2013) *The Armenian Genocide: Evidence from the German Foreign Office Archives 1915–1916*. Oxford: Berghahn Books.

Guyonnet, Damien (2011) 'The Insult in Psychosis'. *Recherches en psychanalyse* 12: 189–95.

Güzel, Hasan Celal (2007) 'İşte, ABD Ermeni Soykırım Taslağın'daki Yalanlar'. *Radikal*, 25 Şubat.

Hacking, Ian (1995) *Rewriting the Soul: Multiple Personality and the Science of Memory*. Princeton: Princeton University Press.

Hakan, Ahmet (2015) 'Ermeni meselesi üzerine 7 Tez'. 25 April. https://www.hurriyet .com.tr/yazarlar/ahmet-hakan/ermeni-meselesi-uzerine-yedi-tez-28831022 (accessed January 2015).

Halaçoğlu, Yusuf (2008) *Story of 2015: What Happened to the Ottoman Armenians*. Ankara: Türk Tarih Kurumu.

Halbwachs, Maurice (1997) *La mémoire collective*. Paris: Albin Michel.

Halbwachs, Maurice (2015) *La psychologie collective*. Paris: Champs classiques.

Han, Byung-Chul (2018) *The Expulsion of the Other*. London: Polity.

HDV (2018) *Turkey Cultural Heritage Map*. https://hrantdink.org/en/bolis/activities/ projects/cultural-heritage/12-turkey-cultural-heritage-map (accessed September 2023).

HDV (Hrant Dink Vakfı) (2015) *Müslümanlaş(tırıl)mış Ermeniler*. İstanbul: Hrant Dink Vakfı Yayınları.

Hinton, Alexander L., T. La Pointe, and D. Irvin-Erickson (eds.) (2014) *Hidden Genocides: Power, Knowledge, Memory*. London: Rutgers University Press.

Hulse, Carl 2007. 'Support wanes in House for Genocide Vote'. *New York Times*, https:// www.nytimes.com/2007/10/17/washington/17cnd-cong.html (accessed June 2022).

Hür, Ayşe (2009) 'İttihat ve Terakki'nin Çocuk Askerleri'. *Taraf*, 12 April. https://hyetert .org/2009/04/12/ittihat-ve-terakkinin-cocuk-askerleri/ (accessed February 2023).

Hürriyet (2004) 'Sabiha Gökçen's 80 Yıllık Sırrı'. *Hürriyet*, 21 Şubat. https://www .hurriyet.com.tr/gundem/sabiha-gokcen-mi-hatun-sebilciyan-mi-38571233 (accessed February 2019).

Hürriyet (2010) 'Gürbüz Cocuklar Ordusu Aranıyor'. *Hürriyet*, 8 October. https://www .hurriyet.com.tr/gundem/gurbuz-cocuklar-ordusu-araniyor-15990854 (accessed March 2019).

İbrahim, Necmi (1934) 'Özledigimiz Yazı Dili [Language of Writing we Missed]'. *Zaman*, 26 September No 108. https://www.gastearsivi.com/gazete/zaman/1934-09-26/1 (accessed 23 November 2022).

Ilıcak, Nazlı (2009) 'Kürt Azinlik Var mi?'. *Sabah*, 9 April. http://www.sabah.com.tr/2009/04/09//ilicak.html (accessed January 2023).

Karabekir, Timsal (2010) 'Gürbüz Çocuklar Ordusu aranıyor'. *Hürriyet*, 8 October. https://www.hurriyet.com.tr/gundem/gurbuz-cocuklar-ordusu-araniyor-15990854 (accessed February 2023).

Karaca, Nihal Bengisu (2015) 'Gelecek 24 Nisan'a kadar rahatmiyiz?'. *Habertürk*, 25 April. https://www.haberturk.com/yazarlar/nihal-bengisu-karaca/1069941-gelecek-24-nisana-kadar-rahat-miyiz (accessed January 2023).

Karakaş, Burcu (2015a) 'Hafıza Taşı Anıları Yaşatacak'. *Milliyet*, 25 April, 20.

Karakaş, Burcu (2015b) 'Konsolosluk önünde oturma eylemi'. *Milliyet*, 25 April, 20.

Karayumak, Ömer (2007) *Ermeniler, Ermeni İsyanları, Ermeni Katliamları*. İstanbul: Vadi.

Keleş, Pınar (2009) 'Genelkurmay Filmi Sarı Gelin Tüm Okullarda Gösterimde'. *Habervesaire*. https://www.habervesaire.com/genelkurmay-filmi-sari-gelin-tum-okullarda-gosterimde-2/ (accessed May 2019).

Keskin, Hakki (2015) 'Obama Soykırım diyecek mi?'. *Aydınlık*, 23 April, 8. https://egazete.aydinlik.com.tr/sites/default/files/dergi-arsivi/2015/04/23_04_2015.pdf (accessed December 2022).

Kırıkkanat, Mine G. (2015) 'Bir Yüzyılın Otuz İkinci Dönümü'. *Cumhuriyet*, 22 Nisan. https://www.cumhuriyet.com.tr/yazarlar/mine-g-kirikkanat/bir-yuzyilin-otuz-ikinci-donumu-259821 (accessed December 2022).

Klemperer, Victor (2013) *The Language of The Third Reich*. London: Bloomsbury.

Köker, Osman (ed.) (2005) *Orlando Carlo Calumeno Koleksiyonu'ndan Kartpostallarla, 100 Yıl önce Turkiye'de Ermeniler*. İstanbul: Birzamanlar Yayıncılık.

Koru, Fehmi (2015) 'İsme takılıp kalmayalım, sorunu bizler çözelim'. *Habertürk*, 22 April. https://www.haberturk.com/yazarlar/fehmi-koru/1068785-isme-takilip-kalmayalim-sorunu-bizler-cozelim (accessed December 2022).

Kubilay, Çağla (2004) 'Türkiye'de Anadillere Yönelik Düzenlemeler ve Kamusal Alan: Anadil ve Resmi Dil Eşitlemesinin Kırılması'. *İletişim: Araştırmaları Dergisi*, 2004, 56–83. https://dspace.ankara.edu.tr/xmlui/bitstream/handle/20.500.12575/62341/T%C3%BCrkiye%27de%20Anadillere%20Y%C3%B6nelik%20d%C3%BCzenlemeler.pdf?sequence=1&isAllowed=y (accessed November 2022).

Kurt, Ümit (2021) *The Armenians of Aintab: The Economics of Genocide in an Ottoman Province*. Boston: Harvard University Press.

Lemieux, Cyril (2009) *Le Devoir et la grâce*. Paris: Economica, coll. Etudes Sociologiques.

Lemkin, R. (1944) *Axis Rule in Occupied Europe: Laws of Occupation, Analysis of Government, Proposals for Redress*. Carnegie Endowment.

Levi, Primo (2013) *The Drowned and The Saved*. London: ABACUS.

Lewis, Bernard (1961) *The Emergence of Modern Turkey*. London: Royal Institute of International Affairs.

Lewis, Geoffrey (2002) *The Turkish Language Reform: A Catastrophic Success*. Oxford: Oxford University Press.

Luhmann, Niklas (2000) *The Reality of the Mass Media*. Stanford: Stanford University Press.

Marian, M. and A. İnsel (2010) *Ermeni Tabusu Üzerine Diyalog*. İstanbul: İletişim.

MEB (1973) *Milli Eğitim Temel Kanunu*. https://www.mevzuat.gov.tr/mevzuatmetin/1.5.1739.pdf (accessed April 2019).

MEB (2002/2) "Ermeni, Yunan-Pontus ve Süryaniler ile İlgili KonularınOrta Öğretim Tarih 1, Tarih 2 ve T.C.İnkılâp Tarihi ve Atatürkçülük Dersi Öğretim Programlarında YerAlması Hakkında MEB Talim ve Terbiye Kurulu Başkanlığı'nın 14.06.2002 Tarih ve272 Sayılı Kararı", MEBTebliğler Dergisi, Temmuz 2002, sy.2538, ss.530–544.

Mengi, Güngör (2004) 'Kitle ikna Silahı'. *Vatan*, 23 February. https://www.gazetevatan.com/yazarlar/gungor-mengi/kitle-ikna-sil-hi-23048 (accessed April 2019).

Metin, Erhan (2015) *Türk Ders Kitaplarında 'Ermeniler' Cumhuriyet'ten Günümüze*. Ankara: TEPAV Yayınevi. https://www.tepav.org.tr/upload/files/1448284085-5.TURK_DERS_KITAPLARINDA____ERMENILER____Cumhuriyet___ten_Gunumuze.pdf (accessed February 2023).

Michel, Johann (2018) *Le Devoir de Mémoire*. Paris: Que sais-je?

Mısıroğlu, Kadir (2015) *Tarihten Günümüze Ermeni Meselesi ve Zulümler*. Istanbul: Sebil.

Mouradian, Claire (2021) '"Dis mémé, raconte moi les massacres": Histoire de ma grand-mère'. In *Penser Les Génocides: Itineraries de recherche*. Paris: CNRS edition, 53–64.

Musa, Isamil Hakki (2018) 'Lettre de L'Ambassadeur de Rurquie en France et Dossier remis au Oresident de la Mission le 14 September 2017'. *Rapport de la Mission d'étude en France sur la recherche et l'enseignement des génocides et des crimes de masse*, 348–50. https://webaram.com/app/uploads/2019/01/mission-genocides-duclert.pdf (accessed June 2019).

Navarro, Yael (2020) 'The Aftermath of Mass Violence'. *Annual Review of Anthropology* 49: 161–73.

Nichanian, Marc (2002) *Catastrophic Mourning – From the Loss*. Berkeley: University of California Press.

Nichanian, Marc (2015) *Le Sujet de l'histoire*. Paris: Linge.

Nobles, Melissa (2008) *The Politics of Official Apologies*. Cambridge: Cambridge University Press.

Obama, Barak (2009) 'Remarks by President Obama to the Turkish Parliament April 6'. https://obamawhitehouse.archives.gov/the-press-office/remarks-president-obama-turkish-parliament (accessed May 2023).

Odyan, Yervant (2022) *Lanetli Yıllar: İstanbul'dan Der Zor'a Sürgün ve Geri Dönüş Hikayem 1914–1915*, Translated by S. Malhasyan and K. Taşkıran. İstanbul: ARAS.

Onedio (2015) 'Melih Gökçek'ten Hayko Bağdat'a "Ermeni Davası"'. https://onedio.com/haber/gokcek-ten-hayko-bagdat-a-ermeni-davasi-476159 (accessed February 2019).

Ophir, Adi (2005) *The Order of Evils: Towards an Ontology of Morals*. New York: Zone Books.

Oranlı, Imge (2021) 'Epistemic Injustice from *Afar*: Rethinking the Denial of Armenian Genocide'. *Social Epistemology* 35(2): 120–32.

Oruç, Merve Şebnem (2015) '24 Nisan ve İttihat ve Terakki'. *Yeni Şafak*, 23 April. https://www.yenisafak.com/yazarlar/merve-sebnem-oruc/24-nisan-ve-ittihat-ve-terakki-2010330 (accessed December 2022).

Över, Kıvanç Galip (2007) *Alman Belgelerinde Ermeni Meselesi 1915*. İstanbul: Kaknüs.

Öz, İlkay (2020) *Mülksüzleştirilme ve Türkleştirilme: The Case of Edirne*. İstanbul: İletişim.

Ozan, Hüseyin and Zafer Kuş (2021) 'Meşrutiyet'ten Cumhuriyet'e Vatandaşlık Öğretim Programlarında Kimlik İnşası'. *Eğitim ve Toplum Araştırmaları Dergisi* 8(2): 237–57.

Özçakmak, Şükran (2000) 'Karabekir' in Çocukları'. *Milliyet*, 16 May, 15.

Özdemir, Ali Ulvi (2021) *Ermeni Soykırımı İddalarina Karşı Bir Yanıt*. Istanbul: Akıl Fikir Yayınları.

Özel, Soli (2015) 'Diplomasiyi ıskalarsınız'. *Habertürk*, 22 April. https://www.haberturk.com/yazarlar/soli-ozel/1068764-diplomasiyi-iskalarsaniz (accessed December 2022).

Özer, Verda (2015) 'ASALA kurbanından Ermenilere dostluk mesajı'. *Hürriyet*, 25 Nisan. https://www.hurriyet.com.tr/yazarlar/verda-ozer/asala-kurbanindan-ermenilere-dostluk-mesaji-28830440 (accessed December 2022).

Özgürel, Avni (2009) 'Van'da gördüklerimi saklayamam'. *Radikal*, 26 April, 15.

Özkök, Ertuğrul (2015) 'Bu afişi inkâr ediyorum'. *Hürriyet*, 25 April. https://www.hurriyet.com.tr/yazarlar/ertugrul-ozkok/bu-afisi-ink-r-ediyorum-28831171 (accessed January 2023).

Paçal, Mustafa (2015) 'Yüzyıllık Acı: Ermeni Soykırımı'. *Taraf*, 23 April. https://www.bahrainair.net/yazarlar/yuzyillik-aci-ermeni-soykirimi/ (accessed December 2022).

Palabıyık, Serdar Mustafa (2015) *1915 Olaylarını Anlamak:Türkler ve Ermeniler*. Istanbul: Beta.

Paylan, Garo (2017) https://www.youtube.com/watch?v=ToIxiQd7E5U (accessed January 2019).

Pazarcı, Hüseyin (2014) 'Perinçek vs. Switzerland Case (ECHR, 17 December 2013)'. *Review of Armenian Studies* 29: 27–63.

Perinçek, Doğu (2012) *Perinçek-İsviçre Davası: "Ermeni Soykırımı" Yalanı AİHM'de*. İstanbul: Kaynak.

Perinçek, Doğu (2016) 'AIHM Karsışında emperyalistlerin yeni mevzisi'. *Aydınlık*, 24 Nisan. https://www.aydinlik.com.tr/koseyazisi/aihm-karari-karsisinda-emperyalistlerin-yeni-mevzisi-6337 (accessed June 2023).

Perinçek, Mehmet (2007) *Rus Devlet Arşivlerinden 100 Belgede Ermeni Meselesi*. Istanbul: Doğan Kitap.

Perinçek, Mehmet (2012) *Rus Devlet Arşivlerinden 150 Belgede Ermeni Meselesi*, 3rd ed. İstanbul: Kirmizi Kedi.

Polatel, Mehmet, Nora Mildanoğlu, Özgür Leman Eren, and Mehmet Atılgan (2012) *2012 Beyannamesi, İstanbul Ermeni Vakıflarının el Konan Mülkleri, 2012 Declaration, the Seized Properties of Armenian Foundations in Istanbul*. İstanbul: Hrant Dink Vakfı Yayınları.

Potter, W. James (2013) 'Synthesising a working definition of "Mass" Media'. *Review of Communication Research* 1 (1): 1–30.

Pulur, Hasan (2015) 'Evet Tehcir'. *Milliyet*, 25 April. https://www.milliyet.com.tr/yazarlar/hasan-pulur/evet-tehcir-2049333 (accessed January 2023).

Purtul, Burcu and Fırat Alkaç (2015) 'Taksim'de anma ve protesto'. *Hürriyet*, 25 April.

Radikal (2009a) 'Washington memnun, Ermeni lobisi rahatsız'. *Radikal*, 24 Nisan, 9.

Radikal (2009b) 'Ankara'da "büyük" hayal kırıklığı'. *Radikal*, 26 April, 10.

Ricouer, Paul (2004) *Memory, History and Forgetting*. Chicago: The University of Chicago Press.

Ricouer, Paul (2005) *The Course of Recognition*. Cambridge, MA: Harvard University Press.

Rubin, Joan and Jernudd H. Björn (1971) 'Introduction: Language Planning as an Element in Modernization'. In Rubin and Björn (eds), *Can Language be Planned? Sociolinguistic Theory for Developing Countries*. New York: University of Hawaii Press, xi–xxiii.

Sadoğlu, Hüseyin (2003) *Türkiyede Ulusçuluk ve Dil Politikaları*. Istanbul: Istanbul Bilgi Universitesi Yayınları.

Sakin, Orhan (2015) *Ermeni Isyan Gunlugu 1915: Osmalı Arşivleri Yeminli Tanık İfadeleri*. İstanbul: Yeditepe.

Sands, Philippe (2017) *East West Street*. London: Weidenfeld & Nicolson.

Sarafian, Ara (2011) *Talaat Pasha's Report on The Armenian Genocide 1917*. London: Gomidas Institute.

Sari, Selay (2015) 'Ermeni Aydınlar Anısına Görkemli Konser: Adalet icin birlikte mücadele etmeliyiz'. *Milliyet*, 24 April, 8.

Sarıkaya, Makbule (2004) 'Bir "Çocuk Kasabası" Sarıkamış'. *A.Ü. Türkiye Araştırmaları Enstitüsü Dergisi* 11(23): 237–43. https://turcology.org/en/bir-cocuk-kasabasi-sarikamis-162167 (accessed February 2023).

Sarıkaya, Muharrem (2015) 'Etekteki Taşlar'. *HaberTürk*, 23 April. https://www.haberturk.com/yazarlar/muharrem-sarikaya/1069192-etekteki-taslar (accessed December 2022).

Savelsberg, Joachim J. (2021) *Knowing About Genocide: Armenian Suffering and Epistemic Struggles*. California: University of California Press.

Seckinelgin, Hakan (2006) 'Civil Society Between the State and Society: Turkish Women with Headscarves?'. *Critical Social Policy* 4: 748–69.

Seckinelgin, Hakan (2016) 'Social policy and conflict: The Gezi Park–Taksim demonstrations and uses of social policy for reimagining Turkey'. *Third World Quarterly* 37 (2): 1–17.

Seckinelgin, Hakan (2023) 'Institutional Denialism as Public Policy: Using Films as a Tool to Deny the Armenian Genocide in Turkey'. *Ethnic and Racial Studies*. https://www.tandfonline.com/doi/full/10.1080/01419870.2023.2176249?src= (accessed May 2023).

Serdar, M. Törehan (2015) 'Ermeni Sevk ve Iskanin (Tehcirin) Altinda Yatan Nedenler (Reasons Behind the Relocation of Armenians)'. *Ermeni Arstirmaları* 52: 221–64.

Sertçelik, Seyit (2015) *Rus ve Ermeni Kaynakları Işığında Ermeni Sorunu: Sömürge Savaşı 1915–1923*. İstanbul: SRT Yayınları.

Seyrek, Ahmet (2015) *Ermeni Meselesi ve Tehcir*. İstanbul: Bizim Kitaplar.

Shanken, Andrew M. (2022) *The Everyday Life of Memorials*. New York: Zone Books.

Sirmen, Ali (2004) 'Ermeni olsaydı sembol olamayacak mıydı?'. *Cumhuriyet*, 24 February.

Solak, Mustafa (2015) '"Soykırım" iddiasına nasıl yaklaşmalı'. *Aydınlık*, 24 April, 2 https://egazete.aydinlik.com.tr/sites/default/files/dergi-arsivi/2015/04/24_04_2015.pdf (accessed December 2022).

Su, Mükerem K (1982) *Türkiye Cumhuriyeti İnkilap Tarihi*, 2nd ed. İstanbul: MEB.

Suny, Ronald Grigor, Fatma Müge Göçek, and Norman M. Naimark (2015) *Soykırım Meselesi Osmanlı İmparatorluğu'nun Son Döneminde Ermeniler ve Türkler*, Translated by A. E. Pinar. Tarih Vakfı Yurt Yayınları.

Szurek, Emmanuel (2013) 'Dil Bayramı. Une lecture somatique de la fête politique dans la Turquie du parti unique'. In N. Clayer and E. Kaynar (eds), *Penser, agir et vivre dans l'Empire ottoman et en Turquie. Études réunies pour François Georgeon*. Louvain: Peeters, 497–523. https://www.peeters-leuven.be/detail.php?search_key=9789042925984&series_number_str=19&lang=fr (accessed April 2023).

Szurek, Emmanuel (2014) 'Le linguiste et le politique. La Türk Dil Kurumu et le champ du pouvoir dans la Turquie du parti unique'. In Marc Aymes, Benjamin Gourisse, and Élise Massicard (éds), *Ordonner et transiger. Modalités de gouvernement et d'administration en Turquie et dans l'Empire ottoman depuis les Tanzimat*. Paris: Karthala, 75–101.

Şerbetçi, K. (2019) 'Koray Şerbetçi ile An ve Zaman'. *24TV*, 27 January. https://www.youtube.com/watch?v=6JUChD_s-KY (accessed 20 January 2023).

Şimşir, Bilâl N. (2014) *Ermeni Meselesi 1774–2005*, 6th ed. İstanbul: Bilgi.

Snyder, Timothy (2011) *Bloodlands: Europe between Hitler and Stalin*, London: Basic Books.

Tachjian, Vahé, Adjemian Boris, and Davidian Vazken (2021) 'Place, Belonging and History: Reflections on the Ottoman Armenian Past and Heritage'. *Etudes Armeniennes Contemporaiens* 13. https://journals.openedition.org/eac/2653 (accessed 11 November 2022).

Takvim (2015) 'Yüzsüzler'. *Takvim*, 24 Nisan. https://www.gazeteoku.com/gazeteler/2015-04-24/takvim-gazetesi-manseti (accessed December 2022).

Taşçı, Selcan (2015) 'Türklerin pişmanlık duyucağı birşey yok'. *Yeniçağ*, 24 April. https://www.yenicaggazetesi.com.tr/yazi-arsivi-384759h.htm (accessed December 2022).

Tate, Jahnisa (2014) 'Turkey's Article 301: A Legitimate Tool for Maintaining Order or a Threat to Freedom of Expression?'. *Georgia Journal of International & Comparative Law* 37: 181–217.

Tayiz, Kurtulus (2015) '"Soykırım" kampanyasının güncel sebepleri'. *Akşam*, 25 April.

Tekin, Arslan (2013) *Türk Adını Silme Planı: Sark Meselesinin Son Aşaması*. İstanbul: Paraf Yayınları.

Tekin, Arslan (2015) 'Bana düşmanlık edene düşmanım'. *Yeniçağ*, 24 Nisan. https://www.yenicaggazetesi.com.tr/yazi-arsivi-384758h.htm (accessed January 2023).

Tepeli, Selçuk (2015) 'Soykırım tasarısına imza atan kongre üyelerinin sayısı düştü'. *Habertürk*, 23 April, 19.

Ter Minassian, Taline (2015) 'Le patrimoine arménien en Turquie: De la négation à l'inversion patrimoniale'. *European Journal of Turkish Studies [Online]*. http://journals.openedition.org/ejts/4948 (accessed March 2023).

Tetik, Ahmet and Güneş Cihan (2014) *Halep Sığınma Evi 1922–1927*. Istanbul: Alfa Yayınları.

Tonga, Deniz (2015) 'Ermeni Tehcirinin 100.Senesinde öğretim Programlarımızda Ermeni Meselesi'. *Adıyaman Üniversitesi Sosyal Bilimler Enstitüsü Dergisi* 21: 871–907. https://dergipark.org.tr/tr/download/article-file/265910 (accessed February 2023).

Trouillot, Michel-Rolph (2015) *Silencing the Past: Power and Production of History*. New York: Beacon Press.

Tuncer, Günay (2004) *Misyonerlik Örgütleri ve Misyonerlik Faaliyetleri*. Ankara: Ankara Ticaret Odası.

Turan, Ömer and Güven Gürkan Öztan (2018) *Devlet Aklı ve 1915: Türkiye'de 'Ermeni Meselesi' Anlatısının İnşası*. İstanbul: İletişim.

Turan, Rahmi (2015) 'Obama "Soykırım" Demezse Hatırım Kalır!'. *Sözcü*, 23 April. https://www.sozcu.com.tr/2015/yazarlar/rahmi-turan/obama-soykirim-demezse-hatirim-kalir-811398/ (accessed November 2022).

Turan, Refik (2015) 'Türkiye'de Lise Tarih Öğretiminde Ermeni Sorunu ve Tehcir (1950–2015)'. *International Periodical for the Languages, Literature and History of Turkish and Turkic* 10/11: 1471–500.

Turan, Refik, Mustafa Safran, Necdet Hayta, Muhammet Şahin, M. Ali Çakmak, and Cengiz Dönmez (2006) *Atatürk İlkeleri ve İnkılap Tarihi*. Ankara: Beta yayınları.

Uluç, Hıncal (2004) 'Ermeni ...'. *Sabah*, 24 Şubat. https://www.sabah.com.tr/yazarlar/uluc/2004/02/24/ermeni (accessed February 2023).

Uluç, Hıncal (2007) 'Kizilderililere degil, Amerikan Halkina yaptiklari'. *Sabah*, 11 February. https://www.sabah.com.tr/yazarlar/uluc/2007/02/11/kizilderililere_degil_amerikan_halkina_yaptiklar (accessed February 2023).

UNHR (2019a) *The letter from the Working Group on Enforced or Involuntary Disappearances*. https://spcommreports.ohchr.org/TMResultsBase/DownLoadPublicCommunicationFile?gId=24294 (accessed 15 December 2022).

UNHR (2019b) *The Response Letter*. https://spcommreports.ohchr.org/TMResultsBase/DownLoadFile?gId=34685 (accessed 15 December 2022).

Üstel, Füsun (2004) *'Makbul Vatandaş'ın Peşinde: II. Mesrutiyet'ten Bugüne Vatandaşlık Eğitimi*. Istanbul: İletişim.

Üstel, Füsun (2021) *'Makbul Vatandaşın' Peşinde: II. Meşrutiyet'ten Bugüne Vatandaşlık Eğitimi*. İstanbul: İletişim.

Wharton, Alyson (2015) *The Architects of Ottoman Constantinople: The Balyan Family and the History of Ottoman Architecture*. London: IB Tauris.

Yalçın, Soner (2015) 'Başkaşının kafasıyla düşünenlere yanıt'. *Sözcü*, 22 April. https://www.sozcu.com.tr/2015/yazarlar/soner-yalcin/baskasinin-kafasiyla-dusunenlere-yanit-810407/ (accessed December 2022).

Yeni Şafak (2007) *Çocuklarınızı nefret ve kinle büyütmeyin!* Yeni Şafak 24 April. https://www.yenisafak.com/dunya/cocuklarinizi-nefret-ve-kinle-buyutmeyin-42267 (accessed June 2019).

Yeni Türkiye: Stratejik Araştırma Merkezi (2014) *Ermeni Meselesi Özel Sayısı*. https://yeniturkiye.com/ermeni-meselesi-ozel-sayisi/ (accessed November 2022).

Yıldız, Pınar (2021) *Kayıp Hafızanın Peşinde*. Istanbul: Metis.

Yılmaz, Mehmet (2009) 'ADD'nin Cumhuriyet mitinginin amacı ne?'. *Zaman*, 24 April, 22.

Yılmaz, M. S. (2014) 'Ortaokul Türkiye Cumhuriyet İnkılâp Tarihi ve Atatürkçülük Ders Kitaplarında Ermeni Meselesi ve Tehcir Olayi (2008–2015)'. *Yeni Türkiye: Stratejik Araştırma Merkezi* 60. https://docplayer.biz.tr/68682718-Turkiye-cumhuriyeti-inkilap-tarihi-ve-ve-ataturkculuk-ders-kitaplarinda-ermeni-meselesi-ve-tehcir-olayi-mehmet-serhat-yilmaz-giris.html (accessed November 2022).

YouTube (2022) *Documentary Sarı Gelin*. https://www.youtube.com/watch?v=XlVAAh58DGw (accessed 18 November 2022).

Yurttagül, Ali (2015) 'Türkiye 1915'i diplomatik kriz grekçesi yapmamalı'. *Zaman*, 22 April.

Zerubavel, Eviatar (2007) *Elephant in the Room: Silence and Denial in Everyday Life*. Oxford: Oxford University Press.

Index

100 Years Ago: Armenians in Turkey (*100 yıl önce Türkiyede Ermeniler*, Köker) 6
'the 1893 Armenian rebellion' 143
1914/1915 documentary (Akyol) 150, 153–66
   Armenian
      atrocities 162
      deaths 161, 165
      deportations 153, 155–7, 159–65
      events from 1905 to 1915 158–9
      experience 153, 163
      lives 157
      nationalist terrorist attacks 162
      pain 162, 163, 167
      suffering 159–63, 165, 167
   'the Armenian issue' 154
   humanitarian disasters 161
   massacre of Muslims 155–6, 160, 164
   Ottoman-European alliances 155
   Ottoman experience on Caucasus, Suez and Çanakkale 155
   politics 154
   Van rebellion 155–6
   violence against Muslim 154, 162

Abdülhamit II 1, 125, 144, 157, 158
absence 31–2, 39, 84
   of living memory 39
academic research in Turkey 141–50, 166–7
Acemoğlu, Daron 177
Adalet and Kalkinma Partisi (AKP) 33, 43, 47, 61
Adana revolt/massacres 125, 157, 158, 162, 180
Agos 68, 82, 92, 98–9, 101–3
Akarca, Mehmet 79–80
Akçam, Taner 22, 185
AKP. *See* Adalet and Kalkinma Partisi (AKP)

Akşam 80
Aktar, Ayhan 68
Aktar, Cengiz 68
Akyol, Taha 153, 155, 156, 158–64, 166
Alphabet Revolution (Harf Devrimi) 50
Altaylı, Fatih 114–15
Altınok, Melih 84
Anadolu Ajansı 66
Anscombe, Elizabeth 34–5, 52
anti-Armenian bias 130
anti-racist sentiments 177
apology 4–6, 149, 182–3
Armenian 103–4
   cruelty 105–10
   rebellion 132, 134, 143
   revolt 131, 141
   and massacres 62
   suffering 153, 159–63, 165, 167
   threat 42–3
   violence 154, 157, 158, 160
Armenian diaspora (*Ermeni diasporası*) 42, 46, 58–60, 64, 67, 69, 76–81, 91, 97, 122, 149
Armenian genocide (1915) 2–6, 8–10, 13–18, 21–6, 32, 34–9, 43–6, 48, 59, 65, 78, 107, 110, 111, 170, 171
   apologies to 182–3
   arrest of Armenians 27–9, 62, 70, 134
   availability of books 178–9
   centennial commemorations 27, 57–8, 70–6, 149–50, 153–4, 157, 164, 172
      marching for 71–5, 78, 147
      newspaper report (*see* newspaper report, on genocide commemorations)
      posters 70–3, 81
      slogans 72–3, 78
   change in the education system 184
   declaration of 24 March 1915 97

denialism 21–2, 181–2
  Twitter exchange 176–8
  UN and the government of Turkey 174–6
deportations 66, 78, 92, 96, 99, 105, 109, 143, 145, 153, 155–7, 159–65
education system and 123
granting citizenship to descendants 183
Habertürk report 60, 63
Huşartsan memorial 68
lobby of United States 94
massacres 1, 10, 15, 20, 62, 78, 82, 83, 92, 95, 97, 109, 126, 155–6, 161, 162, 164, 165
media coverage from the 2000s 88–90
  Agos 92, 98–9, 101–3
  Cumhuriyet 100
  Hürriyet 92–3, 99, 100, 103, 105
  Milliyet 91, 93, 104, 105
  Obama, Barack and 90–1
  Radikal 91, 93, 96, 105
  Sabah 91, 95, 100
  Taraf 105
  Vatan 100
  Zaman 91, 93
memory of 30, 34, 36, 40, 47–9, 54–5, 64
number of losses 92, 95–7
Paylan's parliamentary speech 1–2
publications 22
public debates 3–4, 34
reason to consider as genocide 179–81
recognition of personalities 184–5
restitution of descendants 185–6
silence 22
the so-called (*sözde*) 41, 59, 63, 72, 77, 89, 90, 92, 93, 123, 127, 128, 132, 133, 137, 148, 159, 160, 163
UN Convention 14, 44–6
UN position 67
US resolution 46
Armenian Genocide Resolution 94–7, 114
the Armenian issue (*Ermeni Meselesi*) 9, 10, 13, 22, 41, 58, 77, 79, 83, 94, 95, 98, 115, 118, 122, 124, 128–31, 133, 142, 144–6, 154, 170
the Armenian Problem (*Ermeni Sorunu*) 118–19, 122, 129, 142, 151–3
Armenian Revolutionary Federation. *See Dashnaktsutyun*
Armenian Secret Army for the Liberation of Armenia (ASALA) 21–2, 42, 79, 95, 96, 122, 128, 129
  terrorism 62–3, 122, 130, 132
'*Armenians*' in Turkish Textbooks: From the Republic to Today 129
Assmann, Jan 35
Atatürk, Mustafa Kemal 98–101, 118, 121, 123, 127
Atatürk's Principles and History of the Revolution (Turan, Safran, Hayta, Şahin, Çakmak and Dönmez) 123–6
Atay, Falih Rıfkı 51, 53
Aydınlık 61, 63, 67, 80, 84
Aytar, Mustafa 106

Babacan, Ali 93
Bâbıâli Incident 144, 146
Bağdat, Hayko 83
Bahçeli, Devlet 91
Balian (Balyan) family 185
Balıkçı, Sevag 78
Balkan refugees 158
Balkan Wars 154, 158
Barış, Linda 136
Basic National Education Law (*Milli Eğitim Temel Kanunu*) 123, 136, 138
Batırel, Necmi 177
Bayer, Yalçın 60
Bayraktar, Seyhan 21
Biden, Joe 94
Bitlis rebellions 162, 164
The Blond Bride (*Sarı Gelin*) 151–3
Boggs, Carl 117
Bozkır, Volkan 59, 77

Cemal, Hasan 178
Cemal Pashas 20, 43, 154
centennial commemorations 27, 57–8, 70–6
  marching for 71–5, 78

newspaper report (*see* newspaper
    report, on genocide
    commemorations)
  posters   70–3, 81
  slogans   72–3, 78
Çiçek, Kemal   96, 97
citizenship   100–3, 117, 138, 177, 183–4
Citizenship in Turkey and in the
    World   24
Cıvaoğlu, Güneri   79
CNN   76, 83, 153–4
Cohen, Stanley   48, 97, 149, 167, 182, 187
Çölaşan, Emin   62, 79, 103, 104
collective memory   31, 32, 34, 35, 170
Committee of Union and Progress
    (CUP)   43, 64, 154, 155
Constantinople trials   42, 43, 45, 96, 97,
    170
Convention on the Prevention and
    Punishment of the Crime of
    Genocide (CPPCG)   14, 44–6,
    147
cultural denial   48
cultural memory   35
Cuma, Atacan   91
Cumhuriyet   62, 69, 83–4, 100
CUP. *See* Committee of Union and
    Progress (CUP)

Dashnaktsutyun   16–17, 43, 62, 97, 156
Davutoğlu, Ahmet   36–8, 148
defence   42–4
defensive tactics   61, 173
denialism   12, 13, 16, 19, 21, 22, 25–6,
    48–9, 133, 137–8, 167, 174
  genocide   21–2, 173–8, 181–2
  institutional   22, 61, 182–3, 185
deportation law   125
Dink, Hrant   21, 29, 37, 38, 67, 69, 73, 74,
    76, 78, 82, 153
Dink, Rakel   69, 84
documentaries   150
  1914/1915 (Akyol) (*see 1914/1915*
    (Akyol))
  The Blond Bride (*Sarı Gelin*)   151–3
Dündar, Can   69

education   53, 184
  documentary series in   152–3
  formal   117, 135, 137, 174

  public
    1914/1915 (Akyol)   150, 153–66
    The Blond Bride (*Sarı Gelin*)
      151–3
education system   113, 115, 136–9, 172,
    174
  secondary education textbooks   116,
    127–33
    anti-Armenian bias   130
    the Armenia issue   118, 121–2,
      124, 128–31, 133
    Armenian problem   119, 122
    Atatürk's Principles and History of
      the Revolution (Turan, Safran,
      Hayta, Şahin, Çakmak and
      Dönmez)   123–6
    Basic National Education
      Law (*Milli Eğitim Temel*
      Kanunu)   123, 136, 138
    centralization of   117
    deportations   120, 122, 128–30,
      133
    emotional language   130–1
    genocide of 1915   128–9, 132–3
    History 10 (*Tarih 10*, Turan, Genç,
      Çelik, Genç, Türedi)   131–2,
      135, 137
    History of the Revolution of the
      Turkish Republic (Su and
      Mumcu)   118–23
    Metin's review   129–33
    new approach/curriculum   127–8
    old approach   128
    self-evaluation of   127–36
    situation of Armenians   124
    teaching material   122, 123, 128,
      133, 152
    Turan's review   128–9
    War of Independence   118–19
    Yilmaz's review   127–8
Ehrhold, Käthe   93
Ekşi, Oktay   92, 100
Eldem, Ethem   138
Enver Pasha   20, 43, 154
epistemic power   50, 52, 54
erasure   32, 39, 53, 79, 85, 109, 111, 132,
    164, 166, 170–2, 181, 182, 187
Erdoğan, Recep Tayyip   33, 36–8, 47, 60,
    66, 77, 79, 80, 148
Eroler, Elif Gençkal   117

Ether, Şeref 185
ethnic blindness 101–2
ethnicity 100–2
existential insecurity 43, 46, 49, 50

forced migration 125, 126, 131
forgetting 31, 36, 171
formal education 117, 135, 137, 174
Frisch, Amália 185

Gallagher, Charles F. 51
genocide 9
 Armenian (*see* Armenian genocide (1915))
 concept of 13–18, 64, 179–80
 denialism 21–2, 173–8
 use of the term 63–5, 84
Gensburger, Sarah 34
geopolitical power 92
Gillespie, Alex 173, 174
Göçek, Fatma Müge 3, 9, 21, 22, 53
Gökçek, Melih 33
Gökçen, Sabiha 98–100, 102–5, 109
Gomidas (Komitas) Vartabet 27, 70, 149, 184–5
Görke, Alexander 103
grammar 19, 49, 113, 115, 169, 184
 of denialism 137, 174
group memory 31
group thinking 32
Gül, Abdullah 92–3
Güller, Mehmet Ali 61
Güneş, Cihan 22
Gürkan, Uluç 80
Güzel, Hasan Celal 96, 97

Habertürk 59, 60, 63, 65, 66, 77, 79
Hacking, Ian 35
Hakan, Ahmet 82–4
Halaçoğlu, Yusuf 114
Halbwachs, Maurice 32–5, 39
Hamidian massacres 144, 180
Han, Byung-Chul 84, 85
hegemony 117
History 10 (*Tarih 10*, Turan, Genç, Çelik, Genç and Türedi) 131–2, 135, 137
History of the Revolution of the Turkish Republic (Su and Mumcu) 117–23

history teaching 117–23. *See also* education system
Holocaust 14, 15, 48, 81
Hripsime Hanım 99
Hür, Ayşe 105, 109
Hürriyet 60, 77, 78, 81, 82, 92–3, 99, 100, 103, 105
Huşartsan memorial 68

İmam, Sütçü 120–1
İnsel, Ahment 14–15
institutional denialism 22, 61, 182–3, 185
instructed memory 36
Istanbul Bar Association 147–8, 158
Istanbul University symposium 141–3, 145–8

justice 66
Justice and Development Party. *See* Adalet and Kalkınma Partisi (AKP)
just memory 36, 38, 77

Kaçznuni (Katchaznouni), Hovhannes 67, 79
Kaplan, Hilal 84
Kara, Kemal 130
Karabekir, Kazım 104–10
Karaca, Nihal Bengisu 79
Kardaş, Ümit 83
Kavalcıyan, Zaruhi S. 185
Kemal, Mustafa 7
Kemalism 51, 69
Keskin, Hakkı 61
Kévorkian, Raymond H. 21, 23
Kılıçdaroğlu, Kemal 176–7
Kırıkkanat, Mine G. 62
Klemperer, Victor 171
Köker, Osman 6, 20–1
Koru, Fehmi 63
Kubilay, Çağla 52
Kurt, Ümit 185

language 25, 34, 38–41, 102, 130, 169–71
 Armenian genocide claim 89–90
 of Armenian issue (*Ermeni Meselesi*) 9–10, 79, 87
 emotional 130–1, 134, 137
 and history 52–4, 117, 172, 173, 180
 media 98

national 51–4, 117, 137
  policies 51–2, 54, 172, 173, 180
  public 55
  of public memory repertoire 63, 113
  revolution (*devrimi*) 50–1
  Turkish 1–53, 79, 137, 138
  use of 19, 54, 59
Lemkin, Raphael 13–18, 46, 83, 179–80
Levi, Primo 13
living memory 39–40
Luhmann, Niklas 88–90, 101, 109–11

McCarthy, Justin 97
Marian, Michel 14, 15
martyrdoms 131
mass killings/murder 17–18, 45, 49, 97
mass media 57–9, 82–5, 87–8, 98, 101–3, 110–12, 138, 172
  content of the reality 89
  coverage from the 2000s 88–90
    Agos 92, 98–9, 101–3
    Cumhuriyet 100
    Hürriyet 92–3, 99, 100, 103, 105
    Milliyet 91, 93, 104, 105
    Obama, Barack 90–1
    Radikal 91, 93, 96, 105
    Sabah 91, 95, 100
    Taraf 105
    Vatan 100
    Zaman 91, 93
  definition 88–9
media language 98
Meds Yeghern 92
memorials 57, 69, 184
memory 5–8, 13, 28, 170, 171
  Armenian genocide (1915) 30, 34, 36, 40, 47–9, 54–5, 64
  collective 31, 32, 34, 35, 170
  concept of 30
  cultural 35
  Davutoğlu, public statements of 37, 38
  eradication of genocide 182
  Erdoğan, public statements of 36–8
  just 36, 38, 77
  living 39–40
  of personalities 184–5
  as a process 32–6
  public (*see* public memory)
  reconstruction of 33–4
  of Turkish victimhood 49

Mengi, Güngör 100, 103
Mert, Timuçin 67
Metin, Erhan 115–16, 129–33
Michel, Johann viii, 9
migration 119–20
Milliyet 65, 77–9, 91, 93, 104, 105
Mumcu, Ahmet 118

Nakhashian, Avedis 27, 70
national
  history 51–4
  identity 52, 54, 173–4
  language 51–4
Necmi, İbrahim 51, 53
Nergararyan-Kasabyan, Ofelya 185
newspaper report, on genocide commemorations in 2015
  Agos 68, 82
  Akşam 80
  Aydınlık 61, 63, 67, 80, 84
  Cumhuriyet 62, 69, 83–4
  Habertürk 59, 60, 63, 65, 66, 77, 79
  Hürriyet 60, 77–8, 81, 82
  Milliyet 65, 77–9
  Özgür Gündem 84
  Sabah 77, 84, 91
  Sözcü 61–2, 79
  Takvim 67, 79
  Taraf 65, 68, 83
  Vatan 61, 67
  Yenicağ 67
  Yeni Şafak 64
  Yurt 82
  Zaman 60, 64
Nichanian, Marc 29, 166
Nişanyan, Sevan 114–15

Obama, Barack 80
  not using the word 'genocide' 59–61, 90–3
  presidential statement 92–4
  speech to the Turkish parliament 90–1
  Turkey' angry on 92–3
orphans 102–6, 108–10
Oruç, Merve Şebnem 64
Özal, Turgut 47
Özel, Soli 65
Özer, Verda 81
Özgürel, Avni 93

Özgür Gündem 84
Özkök, Özkök 81

Paboudjian, Paul B. 21
Paçal, Mustafa 65
Partiya Karkeren Kurdistan (PKK) 80
Pastermadjian, Karekin 156
Patriotic Party 63, 72, 76, 80
Paylan, Garo 3, 30
   parliamentary debate about genocide 1–2
Pelosi, Nancy 94
Perinçek, Doğu 45, 63, 80
Perinçek, Mehmet 43
PKK. *See* Partiya Karkeren Kurdistan (PKK)
Potter, W. James 88
public language 55
public memory 3, 19, 28–33, 35–9, 55, 170
   denialist 54–5, 110, 187
   of ethnic groups 88
   remember through 35–40
   repertoire 40–50, 57–9, 63, 64, 66–9, 79, 80, 82–5, 87–90, 94, 96–8, 101–4, 106, 110, 112, 115, 123, 135, 138, 145–9, 170–2
   1914/1915 150, 153–66
   The Blond Bride (*Sarı Gelin*) 151–3
   massacres of Muslim Turks 164
   media coverage (*see* mass media, coverage from the 2000s)
   Turkishness and 50–4
Pulur, Hasan 79

racism 177
Radikal 91, 93, 96, 105
recall 31, 88
religious minorities 46, 47
remembering 5–9, 13, 25, 28–31, 41–4, 46–8, 88, 171
   commemoration of Dink's murder 37, 38
   individual 32
   praxiological process of 39
   as a process 32–6
   social nature 34–5
   through public memory 35–40

Republic of Turkey 44, 46
Research on Social and Political Trends in Turkey 88
restitution 185–6
Retired Officers 106
Ricoeur, Paul 30, 31, 34–6, 39–41, 54, 55, 58, 112, 171, 187

Sabah 77, 84, 91, 95, 100
Sarıkamış disaster 155
Sarıkaya, Makbule 105
Sarıkaya, Muharrem 60
Savelsberg, Joachim J. ix, 50, 87
Scholl, Armine 103
security 42–4
Selçuk, İlhan 101
Sevag (Çilingiryan), Rupen 28
Shanken, Andrew M. 57
shared memory 77
shared suffering 36–8, 47, 148, 153
silence 22, 32, 39, 49, 65, 77, 104, 109, 163
Şimşek, Murat 84
Sirmen, Ali 100
Snyder, Timothy 179
'the so-called (*sözde*) Armenian genocide' 41, 59, 63, 72, 77, 89, 90, 92, 93, 123, 127, 128, 132, 133, 137, 148, 159, 160, 163
Solak, Mustafa 67
Sözcü 61, 62, 79
Su, Mükerrem K. 118
Sultanahmet Square 70

Taksim Square 68, 72–4, 78, 80
Takvim 67, 79
Talat Pasha 20, 43, 154, 161, 165
Talat Pasha Committee (Talat Paşa Komitesi) 63
Taraf 65, 68, 83, 105
Taşçı, Selcan 67
Tayiz, Kurtuluş 80
tehcir (deportations) 13, 15, 16, 18, 23, 64, 66, 69, 78, 79, 82, 83, 92, 95–6, 99, 105, 109, 120, 123, 128–33, 142–3, 145, 148, 153, 155–7, 159–65, 184
Tekin, Arslan 67

Tetik, Ahmet 22
Tonga, Deniz 128
trained memory 36
Treaty
  of Brest-Litovsk 120, 124
  of Lausanne 46, 123, 132
  of Sèvres 42, 43
Turan, Rahmi 61
Turan, Refik 121–2, 128–9
Turkish
  linguistic identity 53
  nationalism 53, 123
Turkish Linguistic Association (Türk Dil Kurumu) 50–1
Turkishness 12, 50–4, 98, 100–2, 104, 106, 136–8, 172, 173, 177–8, 183, 187
Turkish War of Independence 18, 106, 117, 118, 124, 145, 180
TV broadcasting 68

Uluç, Hıncal 95–6, 100
Uluengin, Hadi 68
Üstel, Füsun 116, 117, 137

Van rebellion 155–6, 162, 164
Vatan 61, 67, 100

Wood, Robert 91
World War I 36, 38, 42, 43, 47, 62–4, 66, 97, 124, 142, 144–5, 153, 154, 162, 163, 180
  security problems during 42–4

Yalçın, Soner 62
The Years of Ottoman and Armenian Disaster 153
Yeniçağ 67
Yeni Şafak 64
Yıldıran, Timsal Karabekir 106–8
Yılmaz, Mehmet Serhat 91, 127, 128
Young Turk Revolution 158
Yurt 82
Yurttagül, Ali 64

Zaman 60, 64, 91
Zerubavel, Eviatar 49
Zeytun
  deportations 145
  uprising 144, 146, 157

www.ingramcontent.com/pod-product-compliance
Lightning Source LLC
Chambersburg PA
CBHW052111300426
44116CB00010B/1625